Representing Organization

Representing Organization

Knowledge, Management, and the Information Age

Simon Lilley

Geoffrey Lightfoot

Paulo Amaral M. N.

OXFORD
UNIVERSITY PRESS

*This book has been printed digitally and produced in a standard specification
in order to ensure its continuing availability*

OXFORD
UNIVERSITY PRESS

Great Clarendon Street, Oxford OX2 6DP

Oxford University Press is a department of the University of Oxford.
It furthers the University's objective of excellence in research, scholarship,
and education by publishing worldwide in

Oxford New York

Auckland   Cape Town Dar es Salaam   Hong Kong   Karachi
Kuala Lumpur Madrid Melbourne Mexico City   Nairobi
New Delhi Shanghai Taipei Toronto
With offices in
Argentina Austria Brazil Chile Czech Republic France Greece
Guatemala Hungary Italy Japan South Korea Poland Portugal
Singapore Switzerland Thailand Turkey Ukraine Vietnam

Oxford is a registered trade mark of Oxford University Press
in the UK and in certain other countries

Published in the United States
by Oxford University Press Inc., New York

ISBN 978-0-19-877542-3

◼ ACKNOWLEDGEMENTS

As our (very) long-suffering editors at Oxford University Press are more than aware, this book has been a long time in gestation and thus it seems appropriate that our first thanks go to them. Specifically, we would like to thank Matthew Derbyshire, whose recent addition to the editorial team finally sparked some meaningful activity on our part, but the greatest of our thanks must go to David Musson for his patience and good humour. Emails entitled 'The work of fiction?' not only kept us smiling, but eventually got us to deliver, for good or ill, the manuscript that is currently before you. In terms of the content of the manuscript, our debts are of course too innumerable to mention in their entirety, but we will nevertheless have a go at identifying our greatest creditors. Much of Chapter 8 would not have been possible without the delightful collaboration of Steve Brown, particularly his work with Geoff under the auspices of the ESRC's *Virtual Society*? Programme (Award number: L132251042). Similarly, Simon is indebted both to Mahmoud Ezzamel and Hugh Willmott, and to Adrian Wilkinson (as well as the Chartered Institute of Management Accounting and Institute of Chartered Accountants in England and Wales) for some of the material included in Chapters 1 (Ezzamel, M., Lilley, S. Wilkinson, A., and Willmott, H. (1996). 'Practices and Practicalities in Human Resource Management'. *Human Resource Management Journal*, 6/1: 63–80) and 6 (Ezzamel, M., Lilley, S., and Willmott, H., (1994). 'The New Organization, The New Managerial Work'. *European Management Journal*, 12/4: 454–61). We should also note here that some of the material that appears in Chapters 4, 5 (Lilley, S. (1998). 'Regarding Screens for Surveillance of the System'. *Accounting, Management and Information Technologies*, 8: 63–105), and 7 (Lilley, S. (1996). 'Refining Accountabilities: Opening the black box of management systems success', in R. Munro and J. Mouritsen (eds.), *Accountability: Power, Ethos and the Technologies of Managing*. London: Chapman and Hall) has previously appeared elsewhere, albeit in different form. Finally, we would like to thank in particular those writers whose work and ideas have substantively informed a number of key chapters in this collection. Chapter 1 would not have been possible in the form it is without the expansive contribution to the literature on technology made by David Noble. Similarly, we could not have written Chapter 3 without the seminal contribution of Bob Cooper, whose ideas inform and inspire much of the text as a whole. Brian Bloomfield's meticulous work on the activities of Forrester and the Systems Dynamics group at MIT made the argument we articulate in Chapter 4 conceivable while without Jannis Kallinkos's insightful reading of Calvino, we would be without Chapter 9. In short, the book has only been made possible by the extensive work of others and we give grateful thanks to all of them, especially those we have forgotten in this acknowledgement! Having said that, we do of course close with that hoary old chestnut: the errors that remain are all our own work.

▓ CONTENTS

▓ NOTES ON AUTHORS

Simon Lilley Reader at the Management Centre, University of Leicester. He is less informed about key contemporary issues than he should be and is knowledgeable about nothing.

Geoffrey Lightfoot Visiting lecturer in Accounting and Entrepreneurship, Centre for Social Theory and Technology and Department of Management, Keele University. Course Leader for MBA Option in Management Information Systems.

Paulo Amaral M. N. Associate lecturer in Management Information Systems, Accounting, Marketing and Management, Centre for Social Theory and Technology and Department of Management, Keele University.

▓ LIST OF INSERTS

Introduction

Information *as if it mattered*

The breathless talk of the moment is of an 'information economy' and even a 'knowledge economy', or perhaps with still greater immodesty, of an 'information society' and a 'knowledge society' (e.g. see Wiener 1948; Machlup 1962, 1980; Böhme and Stehr 1986; Rubin, Huber, and Taylor 1986; Castells 1989; Poster 1990). Of a world, to use Yeats' (1916) immortal phrase, in which all is 'changed, changed utterly'. But how can we still gasp in the face of the shock of the new? How do we stifle our yawns, and instead show polite surprise, at yet more talk of information revolution? For neither this talk, nor what it refers to, is particularly new: 'In effect we've had an information economy ever since we invented money' (Bey 1996: 372). And we seem to have had money (or at least the tokens of debt that precede it) for over 10,000 years (Schmandt-Besserat 1992), effectively for as long as there has been what we call civilization. Is information, then, merely a particular representation of, or perhaps better, a particular metonym for, civilization; an essential, and thus ever present, ingredient of an organized world?

Well, one answer is a resounding 'yes' and it is certainly an answer that animates much of what follows in this text. But such an answer fails adequately to come to grips with the (seemingly) more recent hold that talk of the information revolution has upon us. For if there is something about the present that is distinctive, perhaps it is the sheer volume and tenacity of the heralds of the information age who call us all to arms, to join the front, to engage in the fight for a brave new world. Since the advent of the electronic computer in the middle of the last century the persistence of the invitation has made it increasingly difficult to refuse. And such a chronology is informative, for it reminds us of the role of calculating machines in the construction of this Zeitgeist. Might it be merely *technology*, rather than *information* technology that has us in its thrall, as it has had those whom went before? Is there, indeed, anything new about even 'information' technology? For how are we to conceive of accounting and printing if not as technologies of information? (See Exhibit 1, below, for a rather more scathingly direct denunciation of this presentism.)

Well, perhaps, as technologies of *administration* and *organization*, for it is not, in our view, coincidental that talk of information and its revolution rises into a deafening cacophony at just the same time that the cult of the manager takes hold (e.g. see Jacques 1996; Parker 2002). Consider, as illustration of this point, the publication of Burnham's (1941) *Managerial Revolution* and the near simultaneity of the appearance of Drucker's (1947) *Big Business*, Shannon and Weaver's (1949) *Mathematical Theory of Communication*, Wiener's (1948) *Cybernetics*, and the announcements of the

The 'BOOK' is a revolutionary breakthrough in technology: no wires, no electric circuits, no batteries, nothing to be connected or switched on. It is so easy to use, even a child can operate it. Just lift its cover! Compact and portable, it can be used anywhere— even sitting in an armchair by the fire—yet it is powerful enough to hold as much information as a CD-ROM disk.

Here is how it works . . .

Each BOOK is constructed of sequentially numbered sheets of paper (recyclable), each capable of holding thousands of bits of information. These pages are locked together with a custom-fit device called a binder which keeps the sheets in their correct sequence. Opaque Paper Technology (OPT) allows manufacturers to use both sides of the sheet, doubling the information density and cutting costs in half. Experts are divided on the prospects for further increases in information density; for now BOOKs with more information simply use more pages. This makes them thicker and harder to carry, and has drawn some criticism from the mobile computing crowd. Each sheet is scanned optically, registering information directly into your brain. A flick of the finger takes you to the next sheet. The BOOK may be taken up at any time and used by merely opening it. The BOOK never crashes and never needs rebooting, though like other display devices it can become unuseable if dropped overboard. The 'browse' feature allows you to move instantly to any sheet, and move forward or backward as you wish. Many come with an 'index' feature, which pinpoints the exact location of any selected information for instant retrieval.

An optional 'BOOKmark' accessory allows you to open the BOOK to the exact place you left it in a previous session—even if the BOOK has been closed. BOOKmarks fit universal design standards; thus, a single BOOKmark can be used in BOOKs by various manufacturers.

Conversely, numerous bookmarkers can be used in a single BOOK if the user wants to store numerous views at once. The number is limited only by the number of pages in the BOOK.

The media is ideal for long-term archive use. Several field trials have proven that the media will still be readable in several centuries, and because of its simple user interface it will be compatible with future reading devices.

You can also make personal notes next to BOOK text entries with an optional programming tool, the Portable Erasable Nib Cryptic Intercommunication Language Stylus (PENCILS). Portable, durable, and affordable, the BOOK is being hailed as the entertainment wave of the future. The BOOK's appeal seems so certain that thousands of content creators have committed to the platform. Look for a flood of new titles soon.

Source: Built-in Orderly Organized Knowledge Device by Marielle Cartier, then Executive Director, for the then Alliance for Canada's Audio-Visual Heritage. NB: this version was apparently forwarded to the Editor of Abbey Newsletter (Volume 21, Number 8, 1997) by Jim Wheeler. According the Abbey Newsletter it originally came from Association of Moving Image Archivists (AMIA) Listserv, where it had been posted by Marielle Cartier. When she was contacted at brunant@cam.ORG and asked for permission to reprint, she is reported to have said, 'Sure, this is [a] public notice that is now available on many listservs. Go ahead, it supports the preservation of a still well used media, the book!' (details from http://palimpsest. stanford.edu/byorg/abbey/an/an21/an21-8/an21-807.html, consulted on 1 July 2003).

invention of the thinking machine in Manchester, UK, and Pennsylvannia, USA, (e.g. see Large 1984: 36–7), events that all occurred in the momentous era of the 1940s. Indeed, it was also during the 1940s that Herbert Simon, perhaps the god-father of (albeit limited) information processing and certainly the 'father of artificial intelligence',[1] first suggested that the human notion of intelligence might soon be matched or exceeded by its mechanical simulation. And Simon's writing on this subject is illustrative of the rhetorical tricks that allow perpetuation of the breath-lessness that inhabits the hall of mirrors constitutive of the information age. For until his untimely demise, from the publication in 1947 of his classic *Administrative Behavior*, Simon had repeatedly claimed that 'machine intelligence' was just around the corner. 'Each edition promise[d] the almost complete duplication of human intelligence "within a decade". The moving horizon of promised results keeps the image forever young' (Boland 1987: 374). This conjunction of managerialism and informationalism continues to this day in the continuous production of minimally differentiated textbooks and courses parading under mealy-mouthed variations of the title *Management Information Systems*.

So what do informationalism and managerialism share? First and foremost any answer to this question must note the ways in which both of our isms take flight from the phenomenal world, the everyday world of lived experience. They follow lines of flight that although sympathetic are not identical. Managerialism, as Armstrong (2002) has eloquently argued, has, from its inception as a separate discipline at Harvard University at the start of the twentieth century, been distinguished by its lack of attention to the specificity of the tasks and activities it seeks to marshal. Initially just a part of the training provided to railway 'officers' (see also Jacques 1996), clever marketing grew it into a course all of its own, creating a programme without limitations to the domain of its applicability and hence saleability. Indeed, we could and will go further: not only was the new knowledge of 'management' sold as that which could be applied everywhere, it was also the knowledge that guaranteed its bearer distinction from, and superior rewards to, those who actually possessed domain knowledge and real understanding of the specificity of their tasks.

As for informationalism, well, the clue is in the word and its antecedents. The term 'information' can potentially be read as a description of a process, a process of information (see Boland 1987) in which an 'interior' of a person is in some sense transformed as a consequence of interaction with significant aspects of the 'exterior' world. In its more prosaic noun form (generally the only one considered in normal parlance) 'information' represents a nominalization of the verb 'to inform'. Forays into Latin unleash a chain of terms, *informare*—to give form to or to describe—which itself derives from *formare*—to form. And in English, particularly that most denot-ative and etiolated branch of English associated with the analytical wing of the philosophical movement, we discover that 'form' represents 'the essence of some-thing, especially as distinguished from *matter*' (New Collins Concise English Dictionary 1987). Information, then, is the elevation of form and its significance over base matter, mirroring the hiearchization of management over mere labour that we witnessed above. As the quote from Bey which we considered in the first paragraph of this introduction continues, although our information economy has existed since the invention of money, 'we still haven't learnt to digest copper' (Bey 1996: 372). As soon as we leave the idealizations of a Platonic world, information does and must *matter*.

Using *this* book

When we suggest that the heralds of the information age call 'us all to arms', we choose our words with care. For the information revolution is nothing if not individualized, with *personal* computing available to meet our every whim. The term that has come to stand for each and every one of us in all our varieties of forms and needs is that ubiquity of computing and information management, *the user*. The incessant talk about the importance of 'the user' in the field of information systems, while superficially appealing, is often lacking in specificity. At least the sort of specificity that one would normally expect in an engineered product. Indeed, endless deferral to the ill (if ever)-defined notion of the 'end-user' is, on occasion, all that fills this gap. And the end-user is a very strange creature indeed. He or she stands for the human part of a human computer interface, a part that has no need of anything outside of that connection, except of course the desires and needs that impelled connection in the first place. For the end-user is one whose every need has been predicted or who, more realistically, is in effect able to design their own (Robb 1988) system as they use their seemingly endlessly flexible technology. Rather than accepting this phantasm of an information management industry that knows in its heart of hearts that the thing it can never deliver is end-user computing that actually matches this ideal (see 'The Tyre Swing', Figure 1, below), we instead deploy the trope of 'the user' as a consistent way into interrogating the various themes and dimensions of information and its management that we consider throughout this text.

Overall then, the text provides a theoretically informed analysis of the organizational impact of information technologies by examining and commenting upon the myriad ways in which various actors, organizations, and environments are *represented* through these technologies. It deploys a number of different theoretical lenses including systems theory, social constructivism, labour process theory, poststructuralism, and actor network theory, that offer complementary and contrasting insights into the computerization of (managerial) work and its administration, and uses these theories to consider real examples of the development and implementation of knowledge and information systems. It also, symmetrically, uses accounts of practice to reflect upon the theories used to make sense of that practice. Contemporary threats to organizational form and stability are considered alongside the potential that information technologies offer to both exacerbate and overcome them in ways that we hope will foster practical knowledge that is theoretically

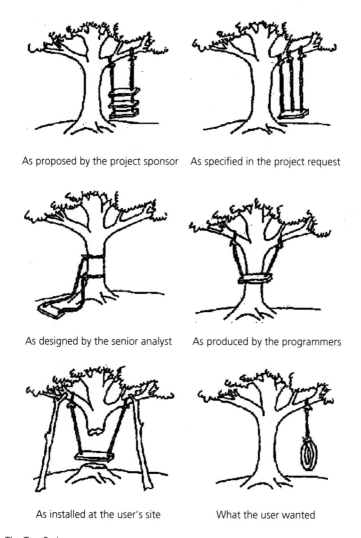

As proposed by the project sponsor   As specified in the project request

As designed by the senior analyst   As produced by the programmers

As installed at the user's site   What the user wanted

Figure 1 The Tyre Swing

informed. In short, the book is an attempt to bridge the gap between the abstractions of current theories of organization and the somewhat excessively grounded material that forms the bulk of literature within the information systems and knowledge management communities.

Following this introduction, Chapter 1 begins to examine some of the historical roots of the implementation of informational technology in an organizational context. To help in this analysis, we work through David Noble's detailed exploration of the management of the introduction of automatically controlled machine tools in the North American engineering, and particularly defence, industry to demonstrate how *Labour Process Theory* focuses attention on the shifting relations between technology and organization. Here, then, we discuss the contention that technological development can best be understood through consideration of the social relations of (capitalist) production.

Chapter 2 introduces the notion of *representation*, a recurring theme throughout our text. It examines how we construct and view ourselves, others, and the material world, when we work, and organize work, through models and information, and considers the implications of doing so. The chapter begins our examination of poststructural approaches to information and organization via the mediating term of representation.

In Chapter 3, *systems theory* explicitly enters the story for the first time. We examine the theoretical roots of this mode of thinking as well as its current role in the *models* that make up the core of many modern managerial information systems. Such models present a world that is other to the world in which we live and face us with a stark set of choices, devil's alternatives we first glimpsed in Chapter 2. Do we eschew the real world, whatever that may be, and choose instead to inhabit the fantasies of the model world, insulating ourselves within our idealizations in the vain attempt to ignore their inability to contain that which they purport to capture? Or do we impose our models on the world with such vigour and sufficient rigour to ensure that the world 'as is' is lost forever, replaced by the comforting images of our conceptualizations?

Chapter 4 presents us with a potential way through, if not out of, this dilemma, at least theoretically! It utilizes the specificities of a detailed example of systems practice from the world of oil refining, to illuminate the material aspects of the so-called information or knowledge revolution. By appealing to the ideas of the *actor network* approach the reader is forcibly reminded of the endless interrelations between, indeed the inseparability of, the social world and its technical or material counterpart and enjoined to avoid the temptation to privilege one over the other.

Chapter 5 both continues with the themes of the actor network approach and the centrality to it of the notion of *translation* between different forms of stability and change and returns to the theme of representation we introduced in Chapter two. We show how *representation*, as an organizing principle, lies at the very core of the mediations that translation seeks to trace. Once again, we illustrate our argument here with reference to the computerization of oil refinery management.

The changes witnessed in oil refining in the previous two chapters can be considered to be early exemplars of the emergence of a new way of managing, one that supposedly exceeds the limitations of the preceding 'command and control' model. We attempt to show the myriad ways in which information systems function as key components of many of the *new management practices* and ideals. Initiatives such as BPR, TQM, JIT, and even 'culture change' rest upon the supposed flexibilities information technologies promise and speak to us in the name of freedom. Chapter 6 subjects these somewhat simplistic assertions to critical scrutiny, through consideration of the use of information systems to enable *empowerment* not in the conventional realm of work and production, but rather in a novel site of application more associated with the pleasures of consumption.

Chapter 7 continues to develop the themes surrounding the management of change and particularly the freeing of initiative that many contemporary forms of the beast promise. Returning once more to the world of refining, we explore in some detail the importance attached to clear *accountability* within these new forms of managerial control. For information systems not only allow accountability to be traced to a point in the organization's hierarchy, the idealizations of their models also provide metrics against which performance can be measured in order to enable that accountability to be made real. Adopting a somewhat cynical twist, we examine how this process occurs in practice through consideration of how accountability for systems delivery is enacted.

In Chapter 8 we begin to bring our story up to date by considering the emergence of the so-called *virtual organization* through a detailed consideration of that ubiquity of modern office life, the email system and associated *groupware* technologies. Such an exploration allows us to continue our focus upon accountability, for despite the techno-boosterism of early proponents of these technologies, who talked of openness, democracy, and free participation, virtual space appears in practice to be if anything one of the most highly regulated media, at least when deployed within organizational borders. The chapter examines both the causes and the implications of this paradox through detailed readings of a number of key cases.

The elimination of *risk and uncertainty* seems to be one of the key objectives underlying systematization. In Chapter 9 we return again to the theme of *representation*, considering the consequences of an instrumental orientation towards representation becoming a dominant way of viewing the world, as has arguably been increasingly the case since the advent of the modern world. But we do so not by examining that modern world explicitly; rather, we follow Jannis Kallinikos as he takes us on a journey to an Ancient China, with Italo Calvino's fictionalization of Marco Polo as our guide. In particular the chapter examines the ways in which, especially within systems of large scale, control is problematized by a tension between the demands of the system to maintain the sense of its contents and the demands of the world to be referred to in requisite specificity. Once again, we witness the key dilemma of representation: to live in order or to live in the world. We conclude by following Kallinikos in his evocation of the powers of experience and natural language to transcend this impasse.

Our final chapter considers that most recent of impertinences surrounding computerized futures, the seemingly imperial realm of *Knowledge Management*. The role of knowledge in organizations has, somewhat ironically, simultaneously become both more apparent and less easy to grasp, as the structures that seek to manage and contain information cum knowledge become more flexible and fluid. Chapter 10 allows us to pull together many of the concerns we have raised throughout the text. For on first sight, a naive reader might believe that knowledge management promises to solve many of what appear to be the perennial problems of organizing, and organizing through, information. However, as we illustrate, it is only a promise that is contained in this burgeoning literature, a promise that is not, cannot be, fulfilled. For knowledge management's promise rests not upon its solution of preceding problems but rather upon its almost total ignorance of the fundamental problems that the notion of knowledge has put before philosophers, social theorists, and indeed thinkers of all varieties, since time immemorial.

As befits a book that insists upon the openness of the world before us and the impossibility of its capture in the simplistic nets of knowledge and information, a conclusion which might confine consideration of matters epistemological and informational either to these pages, or indeed to the ivory towers of academia, seems both inappropriate and impossible to achieve. So we close with a postscript and thus, hopefully, do not close at all.

1 Management, Information, and the Labour Process

KEY CONCEPTS

automation	neo-Fordism
Computer Numerical Control Technology	Labour Process Theory
control over the work process	Numerical Control Technology
Fordism	standardization
empowerment	

KEY THEMES

When you have read this chapter, you should be able to define those key concepts in your own words, and you should also be able to:

1. Explain the relationships between technology and organization.
2. Identify the historical context of information technology.
3. Understand the social relations of (capitalist) production and its connection with technological development.
4. Identify 'users' and 'end-users' of information systems.

Introduction

In this chapter we will apply Labour Process Theory to the shifting relations between technology and organization and begin to put information technology into a historical context. We examine the contention that technological development can best be understood through consideration of the social relations of (capitalist) production.

Who uses information systems?

The incessant talk about the importance of 'the user' in the field of information systems, while superficially appealing, is often lacking in specificity. At least the sort of specificity that one would normally expect in an engineered product. Indeed, the ill (if ever)-defined notion of the 'end-user' is, on occasion, all that fills this gap. This is a particularly interesting trope to which we will return. For now it is enough to point out that it is somewhat odd to sell a product on the basis of its ability to free one from reliance on the producer of that product.[1] In ideal capitalist enterprises one would expect all technologies, indeed all resources, to be deployed to further the ends, the *raisons d'être*, of such enterprises, that is, capital accumulation. This ideal is however complicated by another one, the separation of ownership and control, and thus we see management as agents serving the principal of capital. It surely follows then, that managers, or administrators, are the real end-users of information systems, albeit in their turn serving the ends of another. It is to an exploration of this contention and its consequences that this chapter is devoted.

A substantial literature is associated with such a project: that of Labour Process Theory. We begin with an examination of this tradition which considers the shifting relations between technology and organization in order to begin to put information technology into some sort of a historical context. We elucidate the central argument of Labour Process Theory: that technological development can best be understood through consideration of the social relations of (capitalist) production. To put it crudely, technology is seen as another weapon of capital that is used in its oppression of labour. Although of course this does not mean that the deployment of technology to meet managerial ends goes uncontested. The shapes of the technologies we see in use in organizations today are seen to be crystallizations of the outcomes of prior battles in an ongoing and inevitable war at the heart of capitalist development. The approach is perhaps best captured through the use of an example and we will be focusing upon the following source:

Noble, D. F. (1985). 'Social Choice in Machine Design: The Case of Automatically Controlled Machine Tools', in D. A. MacKenzie and J. Wajcman (eds.), *The Social Shaping of Technology: How the Refrigerator Got its Hum*. Milton Keynes: Open University Press.[2]

Technology and the labour process

Labour process analysis seeks to explain the *dynamics* of organizational and societal change. Such an approach focuses upon the ways in which *social relations* affect the direction of technological change. It seeks . . .

> to conceive of technology in a non-deterministic way, as the result of a process of innovation which is competitive between different firms and between management and workers in each industry and firm, and is also influenced by the general socio-political circumstances in which it occurs. Thus we can hope to gain insights into the relationship between innovation, types of mechanisation and capitalist economic development. (Blackburn, Coombs, and Green 1985: 31)

Blackburn, Coombs, and Green attempt to demonstrate the historical relations between technology and the capitalist economic system. They perceive three dimensions of technological change: changes to the *transformation* dimension of work; changes to the *transfer* dimension of work; and changes to the *control* dimension of work. The first of these dimensions concerns activities such as beating, bending, sawing, grinding, smelting, and moulding; activities designed to alter the shape and indeed the constitution of the material. The transfer dimension concerns activities such as shipping, hauling, carrying, and otherwise conveying both constituent parts and whole products to each other and the marketplace, respectively. Control concerns the administration of these varied constituent activities as meaningful wholes, a process that ideally results in the production of saleable products at profitable prices. Mechanization, from such a perspective, is thus seen to entail 'the replacement of one human-machine combination with another human-machine combination' (1985: 31) along one, or a number, of these dimensions. Blackburn, Coombs, and Green examine the changing importance of each of these dimensions over time.

According to Blackburn, Coombs, and Green, as new sources of power become available and improvements are made in transformation technologies, 'inadequacies' in the ways in which work is organized become more glaringly apparent. Rosenberg (1976) draws attention to the fact that innovative effort is generally focused on those points in the production process that appear as 'bottlenecks', or limiting factors. Changes within the textile industry in the United Kingdom in the eighteenth and nineteenth centuries certainly seem amenable to such a characterization (see, for example, Williams and Farnie 1992). Textile production essentially involves two processes: spinning and weaving.[3] Continuing with this very simplified account, we can see the introduction of John Kay's 'Flying Shuttle' in 1734 as an initial step on a stairway of technological 'evolution'. This improvement in weaving capacity lead to an upstream 'bottleneck' in the preceding process-spinning which could simply not produce quickly enough to meet the weavers' demands.[4] This 'bottleneck' was removed through a number of innovations in spinning (and indeed in the transfer of materials), perhaps most significantly Crompton's 'Mule', which built upon earlier advances embodied in Arkwright's 'Water Frame' and that favourite of all secondary school history teachers, the 'Spinning Jenny'. The scale of equipment subsequently required for 'efficient' spinning itself required some concentration of activities in specifically designed (proto)industrial spaces. And this concentration and concatenation of activities further serves to highlight further bottlenecks.

These exemplary islands of mechanization of the so-called Industrial Revolution were subsequently more directly connected and combined in the mills of the late eighteenth century. This early attention paid to the transfer dimension of work through the emergence of the factory, seemingly overlooked by Blackburn, Coombs, and Green (1985), was subsequently associated with further shifts on the transformation dimension. As steam engines were introduced to power *machine-made* machines a new system of what Marx termed 'machinofacture' was brought into being. This novel arrangement is taken by those following Marx to represent the emergence of a distinct, new production process wherein the 'real subordination' of labour occurred through capital's direct control of the nature and pace of work through its ownership of machinery. This shift is viewed by Blackburn, Coombs, and Green as 'a major . . . step in the *mechanisation of the transformation component* within the three dimensions of the labour process' (1985: 36).

With so many highly effective centres of transformation, at least in historically relative terms, gathered together in the factory, attention started to drift again to other dimensions of production. At around the end of the nineteenth century the emphasis of mechanization in a number of industries shifted towards both transformation *and* transfer problems and away from simple transformation issues alone. Two broad attempts to improve the work flow of production are apparent in this period: a move towards continuous flow processes in industries such as chemicals; and a move towards production line procedures in industries such as engineering. Indeed many businesses in both these industries still operate in this way today. These changes, particularly in the latter group of industries, involved innovations in handling devices, interchangeability of parts through their standardization, improvements in precision manufacture through the use of new transformation technologies, and the introduction of Taylorist forms of work organization (Blackburn, Coombs, and Green 1985). This process perhaps reached its apotheosis in the system of mass production that came to be known as 'Fordism'.

Fordism was expressed in its purest form at the infamous River Rouge plant in Detroit. Although, the 'at' in the previous sentence potentially misses much of the point. For Ford's integrationism extended upstream to rubber plantation holding and downstream to car dealership ownership, with very little in between left 'outside' the system, under the ownership and control of unpredictable others. Within the plant similar attention to complete integration of precisely engineered and standardized people, parts, and procedures was followed to the 'T'. The oft quoted line about 'Any colour so long as it is black' is so oft quoted precisely because it so beautifully captures the trade-off which the Fordist *system* of *standardization* embodies.

As both Ford's systems and those of the early Industrial Revolution in textiles exemplify, developments are often mutually supportive and while the three dimensions put forward by Blackburn, Coombs, and Green are undoubtedly useful, they are not as separate as a naive reading might suggest. Consider, for example, the role of the production line, a transfer technology par excellence, in the control of the labour process. It is also important to remember that these shifts occurred at different times and at different rates in different countries and industries. But even though such a broad-brush approach inevitably involves some simplification, it nevertheless provides a useful framework for consideration of the shifts in the nature of technology in the workplace.

Changing the scale and scope of control

This 'Fordist' production system, seen to be characteristic of the mid-twentieth-century United States, was a combination of process and product technologies,[5] human labour, and a specific form of work organization. Direct *control* of the production process during the period of Fordism's dominance was either achieved through continuous human monitoring and manipulation of powered devices (a system that was introduced in the textile factories in England a century earlier), or via very simple devices in the machine itself. These control devices were inflexible and usually designed for work on only one work-piece, hence their usefulness for mass production, supported by mass consumption. Ford's organization was also instrumental in making the latter possible, providing much higher than average wages to his machine operators, enabling them to purchase examples of the products of their labour themselves. This enhanced payment was also in part offered by Ford's system in exchange for the enhanced control that its overarching rationalism demanded. This somewhat less direct control of the production process, through control of its operators, was provided by supervision and, further up the managerial hierarchy, by various paper and pen techniques, supported by rudimentary office technologies, which were used to manipulate shop-floor data derived from punch cards, time sheets, and the like. It also, at perhaps its most extreme, supported and justified the work of the Ford Sociological Department (see Clarke 1992, for a fascinating account of the weird and wonderful activities of this infamous body).

The machines that made up the production lines of Ford and his imitators were themselves manufactured by machines, in much the same way as those devices that populated the mills and factories we considered earlier. The machines that make the parts assembled to make other productive machines are themselves known as *machine tools*. Machine tools cut away bits of a block of metal to make it into a useful shape, usually to form a part of another machine. Machine tools are really the guts of machine-based industry because they are the means whereby all machinery, including the machine tools themselves, are made (Noble 1985: 110).

Machine tools are traditionally controlled by machinists: skilled craftsmen who transmit their 'skill and purpose to the machine by means of cranks, levers, and handles' (1985: 110). This control involves complex and ongoing decision-making about how the work should proceed to achieve the end product, which must itself be visualized by the machinist. A range of highly developed skills is involved, with tacit knowledge (of which a longer discussion must wait until Chapter 10) built up through a lengthy apprenticeship and experience being of particular importance. Noble notes that during the nineteenth century a number of technical advances in machining occurred, some of which 'built some intelligence into the machine tools themselves' (1985: 110). Such innovations included 'automatic feeds, stops, throw-out dogs [and] mechanical cams' (1985: 110) which made the machines partially 'self-acting'. These changes relieved the operator of some manual tasks and, together with holding fixtures and jigs to guide the movement of the cutter, they did allow 'less skilled operators to use the machines to cut parts after they had been "set up" by more skilled men; but the source of intelligence was still the skilled machinist on the floor' (Noble 1985: 110).

Numerical Control (N/C) of machine tools (see also Noble 1979) that allowed the modifiable specification of work-piece dimensions was first introduced commercially in the United States in 1955 and its diffusion has carried on steadily since then. The system allowed 'the user' to control the path of a cutting tool by inputting a reprogrammable description of required tool movements. Thus metalworking began to undergo *direct* mechanization of the control dimension of the production process. These changes allowed small batch metalworking production to potentially be amenable to the same levels of mechanization and unit-cost reduction formerly restricted to mass production and 'hard automation' (Blackburn, Coombs, and Green 1985: 54).

More recently similar transformations have occurred, through computerization, within the clerical and other labour processes. The flexible production processes that such technologies are associated with, along with the more variegated patterns of consumption that they seek to meet, have been labelled 'neo-Fordism' (Aglietta 1979). Aglietta sees neo-Fordism as a system encompassing flexible technologies, such as N/C machine tools, along with a recomposition of the tasks involved in the production process. This recomposition, frequently appearing under the banner of 'job enrichment', is seen as a consequence of the removal of much of the heavy manual jobs at one end of the scale, along with removal of much of the skilled craft control and supervisory roles at the other. What remains are a number of interchangeable semi-skilled tasks that can be assigned, *by an appropriately informed managerial function*, to individuals and groups of workers in a number of ways. According to Labour Process Theory, this recomposition of tasks will reflect the dynamics of the capitalist social relations of production wherein these changes occur. We thus continue by focusing upon Noble's account of the development of N/C and CNC (Computer Numerical Control) of machine tools, which puts these capitalist relations of production centre stage.

Transforming work and informing management

Noble draws specific attention to the choices that were available, and those that were taken, in the design of automatically controlled machine tools. These choices are understood in terms of the social relations of capitalist production. According to Noble, the introduction of N/C and CNC machines led to a reorganization of the production process in metalworking 'in the direction of greater managerial control' (1985: 109). He identifies changes in both horizontal and vertical relations of production within metalworking. The former resulted in a shift towards concentration in the industry, towards a small number of large firms, with a large number of small firms falling by the wayside. The latter entailed 'a dramatic transfer of planning and control from the shopfloor to the office' (1985: 109). For the technological determinist, who sees technology both as *the result* of the application of knowledge of the material world in an effort to bend that world, and as *the cause* of the consequent organization of production necessitated by its use, these are simply the facts of life. N/C and CNC are seen to be more efficient and effective than the mechanizations of direct control of production (or the lack thereof) that they replaced; as merely more cunning ways of controlling devices which change the shape of metal which themselves require an appropriate organizational context to realize their promise. These 'other' changes in the organization of production—the creation of a smaller number of larger engineering firms; a new range of technical/managerial positions within them at various elevations within a consequently taller organizational hierarchy; and the consequent subversion of the craft skills of traditional machinists—are seen by the determinist as simply the by-products of seemingly inevitable technological change. Their realization is not seen to constitute one of the intentions behind N/C and CNC introduction. But such a view will not do for Noble. He seeks to follow the detail of the development of N/C and CNC in order to show how these shifts in relations are the result of deliberate strategies and choices—strategies and choices that sought, through managerial action, to increase capital's control of labour through the vehicle of technology. They thus cannot to be seen as mere by-products. Their achievement was, at least according to Noble, one of the key aims of the technology's introduction. He notes that 'this new technology was developed under the auspices of management within the large metalworking firms' (1985: 109). This alerts him to the possibility that the outcome was not purely driven by chance or efficiency. He seeks to answer the following questions:

> Is it just a coincidence that the technology tends to strengthen the market position of these firms and enhance managerial authority in the [machine] shop? Why did this new technology take the form that it did, a form which seems to have rendered it accessible to only some firms, and why only this technology? Is there any other way to automate machine tools, a technology, for example, which would lend itself less to managerial control? (1985: 109–10)

And, as Noble goes on to note: 'To answer these questions [we need to] take a closer look at the technology' (1985: 110).

Automating the control of machine tools

The first seemingly serious attempt to automate the control of machining occurred during the 1930s and 1940s when the so-called 'tracer technology' was developed. This allowed a recording of the movements of a skilled machinist to be made via the use of a sensor. This trace could then be 'played-back' to control the machine to cut a similar piece on its own. Since machine tools are general-purpose machines that are used to cut a huge variety of parts, a separate trace was required for each new part and the source of this trace remained embodied in the skills, tacit knowledge, and abilities of a machinist. The war spurred on these developments and the emergence of new sensing and moving devices held out the promise of complete automation of machine control. The trick, as far as manufacturers were concerned, was to do this without losing the versatility that currently resided in the inherently flexible technology and its craft based production process. They aimed to make the machine 'self-acting' without restricting its possible uses. Record-playback could provide such a system if recording and replay could be made sufficiently precise, but, as we have noted, it still left control in the hands of a machinist.

In the late 1940s an alternative mode of automation emerged, supported by the US Air Force and the Massachusetts Institute of Technology. This was the N/C system. In this system:

> The specifications for a part—the information contained in an engineering blueprint—are first broken down into a mathematical representation of the part, then into a mathematical description of the desired path of the cutting tool along up to five axes,[6] and finally into hundreds or thousands of discrete instructions, translated for economy into a numerical code, which is read and translated into electrical signals for the machine controls. The N/C tape, in short, is a means of formally circumventing the role of the machinist as the source of intelligence of production. (Noble 1985: 111)

The key question for Noble then is why N/C technology was developed in favour of record-playback technology. And one answer is immediately apparent from the statistics he mobilizes. Noble notes that between 1949 and 1959 (when the air force ceased its formal support of the development of N/C software), the military spent at least US$62 million on the research, development, and transfer of N/C. Only one commercial company put their own money into this research. In 1955, the air force 'undertook to pay for the purchase, installation, and maintenance of over 100 N/C machines in factories of prime subcontractors; the contractors, aircraft manufacturers, and their suppliers would also be paid to learn to use the new technology. In short, the air force created a market for N/C' (1985: 113).

Noble's key point here is that the air force support that made the development of N/C possible 'also helped determine the shape the technology would take' (1985: 113). The software for controlling these machines turned out to be the biggest problem that needed solving. It proved very difficult to replace the tacit, craft skills of the operators with mathematically derived, logical instructions. Various sites had differing levels of success in their attempts to make this transformation, with a variety of simple 'higher level' computer languages being invented for this purpose at a local site. However, a standard, but complex, software system, 'APT' (Automatically Programmed Tools), was developed that usurped locally developed languages. It was flexible and made up of very basic fundamental 'skeletons' of shapes of actions that were fleshed out for each particular case. This fleshing out required complex programming skills (not generally possessed by current workers) and large computers. Despite these problems, the . . . 'air force loved APT . . . it seemed to allow for rapid mobilization, for rapid design change, and for interchangeability between machines within a plant, between users and vendors, and between contractors and subcontractors throughout the country (presumably of "strategic importance" in case of enemy attack)' (1985: 114).

This usurping of local, simpler but less generic and hence less widely applicable, computer languages was initially resisted, but resistance was eventually overcome by 'higher level management, who had come to believe it necessary to learn how to use the new system for "business reasons" (cost-plus contracts with the air force)' (1985: 114). There were still huge problems with APT for all concerned, but these problems were most apparent for small manufacturers. Standardization retarded the development of simpler, alternative languages (which would have favoured smaller firms) and forced those who wanted to use N/C into dependence upon the controllers of APT development, upon large computers, and upon mathematically sophisticated programmers. Problems could be overcome by the large manufacturers through their receipt of air force subsidy, built in to the cost-plus invoicing system. Commercial users were not so fortunate. Any company that wanted military contracts had to use APT and together we can see how these changes served, over time, to concentrate the industry into a small number of large firms. As Noble notes: 'APT served the air force and the aircraft industry well, but at the expense of less well endowed competitors' (1985: 115).

Record-playback, it would seem, would have been an even better bet for small manufacturers, yet it was abandoned by their large competitors and small companies never even got to see it. The company producing the system was bought out by one of the major N/C manufacturers, who promptly shelved record-playback in order to continue their focus upon N/C systems. Many of the air force part specifications were, it has to be noted, too complex for either manual or record-playback production. N/C also promised to reduce manufacturing costs by reducing the need for both storage of dedicated jigs and traces and of employment of highly skilled and hence expensive machinists. But costs were not the only criterion. N/C also represented the computer age and the advent of the brave new world. Perhaps most importantly, it furthered an ideology that sought to remove control from unpredictable and belligerent workers and place it in the hands of the far more trustworthy and dependable management. It provided an automated route to the Taylorist goal of complete *management* control. And members of management were the ones taking the decision, with the support of the air force, to go for this technology. As Peter Drucker once observed: 'What is today called automation is conceptually a logical extension of Taylor's scientific management' (1967: 26). A desire for control of the workforce and work was what drove N/C and its successor CNC.

However, as Noble notes, this desire was not entirely satisfied. Tacit craft skills are still frequently required to moderate execution of programmes. Use of 'cheap', unskilled staff was resisted by well organized unions and, even when it could be deployed, unskilled labour proved costly, in particular when machine reliability was not 100 per cent (which it never was) and when errors could lead to the 'smash-up' of a very expensive machine. But the push towards complete automation that would eliminate both the need for, and the power of, skilled craftsmen is plain to see. For example, control panels on machines on the floor were frequently disabled, allowing only remote programming from a central office. This also served to ensure that the potentially 'subversive' (because of their unionization) machinists could not learn the new skills and reassert their power. Plans could also be kept out of the hands of potential spies. It is not an insignificant coincidence that N/C machines were first developed and deployed in the United States during the rabidly anti-Communist McCarthy era.

Creating management through information

Noble's account of the development of N/C and CNC machining is not only a story about managerial ends subverting those of labour in the technological transformation of the labour process, but is also a story about the construction of a place, a need, and the raw material required for managing at a distance. By creating representations of work amenable to remote control, in a language alien to that of those who previously controlled production, managers reveal themselves as the true users of N/C and CNC systems. Indeed, one could go further and suggest that managers, and the 'professional' programmers whose interests seem more similar to their own than those of the traditional shop-floor, are necessitated by the moves described. And this, at least, is a facet of the N/C–CNC story that is not unique to the peculiarities of machine tool control. We have recently come across attempts, to use the current argot, to 'empower' staff through the use of information systems in a number of clerical labour processes, attempts that are perhaps better captured, *pace* Noble, by notions of *managerial* empowerment at the expense of previously autonomous specialists. Consider the following example from a UK subsidiary of a foreign owned insurance company who recently computerized the support provided for their telephone based 'service consultants'.[7]

In this company, work scheduling lent itself to regulation through the sophisticated use of information and communication technologies (ICTs) and the term 'empowerment' was applied to describe how the implementation of such systems would reduce the need for close supervision. The suggestion was that the systems would effectively empower employees to organize and accomplish complex tasks. Instead of being a clerical worker who processes information and refers complex problems to others, the employee becomes a 'service consultant'—a proficient user of sophisticated software packages that take care of most of these problems. As the Assistant General Manager (IT) commented, these clerical workers, now have available to them not only the range of data, but the tool that starts to present it to them in a structured way. So you start to say you don't have your old specialists, you actually do now have people who are more broad in the range of things they can handle, in fact you are starting to develop people who can handle the totality of the interaction with the client. (Ezzamel, Lilley, Wilkinson, and Willmott 1996: 72)

By using ICTs, it is possible to replace (costly) specialists (e.g. underwriters) with software that asks for the relevant information and makes the necessary calculations. In this case, the concentration of diverse activities into the role of 'service consultant' was represented as the 'empowerment' of clerical workers rather than the redundancy of specialists, the achievements of software producers, or the power of new technology. It was apparent that the new role of the 'service consultant' was no less structured, and allowed very little increased discretion, than that of the traditional clerical worker. Indeed, the new technology allowed managers to structure the tasks more precisely and to monitor productivity more accurately. As the Assistant General Manager commented, revealingly reverting to the term 'clerk' to describe the job of the new 'service consultants',

The supervisor has available information about how many clerks have turned up today, and they schedule the work and allocate the work. So step by step they go through the steps. The first thing they do is maybe handle an application for a new piece of business, the system leads through what they do. The data is there, you have to make an underwriting decision. How do I make this decision? I invoke a bit of software . . . The underwriting package is in effect making available to this person the underwriting skills you have within the organisation, but it doesn't make it available to them through having to go and talk to a person. It makes it available through the software. (Ezzamel, Lilley, Wilkinson, and Willmott 1996: 72)

'Empowerment' is seemingly being used here as a code for increased responsibility and accountability, a theme to which we return in Chapter 7. Since commercial pressures necessitated a drive to achieve reductions in costs, improvements in quality, and a greater adaptability to market demands, the 'obvious' way to respond to such pressures was to require employees to absorb tasks (e.g. supervision, specialist skills, development) that had previously been undertaken by others—a process of absorption, rationalization, and in effect, intensification that could be more attractively described as empowerment. By taking a wider view of the processes of technological change, then, we see that the logic of the systems introduced with the industrialization of textile production continues to guide many of the changes that we witness in the contemporary workplace.

SUMMARY

The shapes of the technologies we see in use in organizations today were seen to be crystallizations of the outcomes of prior battles in an ongoing and inevitable war between labour and capital. Labour process analysis allowed us to focus upon the ways in which social relations affect the direction of technological change. It was argued that there are three dimensions of technological change: the *transformation* dimension of work; the *transfer* dimension of work; and the *control* dimension of work. The relative significance of each of these dimensions in directing was seen to shift markedly in the passage from the mechanization of the Industrial Revolution era to the so-called neo-Fordism of the present. The deliberate strategies and choices undertaken in the emergence of the N/C of machine tools and the shift to CNC of those tools allowed us to illustrate the virtue of a labour process analysis that is attendant to the specificities of the situation it seeks to describe. The story of this development was revealed as one in which managers were the real 'users' of information and the machines that generated it through the possibility of managing at a distance, at the expense of previously autonomous specialists, that was enabled through the creation of representations of work amenable to remote control. And it was a story whose plot we saw repeated in the contemporary account of the clerical labour process in which, once again, we saw increased responsibility and accountability being delivered through information technologies. But on this occasion the managerial benefits of that increased responsibility and accountability did not seem to accrue to the clerks who were its bearers. Rather we witnessed a technological process of absorption, rationalization, and intensification of tasks that could more palatably be described through that irrefuseable term, 'empowerment'.

▓ DISCUSSION QUESTIONS

1. Where can we currently see the notion of 'the user' being deployed to justify system specifications over which they have had little or no influence?

2. Are managers always to be seen as villains in stories of technological change? Is it possible to also see them as victims? Can you provide any current examples where such a view might apply?

3. What techniques and practices are used to ensure that managers pursue the ends of capital (accumulation) and not ends of their own?

4. Are the programmers, often mentioned but seldom centre stage in these stories, best seen as elements of a broadening managerial stratum or as the new embodiments of traditional craft labour?

5. Is managerial work really that separate from the work of direct production in a commercial world that is apparently increasingly populated by 'informational' and 'cultural' products?

▓ SUGGESTIONS FOR FURTHER READING

Rosen, M. and Baroudi, J. (1992). 'Computer-Based Technology and the Emergence of New Forms of Managerial Control', in A. Sturdy, D. Knights, and H. Willmott (eds.), *Skill and Consent: Contemporary Studies in the Labour Process Critical Perspectives on Work and Organization*. London: Routledge.

Braverman, H. (1974). *Labour and Monopoly Capital: The Degradation of Work in the Twentieth Century*. New York: Monthly Review Press.

2 | Information, Representation, and Organization

Introduction

In this chapter we will examine how we represent ourselves, others, and the material world, through models and information, as well as consider the implications of doing so. We do so through introducing you to what may be termed post-structural approaches to information, organization, and representation; approaches derived primarily from the work of Robert Cooper, particularly his paper *Formal Organization as Representation: Remote Control, Displacement and Abbreviation* (1992; see also 1993). Initially, these ideas may seem strange and difficult. However, upon reflection what will hopefully become apparent is that it is rather the conventional way which we talk about information and organization that is somewhat strange and that the difficulty initially experienced with post-structural approaches is in large part a resistance towards this recognition. Once again, it is the idea of the user that gives us our way in here.

When we think about the 'user' of an information system, the image that tends to spring to mind is that of an individual sitting in front of a keyboard and screen. However, in the commercial world at least, it is not these users who pay for the machines that they operate. Rather, information systems are built and paid for by organizations in which users work. But what happens when we try to think of *organizations* as the users of information systems? What does a focus upon organization enable? How does the notion of organization help us to understand the ways in which information systems are developed and used? To help us to answer these questions let's take another look at what is distinctive about *information* technologies.

What is special about information technologies?

According to Zuboff, information technology (IT) may be used to *automate* processes, in much the same way as other technologies have affected the workplace. But it may also *informate*.

> Informating technology . . . generates information about the underlying productive and administrative processes through which an organization accomplishes its work. It provides a deeper level of transparency to activities that had been either partially or completely opaque. In this way information technology supersedes the traditional logic of automation . . . Activities, events, and objects are translated into and made visible by information when a technology *informates* as well as *automates*. (1988: 9–10, emphasis in original)

When deployed in the workplace, IT, as its name suggests, provides information on work and *representations* of work that can accommodate the various sources of information within a wider model. This is the heart of its distinctiveness. It encourages, perhaps more than any other sort of technology, reflection upon how work is currently seen and conceptualized, and how it is currently organized. It potentially makes new representations, and the new knowledge and information with which they are associated, widely available. To take just one example (see Robson 1994), when the Ford Motor Company was confronted by problems with its existing and somewhat archaic purchasing system it initially planned to simply automate the manual, partially paper based, processes that had constituted this system. However, as part of the process of generation of alternative models for this task, they examined the practices of Mazda, a company with whom they were forming increasingly close links. Mazda had not only automated purchasing, but also redesigned all the job processes involved. This had resulted in a purchasing department of only five staff. This minuscule staffing made Ford's attempts to automate their processes seem somewhat modest. Ford, starting with a purchasing staff of around 500, had initially intended to *save* around 100 posts through their automation. Following the shocked realization of what Mazda had shown was possible, Ford's informated automation allowed them to reduce *total* purchasing staff to about 100. In the process, some deeply political toes were undoubtedly trodden upon—not least amongst those who found themselves 'empowered' to search for alternative employment outside the newly informated purchasing department! [1]

Representations, knowledge, and information are all intimately related with power. Shifts within these dimensions and particularly different shifts for different individuals are thus profoundly political. They may be understood as changes in the ways in which both we and others see what we and others do. The meaning and importance of various things, people, and events are thus almost inevitably thrown open to question.

Building the pyramids: The informational story of hierarchy

Many writers on organization have, in recent years, conceived of their objects of study as organizers and processors of information (e.g. Simon 1955; Galbraith 1974; Williamson 1975; but see also Boland 1987). The limited information processing capacities, or *bounded rationality* (Simon 1955),[2] of individuals is seen to necessitate organization to enhance and maximize the processing capacity of collectives. Thus the limited information processing capacity of humans appears here as both cause and justification of the extended hierarchies, which until relatively recently, we had been used to seeing as the archetype of organized administration. The argument runs something like this: if each of us can only process a limited amount of infor-mation, then to deal, in a reasonable amount of time, with complex matters that involve processing amounts of information that exceed these limits, we must organize ourselves in ways that enhance our collective information processing powers. In short, we must divide up the complexities of the world into humanly manageable parcels for subsequent reconstitution through the coordination offered by hierarchy. Hierarchy can seemingly solve our problems of bounded rationality through its capacity to ensure that the information processing powers of senior decision-makers are not overloaded: by making subordinates summarize information—passing only its most salient aspects to those above—and by making them apply pre-programmed rules to familiar problems—so that they only need to pass up exceptional cases

(Galbraith 1974; see also, Schotter 1981). Within such a view, it is only formally organized groups of individuals who stand a chance of dealing with the complex problems seemingly set by a modern society.

Representing

The story so far has, however, joined the performance in the middle of the second act. For before information can inform there must be some representation of the world that is altered by the 'new' information (MacKay 1969). A representation may be conceived as 'any structure (pattern, picture, model) whether abstract or concrete, of which the features purport to symbolize or correspond in some sense with those of another structure' (MacKay 1969: 161).

'300 million dollars was wiped off the value of shares yesterday' tells us nothing unless we are already in possession of a representational economy or arrangement in which 'dollars', amounts, and the idea of value (and for that matter its relation to stocks and shares) already mean or indicate something else with which we have some familiarity. In this case, the *relatively* unfamiliar would probably be shocked and worried and the *relatively* familiar annoyed that (yet again) processes in which value is lost are asymmetrically described as aberrations. Information can enhance or reduce the power of a representation but it can do nothing unless some form of representation already exists. Thus organizations do not merely process and organize information, 'they also construct [or at least possess] the forms in which information appears' (R. Cooper 1992: 255), that is, *representations*.

Returning to Zuboff (1988) we may go on to suggest that 'informating' is a process of representation, a process through which, in the case of IT, various aspects of 'the world' are translated into first, electronic impulses and second, traces that appear on our screens and paper documents. 'Things' are literally re-presented, their 'natural' presence being substituted by a technologically mediated presence elsewhere. But only certain sorts of representation will do here. Technologies (and organizations may be considered, following our initial line, as technologies for the processing of information) do not represent for nothing—they are tools for intervention in the world and, as such, one of their key *raisons d'être* is the facilitation of control. They enable control by translating the muddle of the world into the tidiness of information (see, also, D. Cooper 1983).

As Zuboff shows, information technology does precisely that: 'it absorbs and substitutes for the debriefed, implicit knowledge and skills of workers and managers' (R. Cooper 1992: 255).

Think back to the example at the end of the previous chapter. There we saw how the embodied skills of underwriters and other technical experts were captured, disembedded from their hosts, and subsequently realized on a computerized platform that makes no ongoing salary demands, 'it impersonalises the authorship of the system and so makes control less vulnerable to criticism' (R. Cooper 1992: 255).

Again, our financial services example is illuminating. Clerks may well have complained to managers about the way in which their work was being structured. Indeed, they may still complain about the way 'the system' structures their work. But while in the first case they can easily access the author of their instructions, in the latter this is almost always impossible. System designers and programmers are rarely, if ever, still present in organizations once users have taken 'ownership' of 'their' system. But this is only half of the point being made above. Common under-standings of 'technology' render it as a purely 'technical' solution to a pre-existing problem, and often as the 'best' solution that is currently 'technically' possible. To be against technology in such circumstances is to run a significant risk of being seen to be a 'Luddite', 'it makes information transparent and "instant" ' (R. Cooper 1992: 255).

We return here to examples from the rarefied world of high finance. Dealers' screens 'instantaneously' display changing share prices, prices which render the current 'values' of firms transparent, from which the movement of the market can be discerned. They do not, on the whole, display the complex causes of these move-ments at the level of productive activity. Indeed, it is infrequent, to say the least, that they even display causes at the market level, 'when information is uncoupled from its action context and represented symbolically, events can be manipulated and combined in new ways, so enabling greater control' (R. Cooper 1992: 255).

This is the traditional story of accounting, an organizational site, which has been amongst the most amenable to informating technological interventions. It is only through the translation of the complex operations of myriad organizational units into the set of figures taken to represent 'the bottom line' that multi-unit conglom-erates are able to compare performance between divisions and units. And it is upon this basis that they claim to allocate their limited resources in the most efficient and effective manner. Without this recombination of signs from disparate sources the very notion of a multidivisional firm is virtually meaningless.

In short, IT encapsulates a general function of all formal organizations: 'the need to make transparent what is opaque, to make present what is remote, and to manipulate what is resistant' (R. Cooper 1992: 255).

Zuboff (see also R. Cooper 1992) notes three aspects of this process as espe-cially relevant for understanding how technologies of representation function in organizations:

- symbols and devices substitute for direct human involvement with material, thus abstracting thought from action;
- displacements and transformations along informational networks substitute for the coordination of discrete acts; and[3]
- complexity is abbreviated—an easily and instantly read two-dimensional repres-entation on a terminal screen substitutes for a confusing three-dimensional world.

Hence the subtitle of Bob Cooper's 1992 paper—remote control, displacement, and abbreviation. But the main title is also informative—all techniques of representation (and formal organization as embodied in designed institutions is just one example) share these characteristics. IT merely 'hyperbolizes' them. 'Ironically' it is 'their constitutive ordinariness' that 'has led to their neglect in organizational analysis' in the past (R. Cooper 1992: 256).

In this view the inherent limitations or 'boundedness' of the human body is 'a required stimulus for representation' (R. Cooper 1992: 256). Just as we make and acquire chairs to supplement the shape of the human skeleton and compensate for the body's propensity for tiredness, and gloves to compensate for the frailty of the human hand and/or the body's propensity for coldness within temperate and polar climates (Scarry 1985), so do we organize information to compensate for our limited capacity to deal with the complex world with which we are increasingly confronted.

Representational environment and economy

> As representations, techniques, and artefacts are *embodied* . . . processes that remedy and compensate for the body's deficiencies and, at the same time, extend, magnify and make more durable its power. In short, representations embody a principle of economy which turns losses into gains. (R. Cooper 1992: 256–7, original emphasis)

The notion of 'economy' here is intended to indicate the symbiotic exchanges between the three interrelated elements delineated by both Cooper and Zuboff. *Remote control* of 'things' is only possible if 'things' can be made mobile or *displaced*. Through displacement key aspects of a phenomenon, such the performance of an organizational sub-unit, are re-presented in a symbolic form, a form that enables symbols to be moved from the site of their production to other sites where other things may be done. Significant attributes of the objects of our interest are decontextualized and subsequently recontextualized in a symbolic economy in which new meanings and possible actions can be derived. To return to our current organizational example, the condensed 'activities' of a sub-unit, in terms of, say, financial inputs, outputs, and hence 'performance', may be combined with similarly condensed stories about other units. Together these bits of information enable a new, more abstract view of activities that makes up a performance map of a diverse group of activities in common form. On the basis of this new informational arrangement, resource allocation decisions can seemingly be made on the basis of a 'level playing field', or at least a level reporting field. This process is perhaps most pronounced in organizations such as GEC (now known, at least at the time of writing, as Marconi) where Weinstock's (Chairman from 1963 to 1996) notorious ratios, such as rate of return on investment, were the only figures that were taken to count, at least at the corporate level.

What is most striking about these figures is their parsimony. These figures, for Weinstock at least, capture the very essence of a business in the smallest possible space. ROI, 15 per cent. In Cooper's terms, these representations are abbreviated. Made as small as possible, to travel as cheaply as possible, with only the essence of the represented object making it through to the new symbolic economy in which it will be combined with other such figures. Only abbreviated representations can do this. As Cooper notes: 'one may not be able to move the mountain itself but it is easy to move a model or map of it' (1992: 257). Abbreviation . . . 'simplifies the complex, makes the big into the small, converts the delayed into the instantaneous. It works according to a principle of condensation in which as much as is needed is condensed into as little as is needed so as to enable ease and accuracy of perception and action' (R. Cooper 1992: 258).

Within these processes that seek to enable remote control, 'symbols and other prosthetic devices' are substituted 'for direct human involvement of the body and its senses' (R. Cooper 1992: 257).

> Administrators and managers, for example, do not work directly on the environment but on models, maps, numbers and formulae which represent that environment; in this way they can control complex and heterogeneous activities at a distance and in the relative convenience of a centralized work station (R. Cooper 1992: 257)

But there is a price to pay—even in a representational economy there is no such thing as a free lunch. The essence, the aspect of the object that counts, is always defined by the overarching representational economy in which it will become embedded and embodied. The particularities of local circumstance simply will not do here. Consider the case of the Body Shop's continued attempts to create a new model of business exigencies in the face of hostility from a sceptical financial community. For while financiers may be aware that the Body Shop's success depends in part upon attention to such unconventional 'ethical' issues, this does not and cannot matter except to the extent to which it influences the 'bottom line', the only figure(s) that count at the level of investment decision-making.[4] We can say, then, that regardless of what in particular interests us about performance at a lower hierarchical level in our monitoring and control system, we only get to see and compare it at a higher level through similar techniques and logics of representation. Remote control always remains remote. Whenever representation intervenes to ensure that control is exercised, that control will (and must) be exercised at a remove. '[R]epresentation is always a substitution for or re-presentation of the event and never the event itself' (R. Cooper 1992: 257). We finish this chapter by considering one example in more detail.

Representational techniques in practices

We return again to the rarefied world of high finance as it relates, through mortgage bonds, to the financing of home loans; an arena that witnessed an explosion of activity during the mid-1980s.

> Formerly sleepy thrifts became some of the biggest swingers in the bond market. Despite their dwindling numbers, the thrifts as a group nearly doubled in asset size, from $650 billion to $1.2 trillion, between 1981 and 1986. (Lewis 1989: 134)

However, we do not start here. Rather we begin with a more comfortable description of how money used to be made available for home purchase in order to trace the role played by representation in the emergence of a new system of home purchase financing. According to ex-Salomon Brothers salesman, Michael Lewis (1989), prior to the advent of mortgage bonds, the financing of home ownership was carried out principally by 'thrifts': the Savings and Loans organization that fulfil a role in the United States similar to that fulfilled by building societies in the United Kingdom. Up until the end of the seventies thrifts had few contacts with the wider financial community, at least not with its more dynamic and volatile incarnations. And this insulated view was seemingly shared on both sides of the divide.

> [I]n 1978 on Wall Street, it was crazy to think that home mortgages could be big business. Everything about them seemed small and insignificant, at least to people who routinely advise CEOs and heads of state. (Lewis 1989: 97)

Representational techniques had not taken full hold here as they had done elsewhere in the financial jungle. Traders who were used to dealing in stocks, shares, and government and company bonds, and indeed in the endlessly nested international financial instruments that were multiply derived from these bases, did not yet see mortgages as amenable to trading. This, in part, was due to the fact that representations of mortgages, the deals struck between lenders and borrowers, were extremely localized phenomena tied to bricks, mortar, and specific individualized owners and lenders.

> The problem was more fundamental than a disdain for Middle America (sic). Mortgages were not tradeable pieces of paper; they were not bonds. They were loans made by savings banks that were never supposed to leave the savings banks. A single home mortgage was a messy investment for Wall Street, which was used to dealing in bigger numbers. No trader or investor wanted to poke around the suburbs to find out whether the home owner to whom he had just lent money was creditworthy. For the home mortgage to become a bond it had to be depersonalised. (Lewis 1989: 99)

Home mortgages were thus not only too small to be of interest to the big wheelers of Wall Street, they were also too attached to local contingencies. The breaking of these local attachments and the subsequent combination of individual deals were required if mortgage bonds were to emerge as depersonalized investments that could be bought and sold by anyone on an open market. This did not necessarily mean anything directly to those whose mortgages made up these bonds, for the representational moves through which they were constructed were all carried out at an increasing level of remove and abstraction.

> At the very least, a mortgage had to be pooled with other mortgages of home owners. Traders and investors would trust statistics and buy into a pool of several thousand

mortgage loans made by a Savings and Loan, of which, by the laws of probability, only a small fraction should default. Pieces of paper could be issued that entitled the bearer to a pro rata share of the cash flows from the pool, a guaranteed share of a fixed pie . . . Thus standardized, the pieces of paper could be sold to an American pension fund, to a Tokyo trust company, to a Swiss bank, to a tax evading Greek shipping tycoon living in a yacht in the harbour of Monte Carlo, to anyone with money to invest. Thus standardized, the pieces of paper could be traded. All the trader would see was the bond. All the trader wanted to see was the bond. A bond he could whip and drive.[5] 'A line which would never be crossed could be drawn down the centre of the market. On one side would be the homeowner, on the other, investors and traders'. (Lewis 1989: 99–100)

Through such processes, mortgage bonds could potentially be made attractive to investors, although it is important to note that much more was required before they could assume this position with ease. An initial 'technical' problem centred upon the peculiar nature, compared to other investments, of mortgage redemption, that is, that the loan could be repaid at any time, usually without penalty.

Whoever bought the [mortgage] bonds was, in one crucial respect, worse off than buyers of corporate and government bonds: he couldn't be certain how long the loan lasted. If an entire neighbourhood moved (paying off its mortgages), the bondholder, who had thought he owned a thirty-year mortgage bond, found himself sitting on a pile of cash instead. More likely, interest rates fell and the entire neighbourhood refinanced its thirty-year fixed-rate mortgages at the lower rate.[6] This left the mortgage bondholder holding cash. Cash was no problem if the investor could reinvest it at the same rate interest as the original loan, or at a higher rate. But if interest rates had fallen the investor lost out; for his money would not earn the same rate of return as before. (Lewis 1989: 101–2)

A secondary 'technical' problem was the nature of 'guarantee' offered on the product. Government bonds, backed as they are by an explicit guarantee from the state, tend to offer a lower rate of interest to investors than that available on commercial interest bearing bonds which can offer no such explicit recourse in the event of failure.[7] Given no desire on the part of traders and investors to 'poke around the suburbs' and engage in a personal assessment of investment risk, such a guarantee was seen to be an essential backing for bonds in mortgages, if they were to be 'depersonalized' and thus trade successfully. A small proportion of the loans made by thrifts already possessed such a guarantee. These were the so-called 'Ginnie Mae' backed products. Ginnie Mae, the US Government National Mortgage Association (GNMA), insured the home loans of lower income families against default, ensuring that the thrifts would serve this risky end of the market. It was this seemingly precise form of guarantee that was required to turn what were previously mere collections of varying individual mortgages into standardized bonds. Indeed, other similar guarantee devices have emerged to cover other US mortgages, although their link to the state is more implicit, but nevertheless seemingly still robust, than that offered by Ginnie Mae. The two principal forms of these guaranteeing organizations in the United States are the Freddie Mac (Federal Home Loan Mortgage Corporation) and the Fannie Mae (Federal National Mortgage Association). While these guarantees were seen to be essential to successful trading of mortgage bonds, they were not seen as ideal by traders, principally because they reinstitutionalized the borrower's right to (penalty free) early redemption.

These 'technical' considerations were not, however, the sole requirements for the development of a market. For, as Lewis points out:

> [A] trader [was] . . . also needed . . . to make markets in the bonds that [had been] . . . created, and that was a bigger problem. The trader was absolutely crucial. The trader bought and sold the bonds. A big name trader inspired confidence in investors, and his presence alone could make a market grow. (1989: 104)

Well, not quite. For as Lewis' account also makes clear, there was little initial enthusiasm for the bonds on the part of investors. The trader had to go out to investors and sell the market, and sell it hard. But he could only do that once products had been constructed that could be sold. Salomon Brothers was instrumental in all the key steps in this process. Initially, it was they who lobbied government hardest to extend the form of guarantee available through Ginnie Maes to a broader range of mortgages, through the creation of Fannie Maes and Freddie Macs. 'If Lewie [Ranieri, Head of Salomon Brothers' newly formed Mortgage Trading Department] didn't like a law, he'd just have it changed', explains one of his traders (Lewis 1989: 118).

They were also involved in the (albeit partial) solution of the problem of indeterminacy over the length of the loans from which mortgage bonds were derived. According to Lewis (1989):

> The CMO [Collateralised Mortgage Obligation] burst the dam between several trillion investable dollars looking for a home and nearly 2 trillion dollars of home mortgages looking for an investor. The CMO addressed the chief objection for buying mortgage securities, still voiced by everyone but thrifts and a handful of adventurous money managers: who wants to lend money not knowing when they'll get it back? To create a CMO, one gathered hundreds of millions of dollars of ordinary mortgage bonds—Ginnie Maes, Fannie Maes and Freddie Macs. These bonds were placed in a trust. The trust paid a rate of interest to its owners. The owners had certificates to prove their ownership. These certificates were CMOs. The certificates, however, were not all the same. Take a typical 300-million-dollar CMO. It would be divided into three 'tranches' or slices of 100 million dollars each. Investors in each tranche received interest payments. But the owners of the first tranche received all principal repayments from all 300 million dollars of mortgage bonds held in trust. Not until first tranche holders were entirely paid off did second tranche investors receive any prepayments. Not until both first and second tranche investors had been entirely paid off did the holder of a third tranche certificate receive prepayments . . . Now, at last, investors had a degree of certainty about the length of their loans. (Lewis 1989: 160–1)

Markets such as these are the result of intensive representational design and marketing on the part of those who act as intermediaries in 'the market' and its constituent 'commodities' that are created in this process. This point becomes even more explicit when one considers developments, or 'refinements', in the 'instruments' (to use the appellation of the financial community) traded on such markets:

> After the first CMO (collateralised mortgage obligation), the young Turks of mortgage research and trading found a seemingly limitless number of ways to slice and dice home mortgages. They created CMOs with five tranches, and CMOs with ten tranches. They split a pool of home mortgages into a pool of interest payments and a pool of principal payments, then sold the rights to the cash flows from each pool (known as IOs and POs, after interest only and principal only) as separate investments. The homeowner didn't know it, but his interest payments might be destined for a French speculator, and his principal repayments for an insurance company in Milwaukee. In perhaps the strangest alchemy, Wall Street shuffled the IOs and POs around and glued them back together to create home mortgages that could never exist in the real world. (Lewis 1989: 163)

As the process continued other 'benefits' became apparent, benefits only realizable within the idealizations of space and time that make up a representational economy:

> Many 'new products' invented by Salomon Brothers were outside the rules of the regulatory game; they were not required to be listed on thrift balance sheets and therefore offered a way for thrifts to grow. In some cases, the sole virtue of a new product was its classification as 'off-balance sheet' . . . To attract new investors and to dodge new regulations, the market became ever more arcane and complex. (Lewis 1989: 163–4)

So what we witness here is a series of policies, both governmental and private, that seek to influence and/or benefit from the provision of loan finance to home buyers. However, these 'policies' are not directly applied to the processes of exchange that constitute the loan-financed house buying. Rather they seek to control and exploit the movement of sets of figures that stand for the overall economy of home financing. But CMOs and their complex recombinations are not that economy. They remain at a huge remove from the multifarious complex of processes that contribute to our ability to purchase a property. This level of remove is perhaps made most tellingly apparent when we begin to witness the 'failure' of many thrifts towards the end of the 1980s. For while many problems of a significant size and nature certainly resulted from this crisis, it is also pretty apparent that Americans did not suddenly stop buying themselves homes and that these purchases continued to be financed, in the main, by borrowed capital.

Representational devices and power

This case is not a particularly unusual one. Economic management, indeed all manner of modern government and management, is conducted through the conduit of representational devices. But control that remains remote is not the only cost to be borne by those who retreat into a representational economy. As we have already hinted, modern technologies and the representations on which they depend are productive of power[8] through their 'technical' detachment from the messiness of the world and its relatively *direct* relations with the human body.

So what is the source of the power that we are confronted with here? As our representational devices move into the world, translating its muddle into tidiness, they become imbued with a power that is the consequence of changes in the world that are themselves brought about through the act of representing. In the process of representation the elements that are seen to make up the world and the relations between them are altered. For example, the financial accounts of a company become that company, at least for those who seek to make investment decisions on the basis of such results. Indeed, one can go further: we are starting to be able to see financial analysts' predictions of company 'results' as 'causes' of those self-same results as worried senior managers struggle to make sure that they meet market expectations (see, for example, Macintosh 2002). In effect, the world becomes changed 'in the direction of representational convenience so that the world becomes more like our representations and less like the world' (R. Cooper 1993: 286). Our control, our power, will not remain remote so long as we remake the world in the image of our representations of it. We get to be in control but only of a denatured world, a world of representation, rather than one which is apprehended in its own terms, whatever those may be. And this is perhaps why remote control seems to work best in the sphere of accounting and accountants than in that of the less tightly ordered arenas and actors of the more 'artistic' world of production design (Armstrong and Tomes 1996). It is also why we never finally achieve the control we seem to be seeking. It is always on the horizon of the future, never with us in the here and now.

▓ SUMMARY

Organizations as well as individuals are key users of information systems and technologies. IT may be used, like more traditional technologies, to *automate* processes, but because it is able to generate information about and to provide additional transparency to those processes it may also be said to *informate*. In so doing it may not only provide information on work but also new representations of work, that can accommodate a variety of information from a variety of sources within a wider model. Representations, knowledge, and information are all intimately related with power. For changes in the ways in which things (and people) are seen are likely to simultaneously constitute changes in the ways in which things (and people) are valued. Representations do not just symbolize some other structure, they also 'construct' the forms in which information appears, enabling it to inform. Representation, when allied with information, seems to operate in some fairly consistent ways, which have considerable benefits for organizing. It simplifies and 'abbreviates' complex phenomena and events, allowing them to be 'displaced' to centres of calculation in which 'remote control' can be exercised. But these processes of representation also have costs. We find ourselves dealing with a world that is impoverished and lacking in detail and specificity, which exists either at a remove from the 'real' world or, perhaps worse, comes to replace it. We illustrated these ideas through consideration of the development of the mortgage bond market in the United States in the mid-1980s in order to witness the ways in which control remains remote in representation (at least until we have entirely remade the world in the image of our representations of it).

▓ DISCUSSION QUESTIONS

1. Who are 'the users' of financial representations of commercial activity?

2. Is there any limit to the decoupling of information and context, or does a tether always remain? Consider the ways in which the 'real' economy and financial trading are linked.

3. Is abbreviation a benefit or a cost for those who seek to organize on a grand scale?

4. In what senses does information, in this representational view, inform?

5. Can information ever, as Zuboff claims, be transparent and instant?

▓ SUGGESTIONS FOR FURTHER READING

One of our key sources for this chapter, and one of the best and clearest accounts of this some-what difficult approach to understanding organizational practices around information and technology, is Robert Cooper's (1992) 'Formal Organization as Representation: Remote Control, Displacement and Abbreviation', Chapter 13 in M. I. Reed and M. Hughes (eds.), *Rethinking Organization: New Directions in Organization Theory and Analysis*. London: Sage.

▓ OTHER USEFUL SOURCES INCLUDE:

Baudrillard, J. (1983). *Simulations*. New York: Semiotext(e).

Baudrillard, J. and Poster, M. (1988). *Jean Baudrillard: Selected Writings Stanford*. Stanford, CA: Stanford University Press, particularly chapter 7.

Cooper, R. (1993). 'Technologies of Representation', in P. Ahonen (ed.), *Tracing the Semiotic Boundaries of Politics*. Berlin: Mouton de Gruyter.

Macintosh, N. B. (2002). *Accounting, Accountants and Accountability: Poststructuralist Positions*. Routledge Studies in Accounting Series. London: Routledge.

Poster, M. (1990). *The Mode of Information: Poststructuralism and Social Context*. Cambridge: Polity Press and Basil Blackwell.

Roszak, T. (1986). *The Cult of Information: The Folklore of Computers and the True Art of Thinking*. Cambridge: Lutterworth.

3 | The Conceptual Basis of Information Systems: Modelling the World

---

KEY CONCEPTS

autopoiesis	model
boundaries	living system
complexity	objective
control	output
decision support systems	self-perpetuation
design	simulation
environment	subsystem
General Systems Theory	system
holism	Systems Theory
input	

KEY THEMES

When you have read this chapter, you should be able to define those key concepts in your own words, and you should also be able to:

1. Understand the System Theory approach and systems thinking.
2. Appreciate the historical background of General Systems Theory (GST).
3. Explain the different meanings, uses, and implications of the term 'system'.
4. Explain the links between systems, power, and control.
5. Assess the main characteristics of 'systems' known to you.

Introduction

In this chapter we explore Systems Theory. We examine the theoretical roots of this mode of thinking, as well as its current role in the models that seemingly organize information for contemporary managers, to enable us to discuss the implications of viewing the world from a systems perspective.

From system to System Theory

'System' is a word that seems to have found a huge array of comfortable sites, both within established academic disciplines and within those areas of discourse that are less obviously ordered. We have solar systems, central nervous systems, administrative systems, information systems, gambling systems,[1] school systems, cell systems, admission systems, ecological systems, economic systems, weapons systems, digestive systems, stereo systems, benefits systems, road systems, financial systems, and control systems to name but a few.

However, views about 'systems' seem to be highly ambivalent—we want a system to save our effort, but we hate having to do something because of 'the system'. As such we seem to love 'beating the system' but note with relish, when others fail to do so, that 'you *can't* beat the system'. This sort of talk about systems seems closest to, and is informed by, one strand of 'systems thinking', a relatively explicit engineering view—with a notion of systems as the outcome of (human) design. However, there is also another body of work, in many ways distinct but in many ways related, that sees systems as in some senses beyond design, as entities possessing *emergent* properties that serve, above all else, to self-perpetuate. Whatever the initial 'source' of the system, at a certain point the system takes on a life of its own, or to use the jargon, becomes *autopoietic*. And in the case of systems where humans are involved, those we normally assume to be its masters can become servants instead. 'Negative' views about systems, such as those caricatured above, perhaps reflect the response of an individualistic culture to the nascent realization that even when we think we are in control (in fact, *particularly* when we think we are) it is not 'us' who is *really* in control. We are seemingly, like many state governments, in office but not in power. One only need to consider the potential double meaning of *being in control* to exemplify the point. Are we *within control*, in the periphery, under the central control of something or someone else? Or are we *at the centre* of things, in the position of power, directing the periphery? Where is 'in'? Systems are slippery things, being plagued by these sorts of issues and, consequently, they are worthy of a little more attention.

According to Luchsinger and Dock (1976; reprint 1988: 3)

The term 'system' has five fundamental implications. These are:

1. A system must be 'designed' to accomplish an objective.
2. The elements of a system must have an established arrangement.
3. Interrelationships must exist among the individual elements of a system and these must be synergistic in nature.
4. The basic ingredients of a process (the flows of information, energy, and materials) are more vital than the basic elements of a system.
5. Organization objectives are more important than the objectives of its elements, and thus, there is a de-emphasis of the parochial objectives of the elements of the system.

In the following definition, which clearly bears many similarities to that provided by Luchsinger and Dock, a system is explicitly seen to include a mixture of human and non-human elements, an insight that was most happily seized upon by those researchers who have come to be known as socio-technical systems theorists, most prominently members of the London Tavistock Institute and their associates (see, for example, the work of Frank Emery and Eric Trist 1969, and that of Enid Mumford 2003).[2] Such views draw explicit attention to the human side or nature of systems as their most interesting aspect, advertising the utilitarian nature of much thought in the systems tradition. Systems here are clearly seen to be the product of design on the part of humans who are seen to be anything but 'disinterested'. They may also be seen to lay the foundations for the latter and continuing focus in the field of information systems upon the seemingly ubiquitous body of the user. Jenkins (1969: 6) summarizes the 'main properties of systems' thus:

1. A system is a complex grouping of human beings and machines.
2. Systems may be broken down into sub-systems, the amount of sub-system detail depending upon the problem being studied. Flow-block diagrams provide a readily understood way of describing these sub-systems.
3. The outputs from a given sub-system provide the inputs for other sub-systems. Thus the performance of a given sub-system interacts with the performance of other sub-systems and hence cannot be studied in isolation.
4. The system being studied will usually form part of a hierarchy of such systems. The systems at the top are very important and exert considerable influence on the systems lower down.
5. To function at all, a system must have an objective, but this is influenced by the wider system of which it forms part. Usually, systems have multiple objectives which are in conflict with one another, so that an overall objective is required which effects a compromise between these conflicting objectives.
6. To function at maximum efficiency, a system must be designed in such a way that it is capable of meeting its overall objective in the best way possible.

Notions of system can be traced a long way back. How far back seems to depend upon how important a 'pedigree' is for the particular devotee in question. In Management theory, Barnard is invoked as an early disciple, in Sociology, Parsons, and in Philosophy the name of Hegel is happily bandied about. Indeed '. . . the philosophical roots of general systems theory go back . . . *at least* to the German philosopher Hegel' (1770–1831) (Kast and Rosenzweig 1972, reprint 1988: 12, our emphasis).

The notion of GST is primarily associated with the name of Ludwig von Betalanffy, who coined the term in 1950. The ideas associated with general systems are often seen as an abstraction of the ideas about living 'systems' that had become fashionable in the biological sciences.[3] Von Betalanffy sought to broaden their applicability, hence the notion of GST. And he was very successful. Indeed, a small industry developed initially around the questions of what GST was or was not and what it could and could not be applied to (see the readings in Wetherbe, Dock, and Mandell 1988) with large numbers of expensive international conferences being devoted to the consideration of these pressing issues. Subsequently, the systems idea, partly through its universal appeal, has continued to command considerable interest and considerable expenditure on the international conference circuit. Much of this appeal has, of course, been given additional impetus by the notion that this idea in some ways belongs to those technologists of information who wish to claim the future as their own. However, for our purposes, the fundamental characteristics of systems themselves described above will do. In short, systems are seen to be organizations of elements through which goal-directed processes occur. We explore the more contradictory aspects of the system metaphor through consideration of information systems. For when we look at the characteristics of systems outlined by Luchsinger and Dock (1976) and Jenkins (1969), a number of questions spring to mind. And, as will soon become apparent, these questions are not amenable to easy answers.

Designed by whom? Or what?

For Jenkins it would seem that the answer to this question must be filled by a human or collection of humans. However, the ultimate systems question that may be seen to motivate the field in its broadest aspects is surely whether there is an ultimate Creator of life, in whose image we are made and from whom we derive our own 'creativity'. Or whether, following Dawkins (1976; but more directly, 1986), we ourselves are simply components or elements within a greater mechanism functioning without purposive direction. Dawkins' claim, that the mechanism which produces 'life' is akin to a 'blind watchmaker', is the same as saying that the resulting products, despite their apparent perfection and complexity, are not 'designed' (in the sense of being a conscious product) at all. Such a view threatens the very heart of Luchsinger and Dock's checklist and its own derivation from very different biological ideals to those favoured by Dawkins, while it totally overwhelms Jenkins' parochial, humanistic concerns. One way out, of course, is to allow almost anything to take the role of designer, including seemingly abstract and sanguine imperatives such as the one that we, following luminaries such as Darwin and Dawkins, term 'evolution'.[4] However, if we accept a broad-based answer to the question of who or what does the designing, other questions open up. In the somewhat more prosaic world of management systems design, the question is seemingly translated into a focus upon 'the user'. We may return to our question as to who uses systems and seek to base our systemic efforts on the answers we receive to this question, attempting to build a system that is both under the user and enables 'user control'. Two points are noteworthy here. The first is the oft-noted separation of user and designer and the problems attendant upon it. That is, that there would be no 'user problem' if users designed their systems themselves. Remember the tyre swing cartoon we encountered in the Introduction! The second is related but, perhaps, more fundamental in nature. It concerns the 'in control' issue we considered briefly earlier. For when a system includes a space specifically designed for a user (however general or specific that space and user might be) we may reasonably ask if the user who fills that space can be seen as anything more than an element within that system. We return to this point, with some empirical detail, in Chapter 7.[5]

Is everything a system?

Obviously, Luchsinger and Dock, are attempting to answer this question by prescribing what will count on the basis of whether their five fundamentals implications can be seen to pertain to the putative system (indeed, Jenkins' checklist functions in a similar way). But as we noted in our introduction to this chapter, many disparate 'things' are deemed to warrant the title of 'system'. And this may be for precisely the reasons we have been considering: that assessments of the applicability of the five fundamental implications or of the existence of the six main properties are not unproblematic or easily achieved. Each implication identified by Luchsinger and Dock and each property described by Jenkins potentially opens up an endless line of inquiry. A hermeneutic circle within which meaning can, at best, be approached but never finally decided upon (see Boland 1987, for an example of the application of the ideas of hermeneutics to the field of information systems design), a circle that can never finally be broken, except, of course, by the arbitrariness of the arbitration of convention. We have each, and in each circumstance, drawing no doubt upon conventions such as those delineated by both Jenkins and Luchsinger and Dock, to judge what is a system and what is not. For a list of rules that includes rules of application of those selfsame rules is *theoretically* infinite regardless of how closure is practically enabled (see Gödel's Incompleteness Theorem, and the work of Russell and Wittgenstein (discussed in Chapter 10), mobilized in terms of expert systems by Collins 1987).

What is 'in' the system and what outside? Or, to put it another way, which parts are 'system' and which 'environment'?

For the notion of 'a system' to be meaningful there must be a 'not system', an aspect of reality which functions as a foil against which that entity considered to be 'the system' is displayed. In Systems Theory this space is known as 'the environment' and it is constituted by the world beyond the system, or more precisely, beyond the system boundary. The relation of the system to its environment provides a point of significant bifurcation for systems theory. For on the basis of this relation systems are deemed to be either 'closed' or 'open'. A closed system is one that does not transact with its environment, by virtue of being either self-contained or all encompassing. Most systems that are seen to be of interest, particularly intellectual interest, are, however, 'open'. Indeed, it is their openness that opens up their interest. An open system can, and does indeed have to, transact with its environment. In the process it may give up some of itself to the environment or indeed, consume some of that environment, making it part of the system as both system and environment change, or evolve over time (see, for example, Ashby 1958). Or to put it another way, the boundary of an open system is both permeable and potentially able to move. Such systems are often seen to be coterminous with or to include those systems that are deemed to be 'living', in the broadest sense of the term. It is this mobility between system and environment, both in terms of exchange and transformation, that gives the field of open systems such endless questions to address. Among these is the endlessly moot point over whether the boundary of a system is seen to be part of the system, part of the environment, part of neither, or part of both. Consider, for example, the human body as 'living system'. At first sight the human is clearly contained within a skin that delineates system from environment, a skin that belongs to the body. However, think in a little more detail about digestion. Where does it occur? Somewhat counter-intuitively we find that digestion goes on 'outside' the body, at least if we take the inside to be that which is underneath the skin. Nutrients are extracted from food in a canal that runs from our mouth to our anus.[6] Those nutrients are taken in to the body, but not when we eat them, rather when they are absorbed into those widely extended parts of our tissues that are adjacent to the canal's walls. Topologically then, the human body is a doughnut, a form in which inside and outside are perennially confusable. Or consider the body as it appears with another system, the body of the user of a computerized information system. As Collins (1987) among others has made clear, a system that does not take account of what its user brings to the party is inherently *useless*. A sophisticated medical diagnosis system will not enable an illiterate to engage in any meaningfully enhanced self-diagnosis, neither is it likely to be seen as of much additional use by an 'expert' in the field. It may however significantly enhance the diagnostic powers of a semi-expert, at least to the extent to which diagnosis can be seen as a systematic practice. Where is the user to be located in such circumstances? Is he or she part of the system, part of the environment, or part of both, as constitutor or container of the potentially mobile boundary between them?

Is a system a 'thing' or is 'systems' merely a way of looking at 'things'?

As we noted above, it seems that the endlessly ramifying questions we have to ask in order to judge whether a particular arrangement of elements is a system make the latter possibility more convincing here. However, we undoubtedly do witness arrangements that seem to possess 'a life of their own', irrespective of our descriptions of them. It seems clear that no one *consciously* intends to construct, say, a prison system which produces bands of up-skilled, 'professional' villains.[7] However, such products are certainly one of the most consistent outcomes of Western penal practice, as penal reform groups continually remind us.

Taking the alternative view, that it all depends how and where we are looking, and crucially, for what purpose, does not however save us from difficult questions. Take the most overused words in business courses on the threats and opportunities associated with an information age, the seemingly ubiquitous Management Information System. Is such a notion intended to alert us to issues surrounding the *management* of information? Or are we expected to grasp the ways in which we can use *information* to manage? Are we interested in the Information System—or the Management System? Despite the seemingly straightforward and rational nature of this subject, even the very terms used to describe it as a separate field are unstable. The terms, and no less their referents, once separated and fixed, tend to change positions and invert their relationships. The management of information becomes management through information and vice versa. And it is the idea of system that does the real damage here. For a system must always have an objective to which other aspects are subordinate. In a systemic view we can have information management or we can have management information, but we cannot have both at the same time.

How do we define (or divine) the objective of a system? How do we know that it is the *overall* objective that we have happened upon?

Conventionally the objective of a system, in the enlightened end-user computing times in which we live, is the need that is satisfied in the user by system use. This tautology is, however, never as simple as it seems. Consider a University System and the users of that system. To the student it may appear that the objective of an individual university is to educate the student and his or her peers. However, the academics expected to participate in the fulfilment of this objective may believe and act as though the 'real' objective of the university is to support and promote research of an 'internationally recognized' standard. And cynics may view the arrangement as a societal mechanism for sorting sheep from goats according to criteria that bear little or no relation to capacity or willingness to learn.[8] For professional and political administrators in the sector, we find attempts to balance between these two extremes, usually based upon ensuring the continued financial well-being of the institution. This balancing between two contradictory views is enabled by translating both into the common language par excellence of money. Crucially, then, such attempts to balance 'make sense' only in the context of a capitalistic system of accumulation and only in so far as a university can be seen to be an enterprise like any other business. It is far from clear where we should stand in order to assess the rectitude of the situation, for clearly the University 'System', such as it is, is amenable to multiple meaningful characterizations which may or may not contradict each other. What is not clear is what the overall objective, in Jenkins' sense, might be. We are left with a no-choice choice. Either we cannot decide what the overall objective is, or we are forced to accept an impoverished objective which does little to inform us about the particularities of the specific system that confronts us, for the objective is one which is so 'overall' that it applies to all systems. Obvious candidates include, for those with a disinterested bent, a desire for self-perpetuation, while the interested might favour a desire for perpetuation of capitalist relations of ownership, control, and accumulation.

Within the supposedly more practical world of informational support for business activities it is not surprising to find that similar games may be played.[9] For when we look at the details of any particular example, it soon becomes apparent that opinion is divided over what a particular system is supposed to do between individuals with differing relations to that system. Principals and agents, owners and operators, users and designers can all disagree about what, and indeed who, the system is 'for'.[10]

What counts as an 'established' or 'designed' arrangement? What is being 'established' or 'designed'?

Our reflections above on the unintended consequences of arrangements such as the penal system are key here. Certain outcomes and their causes will undoubtedly be established in the creation of any durable arrangement, but it is not clear that these will always be solely those intended by the designers of the system. Indeed, in extreme cases the intentions of the designers will be notable only by their absence (see, for example, Forrester's comments on counter-intuitive understandings later in this chapter). This may, theoretically, present few problems to systems theorists, particularly those who revel in the elegance of an autopoietic understanding. Such academic (in the most pejorative sense) reflections are, however, likely to be less welcomed by those who actually seek to do things in the world through the systems that they employ. And even the disinterested theorist is still required to judge which of the established arrangements that are potentially discernible is the 'overall' one, the one that counts, the one that dominates, the one that captures *the* nature of the arrangement as a whole through correctly identifying its essential reason.

If we do not know what the 'whole' is, how do we know if it is greater than the sum of its parts?

Where do we start when looking at a system? Designedness and designers seem unable to provide us with any clarity here, and objectives seem only to be subjectively available to us as observers. Perhaps, then, we can grasp the notion of system through the idea of wholeness, of holism, which seems to be of central importance. However, if, as we have noted, it is impossible to definitively define the boundaries of a system with any certainty, or indeed to define *the* overarching purpose it serves, how are we to recognize its wholeness? And this is a problem that persists throughout the *hierarchy* of systems and *subsystems*. Such artefacts merely serve to move the problem around.

How do we distinguish between elements and process flows?

Problems continue when we enter the system itself, as our hints about subsystemic difficulties indicate. Returning to the example of the human body, the question of what is flowing, or being processed, through what is far from easy to answer. And this confusion is not simply the result of the distractions and complexities of 'life'. Consider a relatively simple mechanical system—a hydroelectric dam. In the dam, gravitational forces engender the flow of water through a confined space, and in the process, force a turbine blade to spin. The turbine blade is connected to a shaft, which turns a magnet within a coil of wire. The movement of the magnet within the coil causes a current to flow, a current that may either be directly used to power an electrical device or stored in the chemical potentialities of a battery. Which of these is element and which process flow? One answer, of course, would be to say that it depends upon what aspect of the system is of interest to us—in this case electricity or water—and such a view would be entirely consonant with Jenkins' focus upon the essential human element of design. The elements of the system could be the differences in electrical potentialities embodied by the arrangement of the turbine, magnet, and coil, in which case the process flow would be that of water. Or the elements could be the different energetic potentialities of two bodies of waters, in which case the process flow that would be of electrical current. In the first view electricity is *produced* as energy is transformed, in the latter it is merely *extracted*.[11] But while we have noted that such a view will do for Jenkins, Luchsinger and Dock's demand that process be more important than element necessitates an objective settlement of which is which 'in reality'.

What is system and what is element? Or what is system and what is subsystem? Where does the hierarchy end?

Our earlier reflections on the Marxian view of the overarching nature of capitalistic relations of accumulation are informative here, but consider also the system of and surrounding the internal combustion engine. We could say that the internal combustion engine is itself a system, or perhaps it may be an element or subsystem in a car which is itself an element in a transport system that serves the people we call 'drivers'. Other elements may include roads of various types, traffic lights, and other modes of flow control, garages, mechanics, etc. Some of these elements, most obviously traffic lights, seem to control drivers, but it is these drivers and their intentions that we have just seen as the superordinate purpose of the system. If we are to continue to see traffic lights as elements we need to move to a different level of abstraction, one that sees a transportation system serving not individual drivers, but the ongoing movement of traffic as a whole. This system's working may provide benefits to individual drivers, but they are not its *raison d'être*. As Bob Cooper (1989) has noted, we are driven as much as we drive, which is a very different view on usability than that which we normally find in the systems design literature. The point here is not simply that all systems are nested, which would be fairly easy to deal with if there was just one hierarchy in which all were related. Rather, it is that there may well be multiple hierarchies, in multiple systems, which may not be reduced to one overall 'world' system. And even if one does accept that there is one overall system in which all others may be considered, the choice of which system should be seen as the most encompassing is far from clear, as debates of all sorts continually make clear. Consider, for example, Boulding's (1956) hierarchic ordering of systems in which higher levels presuppose the existence of lower ones: 'Static structures, Clockworks, Control Mechanisms, Open systems, Lower organisms, Animals, Man, Sociocultural systems, Transcendental systems'.

While seemingly giving an 'objective' guide upon which to base the problematic assessment we have been considering, such a hierarchy merely replicates our conventional and long-held views concerning the relative worth of materials, animated materials, self-animating materials, consciously self-animating materials, interconsciously self-animating materials, and the realm of the Almighty from which all animation is seen ultimately to derive. As the literary theorist Kenneth Burke (1996) has noted, echoing these assumptions, 'Men Act, Things but move'. In the world of business such seemingly 'natural' hierarchies abound: Maslow's needs, the distinctions between strategies, tactics, and operations, and between individuals, groups, divisions, and corporations. Each of these distinctions seems wholly meaningful and unproblematic until that is one approaches the details of any specific set of circumstances. Such practical problems are, perhaps, most apparent in the process of provision of informational support for business activities. For when information professionals seek to map these comfortable distinctions on to the shifting complexities of organizational life, they are themselves often discomforted. We find, for example, in the details of the refinery information system that we consider in Chapters 4, 5, and 7 that for those who design information systems issues of strategies, tactics, and plans are discrete, while for those who seek to manage the movement and transformation of oil these distinctions are far from clear, and thus the systems with which they are supposedly supported are far from being immediately usable.

The ideas of systems are crucial for the models upon which many of the computerized platforms that support modern administration depends. It is, therefore, to models that we now turn our attention.

Seeing the future

If we can think of, and represent, aspects of the world as a coherent and connected system; we may produce a model of that world and iterate its cycles of 'behaviour' in order to simulate the passage of time, and hence re-present 'the future'. If we get it 'right' we may get to know in advance what is going to happen. But if we get it wrong, we may still think we know and that could be dangerous, to put it mildly. In this section we examine some of the basic ideas around the notion of modelling and consider briefly some of its more grandiose applications. But it is important to realize that these are not the only sites where modelling techniques are applied. Models, like systems, abound. It seems as though anything that is seen to change can and should be modelled. From windscreen wipers to the world as a whole, everything seems amenable to modelling. Designing has become a process of model construction and refinement; and management, the modelling of processes in order to 'decide' how best to intervene in them. Models of particular 'systems' deemed to exist in the world form the heart of all decision support systems (DSS). And such systems constitute a considerable proportion of the Information Systems in use in organizations today. They are, therefore, worthy of some serious attention.

Historical precedents?

Throughout history various groups have claimed a 'special' relationship with, and knowledge of, the world and its future. We have always had our prophets, usually of doom, and usually with some ulterior motive such as the achievement of privileged status and 'natural' control. These groups have deployed various arcane tools to supply them with the 'information' they require for prediction, and to keep others on the outside of their arts. And the modern world is no exception. With a weakening of beliefs in 'traditional' forms of knowledge, a 'science' of the future has been called into being—that of (computer) modelling. Forecasting, from the weather to world destruction, is now carried out 'legitimately' through use of the tools of science and technology. But the desire behind the techniques remains the same—a 'curiosity about revealing the course of future events' (Bloomfield 1986: p. vii). Brian Bloomfield has investigated one particularly significant group of these modern day prophets—the Systems Dynamics Group at the Massachusetts Institute of Technology (MIT) in the United States. Founded by Jay W. Forrester, the group is most famous for the world models it constructed during the 1970s.

How does modelling 'work'?

Two intimately related answers to the above question seem to be required here. How 'technically' is modelling done? And what 'social' objectives does modelling tend to achieve?[12]

The MIT group models embodied the principles of *system dynamics*:

> Basically, the system dynamics approach involves the building of a computer simulation model to describe the behaviour of any particular system under study, followed by experimentation with the model in order to derive suitable policy options for modifying the behaviour of the 'real' system. (Bloomfield 1986: p. viii)

System dynamics was originally developed at the Sloan School of Management at MIT[13] during the 1950s. It built upon work in systems engineering, feedback control,[14] and 'technological' system design. Indeed, it was the success of the former two theoretical ideals in the latter practical field that led the extension of system dynamics to the design and control of social systems, and hence the sort of GST we encountered earlier in this chapter. Such a tool was deemed to be useful for 'the management and control of all complex feedback systems'. For '. . . it was assumed that the properties of any system, whether technical or social, could be explained on the basis of the same fundamental principles common to all feedback structures' (Bloomfield 1986: p. viii). On the basis of such an understanding, system dynamics was able to move from a restricted applications site in engineering systems to models of industrial enterprises, cities, and eventually, nations and the globe.

Analysis of system dynamics promised to increase understanding of social problems in two key, interrelated ways. First, the laborious tasks of remembering and calculating relationships could be partially automated through the use of computers, enabling more and more complex problems to be studied. And second, the understandings so generated were seen, by systems dynamicists, to provide 'a new and better approach to studying such problems' (Bloomfield 1986: p. ix). Gains attendant upon greater amounts of information being processed were supplemented by further gains, which were themselves seen to be attendant upon the very practice of modelling. It was thought that abstraction of key features from the complex world, their recombination into realistic simulations, and the subsequent comparison of those simulations with 'real world' outcomes together delivered an understanding of problems that was qualitatively different from that associated with other techniques of large-scale control. The system dynamicists suggest

> that the human brain is not adapted to understanding the properties of complex systems—where many variables interact through time—and conclude that computers should be employed to aid in this task. Though the human brain may correctly perceive the structure of a complex system, they contend that it cannot predict how that structure will behave dynamically. (Bloomfield 1986: p. ix)

Thus, the 'technology' that enables the approach and the approach 'itself' are in practice inseparable.

System dynamics focuses upon the feedback structures of complex systems, the ways in which prior states effect present states, and its proponents suggest that knowledge of such structures is necessary for comprehending the behavioural modes of these systems. It is only a small step from here to the assertion that the world being (successfully) modelled in this process is itself made up from the interrelation of elements in complex feedback structures. And then it is no step at all to claim that one has a better understanding of the world than others whose techniques do not mirror it so perfectly. In a similar vein, complex systems were actually seen to be *counter-intuitive*, 'that is "they give indications that suggest corrective action which will often be ineffective or even adverse in its results" '. (Forrester 1969: 9; cited in Bloomfield 1986: 9)

> Here lies much of the explanation for the problems of faltering companies, disappointments in developing nations, foreign exchange crises, and troubles of urban areas. (Forrester 1969: 110; cited in Bloomfield 1986: 9)

The system dynamicists therefore envisage the spread of systems dynamics into all levels of education. They also advocate the education of the electorate in order that people might better appreciate the dynamic properties of social systems and thereby make more 'informed' choices when voting for policies. (Bloomfield 1986: p. ix)

In short, 'system dynamics is not merely a modelling tool or technique, but . . . a theory of the behaviour of social systems' (Bloomfield 1986: p. ix). And, thus, we come to the second sense in which modelling works. Claiming to have 'discovered' the route to the source of the mysteries of the social world, systems dynamicists place themselves in pole position for the construction of new policies to combat the threats they discover. Systems dynamics may be viewed as 'a type of social theory . . . which is explicitly designed for large-scale social engineering' (Bloomfield 1986: p. ix).

And who could resist the appeal? For example

WORLD 2 and WORLD 3 . . . looked at the Earth as a closed global ecosystem and from the computer simulations it was concluded that the world was facing a catastrophic collapse in its life-support systems. Depicting scenarios of mass starvation, the exhaustion of natural resources, global asphyxiation, and over population, the simulations opened a window on a nightmarish future. As an alternative to catastrophe the MIT modellers offered a global equilibrium society where growth in population and industrialization would be halted; a world of harmony between man and nature. The ensuing message was broadcast throughout the world and captured much attention, particularly within Western societies, and the debate which it stimulated still continues in many circles. (Bloomfield 1986: p. viii)

And it did not matter too much if they had got the exact figures wrong in their assumptions, for as we noted earlier in the chapter, for the systems theorist the *structure* of the system was seen to be the important thing.

A complex system was alleged to be *insensitive* to changes in its parameters; in other words, changes in the value of a parameter do not appreciably alter the behaviour of the system. This led to the argument that the structure of a system is more important than the data specifying the values of its parameters, an argument which underscored the system dynamicists' general systems approach—i.e. irrespective of differences in parameters, systems with similar structures tend to have similar behavioural properties, whether those systems be an electronic circuit, a stock-control system, or a city. (Bloomfield 1986: 9)

By examining Forrester's cultural background (initially an electrical engineer of military/technological systems, and subsequently a management scientist interested in 'non-technical' systems), and the ideals embedded within systems dynamics, Bloomfield is able to argue that the latter, and particularly that form of the beast associated with the MIT group, may be seen to be oriented to the 'traditional middle-class concern . . . with the preservation of social order [in the face of these simulated threats], and was similarly committed to society's dominant institutions and values' (1986: p. xi). Considering the development of systems dynamics in relation to social developments within North American society, particularly the urban and environmental crises, Bloomfield suggests that

> it was originally devised in the spirit of furthering American dominance—both economic and political—in the world system, but was later expanded to address the issues of urban decline and environmental degradation . . . [I]n the face of such problems . . . the aim was primarily to maintain social order, and to do so without challenging society's dominant institutions such as capitalism, and the distribution of wealth. (1986: p. xi)

As the techniques were applied to different domains there were a number of extensions to the theoretical content of system dynamics, which Bloomfield interprets in relation 'to the specific threats to social order to which they were a response' (1986: p. xii). For example, the existence of different continuing problems within urban 'systems' despite the best efforts of administrators suggested that system relationships were likely to be 'counterintuitive', and hence that seemingly progressive policies could make things worse.[15]

> Forrester argued that low-rent housing encouraged an 'excessive' influx of underemployed people into cities, with the consequent erosion of the tax base and the fuelling of urban stagnation. The [systems dynamics] suggested remedy was to constrain this inward migration by demolishing the slums and not replacing them with alternative housing. (Bloomfield 1986: 10)

The models could often lead to surprising conclusions, such as this, although the conclusions were not always completely predictable and could certainly not be simply read off from social class positioning. And thus Bloomfield's interpretation also allows for system dynamics to affect the cultural environment in which it is produced. 'This is particularly important in view of Forrester's shifting perspective on capitalism—wherein he (and the other system dynamicists) came to expound the thesis that industrial growth must be halted' (Bloomfield 1986: p. xii).[16]

So a number of shifts can be seen in Forrester's position vis-à-vis his values and aims for the models. Despite these seemingly seismic shifts in position, however, his commitment to the preservation of order remains. As Bloomfield notes, just as reading the entrails of chickens provided our ancestors with some security in an uncertain world, so system dynamics . . . 'like a computerized form of astrology . . . offered to bring structure and certainty into a world that appeared to be rent by contrarieties and mounting global problems' (1986: p. xiii–xiv).

▓ SUMMARY

Opinions on the nature of systems are manifold. That said, systems are often seen to be mixtures of human and non-human elements, designed to accomplish an objective. Systems consist of established arrangements, possess synergy in the interrelationships among their individual elements, and privilege both process over structure and overall 'system' objectives over more parochial ones. Systems are generally seen to form part of a hierarchy, themselves usually being seen to be made up of 'subsystems', with the outputs from a given subsystem providing the inputs for others. Notions of system can be traced back to at least the eighteenth century with the term (GST) being coined in 1950. Opinions on the nature of systems are perhaps so manifold because all of the aspects of systems delineated above can be interpreted in a myriad ways. For example, it is far from easy to establish the location of the boundary of a system and indeed its nature, particularly whether the boundary is to be seen as part of the system. The boundary of a system can be permeable and moveable, enabling exchange with the system's 'environment', and such 'open' systems are deemed to be those worthy of the most attention. Systems ideas are crucial to the construction of models, which are in turn essential elements of many modern information systems. Modelling may be seen primarily to be a way of forecasting events. The work of the Systems Dynamics Group at MIT enables us to consider the complex relationships between the 'technology' of modelling and the theoretical suppositions that constitute it. Embedded within the latter are concepts carrying the marks of the cultural and social circumstances from which they arise, but at least some of these underpinnings are brought into question by the partially unpredictable outcomes of these conjunctions of ideas and their processing.

▒ DISCUSSION QUESTIONS

1. What is a 'system'? How it is defined and designed?

2. In what ways can a system operate in and transact with its surroundings?

3. Do we live in a world made up of systems or is it better to see systems as merely an idea that we apply to help us understand our world?

4. Why did the ideas of the Systems Dynamicists receive so much attention during the 1970s? Whose ideas speak to the present in the same way?

5. What would a system dynamics view of 'globalization' look like?

6. How could Bloomfield's approach contribute to a better understanding of the prophets of the present?

▒ SUGGESTIONS FOR FURTHER READING

von Bertalanffy, L. (1950a). 'An Outline of General Systems Theory'. *British Journal of Philosophy of Science*, 1: 134–64.

—— (1950b). 'The Theory of Open Systems in Physics and Biology'. *Science*, 111: 23–9.

Bloomfield, B. P. (1986). *Modelling the World: The Social Constructions of Systems Analysts*. Oxford: Basil Blackwell.

Roszak, T. (1986). *The Cult of Information: The Folklore of Computers and the True Art of Thinking*. Cambridge: Lutterworth.

An excellent beginning point for exploring the masses of both new and classic material on systems, cybernetics, and modelling that is available on the world wide web is http://pespmc1.vub.ac.be/CYBSYSTH.html.

4 Speaking for Information Systems: Analysing and Prescribing Material Information

---

KEY CONCEPTS

Actor Network Theory	Oil Management Systems
agency	screens
agnosticism	simulation
contextualization	sociotechnical networks
enrolment	social determinism
free association	social reductionism
hyperreality	social shaping of technology
identity	speciesism
interessement	symmetry
linear programming	technological determinism
mobilization	translation

KEY THEMES

When you have read this chapter, you should be able to define those key concepts in your own words, and you should also be able to:

1. Appreciate how 'screens' shape our understanding of the world.

2. Critique the different reasons put forward as explanations for 'technological' changes.

3. Explain how social and technological determinism and/or reductionism give different pictures of the development of Information Systems.

4. Explain the nature and significance of Actor Network Theory.

5. Apply the actor network approach to Information Systems.

Introduction

In this chapter we will describe a variety of methods that may be used to make sense of the technologies that are seen to herald the advent of the information society. In addition to providing an essential grounding in the material aspects of this so-called revolution, herewith we will introduce you to the actor network approach.

More precisely, this and the following chapter interrogate various methodologies and modes of representation that may be employed to study the relationship between ICTs and organization through applying them to the emergence of *refinery-based* Oil Management Systems (OMS) within one of the industry's 'seven sisters'. Using this story as a base, an attempt is made to assess the methodological implications of different approaches to the society/technology imbroglio for those who seek to study information systems in their organizational contexts. Starting from simpler sociotechnical ideas that demand cognizance of the *social shaping* of technology, the chapter goes on to consider the advantages offered by the *translation* approach, advocated by writers such as Law, Callon, and Latour, to the understanding of *sociotechnical networks*. Then, in the following chapter, the key role of *representation* in these processes and its relation to the 'impermanence' of the body is examined in some detail before a discussion which addresses some of the political and existential implications of these insights for researchers in the field for, as our discussion makes clear, researchers and systems analysts are themselves key 'users' of information systems and the techniques that we possess for making them knowable. Such 'users' utilize these resources to make, among other things, the cultural and financial capital that may be seen to accrue from contribution to academic and practitioner literatures.

Different 'screens'

We wish to consider the complex relationships between the so-called social and technical entities of organization. To this end various *screens*, upon which the inter-linkings of 'technology' and 'society' can be 'shown', are examined. Weber's (1996) exegesis of 'screen' in an essay concerning the specificity of televisual media is instructive here for we also regard our systems and their contents through screens.

> A screen is first of all a surface upon which light and shadow can be projected . . . , it . . . allows distant vision to be *watched*. Second, it *screens*, in the sense of *selecting* or *filtering*, the vision that is watched. And finally, it serves as a screen in the sense of standing between the viewer and the viewed, since what is rendered visible covers the separation that distinguishes the *other vision* from that of the sight of the spectator sitting in front of the set. (Weber 1996: 120 and 122–3)

A screen allows us to 'see', but only some things are made visible. Nevertheless, if a screen is effective, if it allows us a seemingly direct and 'natural' line of sight, our 'but' will remain forgotten. For a screen that is 'ready-at-hand' (Heidegger 1962) will also screen ('cover') its own screening (filtering). Such screens also provide defence; they 'shield' and 'protect' our understandings. More broadly, when we screen our defences, we 'surround', 'enclose', and 'fortify' our intellectual possessions and others must respect our defences or invest the energy required to jump them if they want to engage with us. Our screens allow us to define and appropriate fields as we exclude, or better still regulate the movement of, others. And they, too, do so in the name of efficiency, in this case 'analytical' efficiency. Screens or fences provide us with possessions that *represent* our status, along with that of our defined subjects and objects. And our key possession here is authorial and authoritative status as expert witnesses to the process of technological change: experts who have and deserve a say. We examine these screens as the 'facts' of our case unfold.

Managing refining

Our case concerns the diffusion of an innovation[1] in the management of oil refining (see also Lilley 1993*a, b*, 1995, 1996, and in particular, 1998). This innovation emerged during the late 1980s at the Rotterdam refinery of one of 'seven sisters',[2] hereafter referred to as 'Mexaco'.[3] It took the form of a computerized 'Oil Management System' (OMS) that sought to enable *refinery-based* control of on-site oil and oil-product management processes. In 'technical terms' the system was built around the organizing potential of a central database of key refinery data and modelling techniques:

> You can actually visualise a series of building blocks: process control; advance control; on-line optimisation [through the use of Linear Programming modelling techniques]; and OMS basically is dependent on those, and OMS sits above the whole framework of data capture . . . But . . . how do you use the data to your advantage to generate a commercial edge over your competitors? And the idea is basically that you have the data, you have computers that can handle that data and manipulate the data for you, and that basically allows you to shift data from one application, modelling system, whatever, into another. So it's allowing you to integrate the modelling systems. (Interview with a Refining Analyst for Rotterdam Refinery, Manufacturing Development Group, 'Mexaco' Oil Europe)

Here, we have a story of technology and organization. Superficially, at least, it is a rather neat and simplistic one. 'Advances' in technology allow us to deal more efficiently with all the different information that we 'need' to make the 'right' decisions. Indeed, one may read the quote as suggesting that these advances partially determine, or at least enable, a future in which disparate expertises and rationalities (different 'modelling systems') are brought together to provide and service one centralized and coherent view of organizational activity: a 'commercial' view. But this is not the only story that can be told and we will explore the system and its context in more detail as we begin our delineation of different analytic screens.

Our story, as told, may be indicted on the grounds of 'technological determinism', a view of the world in which our knowledge of the nature of technology is 'neutral', as are the 'societal' effects of that technology. Within such a view, the 'Internet', for example, is simply the most effective form of connecting computers currently available. The historical contingencies leading to its development, for example the interests of particle physicists and of the American miltitary–industrial complex, being mere froth adding drama but not substance to the story. But this is not the only way to apprehend technology. We may also ask

> What has shaped the technology that is having 'effects'? What has caused and is causing the technological changes whose 'impact' we are experiencing? (MacKenzie and Wajcman 1985: 2)

And in the process

> Our technology becomes, like our economy or our political system, an aspect of the way we live socially. It becomes something whose changes are part of wider changes in the way we live. It even becomes something whose changes we might think of consciously shaping—though we must warn right at the beginning that to say that technology is socially shaped is not to say that it can necessarily be altered easily. (MacKenzie and Wajcman 1985: 3)

The definition of technology mobilized in this literature is broad, encompassing artefacts, what people do with those artefacts, and what people know. The demands of the approach do not entail an abandoning of research on the effects of technology on society, rather the approach seeks a balance, with 'at least equal time for the study of the effects of society on technology' (MacKenzie and Wajcman 1985: 2). And returning to our example from refining we can see the virtue of this 'corrective'. The Rotterdam OMS may be seen to have emerged out of the specifics of historical contingencies that pertained at and around the site. The complexities of refinery management that the OMS sought to ameliorate were relatively recent phenomena. In the past, the seven sisters had managed the whole of the production process internally, from discovery through to end-user sale. And visions of a coordinated, vertically integrated future that followed experience of a coordinated and vertically integrated past seemingly created a programme of activity by major oil companies. These choices may be seen to have contributed to the shape of the OMS that subsequently materialized. This new story, though, needs a little further consideration:

> there was a vast expansion in crude oil processing capacity in the seventies in anticipation of a rapid growth in oil demand. Now what then happened . . . was we had . . . Yom Kippur . . . in 197[3], we then had the Iranian crisis in 1978/79 . . . [and] because the crude price jumped in two very large steps from effectively $3 a barrel to $30 a barrel . . . what you then had was a dramatic slowdown in growth of demand. The capacity had already been built and hence people found themselves with surplus capacity. What they then had to do if they wanted to move the crude through it was get rid of the products. (Interview with Production Planner and Ex-Trader, Oiltown Refinery)

Accounting systems now emerge in our see-sawing story. These technologies shaped a response to 'environmental' conditions that in turn entailed the use of extant discursive technologies. Notions and techniques of 'marginal economics' contributed to a decision to utilize 'surplus' refining capacity rather than let it stand 'idle':

> the overriding push was that you have all these fixed costs associated with refineries and you need to keep the throughputs up in order to spread those fixed costs around. You've got marginal economics to play and if you make a dollar a barrel in terms of producing an extra amount of refinery product and you can sell it then at least you've got that dollar a barrel. The fact that your total fixed costs might've been two dollars a barrel or more still meant that you were getting a contribution to fixed costs, and that always pushed the economics of throughput up beyond your markets. (Interview with Systems Manager, Oiltown Refinery)

This (over)utilization resulted in the construction of new arrangements that absorbed the surplus that 'surplus capacity' and 'marginal economics' had combined to create. '[R]efineries like Rotterdam were pumping out surpluses into a market, were *generating intermediate markets*' (Interview with Systems Manager, Oiltown Refinery, emphasis added). This marketization of the intermediate stages of a previously integrated production and supply chain was exacerbated by other factors, by 'Independents[4] coming in to see if they [could] play blending games, moving the stock games' (Interview with Production Planner and Ex-trader, Oiltown Refinery). These circumstances created an increase in the complexity of the refinery management task. An increase that would contribute to the 'need' for and shape of a technological solution, the OMS that emerged at Rotterdam.

> you . . . had to control it because for the first time you had a third party interface coming into it. If it was internal there was no sale, you just moved the oil. Whereas what was happening is that we were making sales by barge to third parties. We had to invoice them, we had to control them, had to take orders, and all of a sudden there was a whole new commercial scene to manage. (Interview with Systems Manager, Oiltown Refinery)

But here we see an equally pernicious risk begin to rear its ugly head in the background of our newly enlightened account: that of an overprivileged *social determinism* with technology entirely subservient to the demands of the protagonists. And it is the call for 'balance' that aims to mitigate this extreme. The balanced 'social shaping' approach seeks a mode of analysis that is both open to, and cognizant of, the social in the technological and the technological in the social. An exclusionary emphasis on the 'effects' of technology is counterbalanced by consideration of the 'effects' of society. But a nagging question remains. Can such an approach enable a synergy of positions, an understanding of the world that is not dependent upon the twin simplifications of social reductionism and technological determinism? Or do such moves merely degenerate into 'reciprocal accusation[s] of myopia' (Law 1991*b*) between the established discipline of sociology and the emerging discipline of technology studies?

There are two key objections to such a balancing act. The first concerns the indictment of social science on the grounds of its 'speciesism' (see, for example, Callon 1986, 1991; Latour 1986, 1987, 1988*b*, 1991*b*; Law 1986, 1991*a*, *b*; Haraway 1991; Woolgar 1991); its ignorance of machines.[5] Speciesism is characterized by the desire (or perhaps the linguistic necessity) to separate, and grant different ontological statuses to, 'people' and 'machines'. As Law notes:

> The problem has something to do with the absence of a method for juggling simultaneously with *both* the social *and* the technical. Sociologists . . . tend to switch registers. They talk of the social. And *then* (if they talk of it at all which most do not) they talk of the technical. And, if it appears, the technical acts either as a kind of explanatory *deus ex machina* (technological determinism). Or it is treated as an expression of social relations (social reductionism). Or (with difficulty) the two are treated as two classes of objects which interact and mutually shape one another. (Law 1991*b*: 8)

> We are dealing with a form of distribution built deep into sociology—the distribution between people on the one hand, and machines on the other. (Law 1991*b*: 8)

> Sociology may know about class, or about gender. But how much does it know about speciesism—the systematic practice of discrimination against other species? And how much does it know or care about machines? (Law 1991*b*: 6)

The implication, it would seem, is that it knows and cares very little. But is an awareness of the above provisos and a cognizance of the evil dual imperialisms that we may have been inadvertently perpetuating enough to allow us to bring forth a better account? Can we now safely reopen our case? Let's give it a try.

We are now in a position to see the story we have been telling as something of a simplification, as are all of the stories we 'tell'.[6] But we can usefully make things a little more 'messy' here, for mess may be instructive. The dramatic rise in crude oil prices during the 1970s did not have a uniformly negative effect upon the corporation's ability to generate profits. As we noted earlier, Mexaco was a highly integrated company and the disintegration that occurred during the 1980s was only in terms of trading relationships. Most, if not all, of the constituent activities of the organization remained. The Mexaco group still had, and continues to have, very considerable interests in the exploration for, and production of, crude oil, and the organization as a whole may have derived a net financial benefit from the rising price of oil. It was only the refining and marketing sectors of the business that suffered as a result of the changes in price. However, it is crucial to note that this suffering was not apparent until these 'sectors' had been appropriately segregated through the institutionalization of new social relations. These new social relations were changes in the organizational structure[7] and accounting practices of the Mexaco group. The new structure was to take 'account of the increasing diversity of the group's world-wide operations, [to allow] for greater devolution in decision-making, and [to establish] a basis for further evolution in the 1980s' (Business Press Article).

> Before that we were very much a unified company. We thought that concealed, in a way, where we were good and where we were bad. It was much better to be more transparent

and much better to be more devolved and then businesses could be judged on their own terms, with their own competitors, and not have them concealed by the overall Mexaco. (Interview with Senior Manager, Mexaco Oil International)

In late 1981 a new chairman took control of the group and for the first two years of his stewardship the financial performance of the newly formed 'Mexaco' Oil International (MOI)—the part of the 'new' organization responsible for oil supply, refining, and marketing—was considered unsatisfactory, with substantial losses being made in refining and marketing, particularly in Europe (MOI Annual Report and Accounts 1981). Slicing up activities in new ways revealed 'loss making' areas and practices that were ripe for organizational intervention. Calculative devices were deployed to exploit the new lines of sight made available, surveying the technological base of MOI's activity. At the time of its formation in 1981, there was seen to be some 40 per cent surplus in crude oil distillation capacity in Europe (MOI Annual Report and Accounts 1981). By early 1984, 33 per cent of the company's 'refining capacity' had been closed (Business Press Article), with the majority of these closures occurring in north-west Europe. With a small revival in world oil demand and this removal of some 'overcapacity' in the sector, $125 million in refining and marketing losses in 1982 became $297 million in profits in 1983 (Business Press Article). This progress was not however seen to be sufficient, and further action to reduce overcapacity in Europe continued through 1984, with a series of new 'rationalization' measures being announced in January 1985. Much of Mexaco Oil's European refining capacity was removed. On completion of these changes MOI had reduced its European crude oil distillation capacity to 65 million tonnes per annum, a reduction from the beginning of 1981 of 43 million tonnes. In 1988 MOI had five major refineries in Europe compared with sixteen in 1981 (MOI Annual Report and Accounts 1988).

As a result of these changes, the refining or manufacturing side of the business no longer simply responded to customer needs filtered through a central supply department. Refinery products could now be traded entrepreneurially, apparently increasing the importance of predictability of supply. In the past predictability of supply had meant confidence in one's ability to fulfil customer needs through one's own refineries' production. In the future predictability was seen to be key for the exploitation of (intermediate) market opportunities. Maximization of value added was to depend upon careful combination of manufactured and purchased products. As such, it was seen to be more and more important that the *detailed activities* of refineries and their 'performance' should be made if not perfectly visible, then at least predictable to elements of the Mexaco Oil organization that were remote from refineries. 'Supply' was seen to need more information on 'manufacturing' in order to deal with the increasing complexity arising from huge changes in the nature of product distribution, changes that were seen to result from the increasing importance of both marketing and product exchanges with other oil companies.

From 'managing imbalances' to 'exchanges and modal planning'

Mexaco moved from a situation where occasional crude and product transfers occurred, represented as 'managing imbalances' (Interview with Systems Manager, Oiltown Refinery), to one in which the coordination of distribution and supply through links with other players came to be seen as core to the business. Managers within Mexaco Oil UK's Supply Division saw their 'new' role as one which ensures 'that we supply our markets profitably within the procedural constraints under which we have to operate, and the main function through which we achieve that is exchanges' (Interview with Refinery Programming Manager, Mexaco Oil UK).

As a result of refinery closures exchanges are an extremely significant part of the modern European oil industry. For example Mexaco now operates only one major crude oil refinery in the United Kingdom: 'Oiltown'.[8] Ten years ago Mexaco operated four refineries in the United Kingdom. This capacity, now seen as 'surplus', meant that little exchange of product with other oil companies was required. However, with the partial closure of one refinery and the complete closure of two others, Mexaco had to answer the demands of a market based almost entirely in one part of the country with refining operations that were concentrated elsewhere. Consequently, emphasis shifted away from a primary concern with refinery coordination towards consideration of marketing and exchange issues, or 'Exchanges and Modal Planning' (Interview with Commercial Manager, Oiltown Refinery). Exchanges are made with other oil companies to ensure adequate supply throughout the country. Thus the 1980s not only witnessed an unprecedented increase in the importance of the marketing of refinery products, but also, through the removal of overcapacity, an equally large increase in the importance of product exchanges (Telephone Conversation with Systems Manager, Oiltown Refinery). Mexaco Oil UK now supplies approximately half of its customer demand through exchanges. Together, marketization and exchanges created a massive increase in the complexities surrounding refinery management. And it was these complexities that, as we shall see, OMS eventually sought to assuage.

So how are we to interpret this account? Our story has changed to one where new 'social' arrangements demanded a 'technical' survey of 'technological assets', a survey which then resulted in a removal of these assets through some 'technical' decisions. However, new 'technical' and 'commercial' rationales concerning optimal utilization ('What it did have was . . . a lot of capacity let's say in the Rotterdam refinery, but it was deficit elsewhere as a result of those closures' (Interview with Systems Manager, Oiltown Refinery)) and market presence ('If every one had to supply their own product to all locations from their own refineries you would find companies would pull out of certain areas which would reduce competition . . . There is no doubt therefore that exchanges are a force pulling prices down'

(Company Newspaper Article)) then combine to create pressures for enhanced social contacts between disparate organizational sites. And it is this social complexity and distance that creates a need for an initial technological intervention. So we now run back along our see-saw to the social end to see what the technological requirements of such an intervention might be.

The emergence of the 'commercial scene' and the 'need' to manage refining activities in relation to an intermediate market were apparently particularly marked at Mexaco's Rotterdam refinery. The activities of the refinery were very closely linked to the activities of buyers and sellers on the Rotterdam spot market.[9] Although the Rotterdam refinery had a relatively small local market, it was well placed to deal with north European trading on the spot market (Interview with Senior Manager, Systems Development Unit, Mexaco Corporate Centre). Rotterdam refinery's geographical location in relation to north European trading routes, coupled with the emergence of an intermediate market for refinery products, and later supplies (Interview with Systems Manager, Oiltown Refinery), placed it in a situation that was seen to present significant opportunities in the new commercial world that was emerging. However, as we have already hinted, the benefits of playing in an intermediate market were not cost-free. For in this newly commercial world refining was only one side of the recently segregated Manufacturing and Supply (M&S) activities of an oil company. Refining, the production or manufacturing side, required coordination and management to ensure that customer supply demands could be adequately met. The supply side of the M&S Division of Mexaco Oil seeks to ensure '. . . that we supply our markets profitably within the procedural constraints under which we have to operate' (Interview with Refinery Programming Manager, Mexaco Oil UK). The supply function is concerned with ensuring both that customers are supplied with refined products and that refineries themselves have adequate feedstocks to produce the prescribed product mix to satisfy those customer needs. Within this distribution each refinery's field of competence was almost entirely limited to the running of plant and the blending of components so produced. Decisions concerning the sources of raw materials, amounts of raw materials required, destinations of products, size of production, and product mix were the exclusive concern of the supply function.

'Historically' this supply coordination task had been carried out at Mexaco's corporate centre, a situation that did not seem to be inherently problematic. It had apparently worked adequately while the organization was acting as a 'vertically integrated company', before the emergence of intermediate markets. Rotterdam refinery's manufacturing and supply functions were, and had always been, geographically separate. However, the activities of those concerned with commercial dealings in refinery products and supplies, who worked from the corporate centre, did have a considerable effect on Rotterdam refinery's activities, an effect that was particularly pronounced due to the refinery's proximity to an important trading area on the spot market. Activities at the refinery were consequently very closely linked to those of buyers and sellers on the spot market.

And now our see-saw begins to swing again. For presumably 'social' reasons such as a penchant for hierarchy and bureaucracy,[10] Mexaco was apparently reluctant to relinquish centralized control of its supply function, and thus a computerized system was developed in the early 1980s to 'bridge the gap' between Rotterdam's manufacturing and the corporate centre's supply functions (Interview with Systems Manager, Oiltown Refinery). Mexaco traders who worked within the corporate supply function needed information on the refinery's stocks in order to allow them to play the market:

> theoretically you could sort out the Rotterdam control problem by transposing the commercial control across to the refinery. Now, in fact, what we chose to do as a company was not to do that but actually bridge the gap using technology. (Interview with Systems Manager, Oiltown Refinery)

And so a desire to maintain centralized commercial control led to the introduction of a distribution monitoring system, known as Supply Information System (SIS),[11] to Mexaco's corporate centre. This was a supply *control* information system at the corporate supply centre, 'upstream' of refinery production. The supply division determined production requirements and '. . . then it was downloaded to the refinery, then production would handle it' (Interview with Systems Manager, Oiltown Refinery). Thus, the SIS system provided a technological solution to the social problem of controlling distant production in relation to the demands of an adjacent intermediate market.

So where has our new story taken us? We are certainly talking about both 'people' and 'machines', but in a rather disjointed manner. For, although we can demonstrate an awareness that technology is not *determined* by the social order and that the social order is not determined by technology, we can seemingly do so only by playing a distracting game of ontological[12] tennis. Law (1991*b*) conceives of this problem as one of 'heterogeneity' and sees in it a re-presentation of the age old 'problem' of the social order. The solution to such a problem is to 'find a way of talking about the-social-and-the-technical, all in one breath' (Law 1991*b*: 8).

> The social order is not a social order at all. Rather it is a *sociotechnical order*. What appears to be social is partly technical. What we usually call technical is partly social. In practice nothing is purely technical. Neither is anything purely social . . . [W]herever we scrape the social surface we will find that it is composed of networks of heterogeneous materials. (Law 1991*b*: 10)

The social shaping approach sensitizes us to these issues, but provides only a partial solution. As a slogan and as a research programme it does allow a counterbalancing of the more prominent but often implicit diagnoses of technology's 'effects'. But it does not, in itself, provide 'a way of talking about the-social-and-technical, all in one breath'.

And this brings us on to the second and perhaps more fundamental criticism that one could level against such an approach: the claim that the very use of the terms 'society' and 'technology' (or 'social' and 'technological') can play fundamental roles in the shaping of sociotechnical networks (Latour 1988*a*, 1991*b*; Callon 1991; Bloomfield and Vurdubakis 1992). This move suggests that 'society' and 'technology' must be seen, at least in part, as rhetorical devices that seek to structure and obtain a reality in the process of network building. For example, to describe a market as a technical device is to partially naturalize it, making its perpetuation more likely, its change only being possible once a 'better' technical device is 'discovered'. However, to describe a market as socially constructed potentially opens up many more possibilities for deliberate change to its functioning. The success of conceiving of and creating a reality using terms such as 'technical' and 'social' is, thus, one of the outcomes that requires description and explanation. The terms cannot therefore function as explanatory variables themselves. As Latour (1988*b*) puts it, 'Technology and society are two artefacts created by the analysts' duplicity' (1988*b*: 22).

> This is why, instead of the empty distinction between social ties and technical bonds, we prefer to talk of association. To the twin question 'is it social?/is it technical?' we prefer to ask 'is this association stronger or weaker than that one?' (Callon and Latour 1981; Latour 1986, 1987) (27).

An associology of translation?

The solution proposed to this problem by writers such as John Law, Bruno Latour, and Michel Callon is to apprehend the (re)construction of the sociotechnical through the notion of *translation*, an approach predicated upon three core principles:

> agnosticism (impartiality between actors engaged in controversy), generalised symmetry (the commitment to explain conflicting view points in the same terms) and free association (the abandonment of all a priori distinctions between the natural and the social). (Callon 1986: 196)

The researcher seeks to account for the (always temporary) stabilization of a sociotechnical network through consideration of the elements that make up that network and the relations that hold them in place. This task must be undertaken with the three principles outlined above in mind. The researcher must be alive to the fact that the designations and descriptions of entities and their relational links provided by those actors involved in the network building process are themselves an important facet of that network building process.

> Instead of imposing a pre-established grid of analyses upon these, the observer follows the actors in order to identify the manner in which these define and associate the different elements by which they build and explain their world, whether it be social or natural. (Callon 1986: 201)

The terms used to explain the (re)production of a sociotechnical network are primarily actors and their translations. Actors (be they 'social' or 'technical') are accorded agency in such an approach. Thus, one witnesses the mutual translation of actors by other actors. Utilizing a linguistic analogy, Latour proposes consideration of actors or entities in terms of texts or statements. Actors and their network building programmes are 'read' by other actors and through this reading process readers, text, and indeed author are (potentially) transformed. Thus, 'we are not to follow a given statement through a *context*. We are to follow the simultaneous production of a "text" and a "context"' (Latour 1991*b*: 106).

The extent of agreement between various actors' readings of each other provides us with an indication of the 'reality' of the network that they constitute. 'Reality' is the outcome of network building. In the process of translation reality is created as 'the identity of actors, the possibility of interaction and the margins of manoeuvre are negotiated and delimited' (Callon 1986: 203). Or to put it another way, considering translation allows us to apprehend 'the simultaneous production of knowledge and construction of a network of relationships in which social and natural entities mutually control who they are and what they want' (Callon 1986: 203).

An obvious example we have already encountered is the way in which a number of refineries, particularly in Europe, are transformed from essential equipment into 'surplus capacity' that is ripe for removal. A new view of these refineries emerges simultaneously with a new role for them in the emerging refining network of the future. In this case, this role is at best, that of impediment, and at worst, that of no role at all. In the process, new identities and interests are imputed to those social entities that manage refining. We return to these entities through an expansion of our understanding of translation.

The translation process

Callon (1986) identifies four 'moments' of translation: *problematization, interessement, enrolment,* and *mobilization*; although he is at pains to point out that they do not necessarily occur in a tidy sequence. Through translation actors attempt to impose themselves and their definition of a situation on the other actors implicated in that definition. In the first moment, a primary actor or 'enunciator'[13] *problematizes* an issue. The 'problems' and identities of other actors are defined in such a way as to render the enunciator as an 'obligatory passage point' (Callon 1986) for those problems' solutions. The enunciator defines others and their situation in order to become indispensable to both. The network of relations, or solution to other actors' 'problems', can only be constructed through the enunciator. Thus, the enunciator defines for itself an integral role in the construction of its product (the network) and defines this product as the solution to a problem; a defined problem for defined other actors: 'problematization describes a system of alliances or associations, between entities, thereby defining their identity and what they "want"' (Callon 1986: 206).

So we return to refining to examine problematization there. Indeed we have already been doing so. The key problematization in our case would seem to be the circumstances facing managers at Rotterdam and our whole preceding story has contributed to the reification of this 'situation'. The most salient enunciators of this problematization are, for the purposes of *this* story at least, the members of the Systems Group of Manufacturing and Supply's Business Development Unit (M&S BDU) from Mexaco's Corporate Centre. For it is they who define Rotterdam's 'problem' in such a way that they emerge as the 'obligatory passage point' for its solution. And it is their (reality structuring) account of Rotterdam's situation that seems to inform the accounts given by other organizational participants who are more remote from the site.

As you will probably have already gathered, the SIS at Rotterdam did not entirely 'solve' Rotterdam's 'problems'. In the powerful stories that we can now see as contributing to the development of OMS, the increased ability to play the market that the system provided to the supply division did little to ameliorate an increasingly complex refinery production management task. Indeed 'tensions' developed during the early 1980s as immediate 'electronic trading became more important' (Interview with Senior Manager, Systems Group, M&S BDU, Mexaco Corporate Centre). Apparently Rotterdam refinery's proximity to the spot market's main distribution route, coupled with increasingly dynamic trade, resulted in the refinery using up to fifty different crude supplies a year. Each cargo of crude was throughput in approximately two to three days. Every two to three days the refinery had to respond to changes in its supply side, while at the other end output was extremely variable as it was 'market driven' (Interview with Senior Manager, Systems Group, M&S BDU, Mexaco Corporate Centre). The key tangible 'result' of these 'problems' is Mexaco's inability to honour agreed deals from its own refinery manufacturing. Instead they were forced to buy stocks on the market to meet customer needs to which they were committed. The organization was being forced to act as a 'distressed' purchaser, leaving itself in a vulnerable position (Interview with Senior Manager, Systems Group, M&S BDU, Mexaco Corporate Centre). Traders trading on the spot market were apparently committing the refinery to supply a customer up to one month ahead of delivery. They were seemingly dealing in future production capabilities, while basing their deals on current-rather than future-oriented information. And the result was the distress and vulnerability to which we have referred.

This is *one* story. However, as we noted above, all the entities or actors that describe a network are themselves granted agency in an account based upon translation. And thus, potentially, they may not agree with the designation provided by the primary actor in the problematization statement. To put it simply, they may want to tell another story. The primary actor must work to establish the identities and relations as they are rendered in the problematization. This work is termed *interessement*. 'Interessement is the group of actions by which an entity . . . attempts to impose and stabilise the identity of the other actors it defines through its problematization' (Callon 1986: 207–8).

Traders appear somewhat villainous in the BDU's account of Rotterdam's situation. But it is seemingly enough to provoke a desire to tell their own story, with, of course, appropriate prompting. When an ex-trader is asked about the possibility of SIS and the traders' activities exacerbating Rotterdam's problems, a very different account emerges. In his story traders were, and still are, making 'seat of the pants' decisions. The last thing they would want to be doing is ploughing through reams of 'irrelevant' screens and much of the available information apparently pertains to aspects of manufacturing and supply that lie outside of their field of expertise.

> They don't have the background to understand what the information means. People who understand it best have already seen it. And they don't have the time . . . A lot of those traders are not engineers, they do not necessarily understand the refinery and they are not the people who are dictating how the refinery runs. (Interview with ex-trader)

According to this actor then, traders were working within quite severe constraints set by the supply function.

> Supply people are essentially considering movement of stock and ensuring there is enough stock to go round all the terminals. The traders are . . . trying to balance that when there is a demand to buy in or sell out [and optimise the price paid or received]. [SIS information] enhanced [the traders] understanding of what stocks were available but [they] never saw that information [directly]. It went to the [supply] operational function within the Head Office and they then presented the options to the traders. (Interview with ex-trader)

Interessement seeks to manage these different realities inhabited by different actors in a putative network. In essence, the method by which actors interesse other actors is through the building of devices or networks which can be placed between the actors to be interested and 'all other entities who want to define their identities otherwise' (Callon 1986: 208). These notions of political analysis and (re)synthesis reveal the strategic nature of network building. Strategies and mechanisms are (re)defined *in situ* and are predicated upon interpretations of what those actors yet to be enrolled want and how they are currently defined through their associations with other entities. Just as old links must be broken to form new linkages, so must new linkages be formed to break the old. Interessement is a simultaneous putative breaking and remaking of networks.

> [I]nteressement helps corner the entities to be enrolled. In addition, it attempts to interrupt all competing associations and to construct a system of alliances . . . [S]tructures comprising both social and natural entities are shaped and consolidated. (Callon 1986: 211)

One of the most effective ways to break an entity's link to an old network is to discredit that network. In our case the traders' disagreement with the BDU is consigned to the margins through the use of an appropriate rhetorical scapegoat (Burke 1969) that breaks old links, absorbs old differences in interests, and makes new alignments and associations. Prior network linkages are neatly severed as enrolment in the new network around OMS begins to emerge. The handy new villain here, as you may have guessed, is 'Head Office' and the hierarchical central-ization of the past that it represents (see Lilley 1995).

> The Head Office then, and it's still the case, . . . dictated the plan for the refinery, decided what stock levels should be. They didn't decide what tank should be blended with what tank to make what, but they did decide what the demand levels were and what should be manufactured. (Interview with ex-trader)

A commercial future will be more distributed and cooperative, echoing current pop-management thinking around 'empowerment' and 'the network organisation', despite the persistence in some parts of Mexaco of a more centralized and coer-cive alternative. And, thus, through a rubbishing of a specific instantiation of information technology, the idea of 'advanced information systems', as well as their new instantiation in OMS is able to survive. For our ex-trader such systems can provide

> a great deal more information [but] what it hopefully does is it allows the people who send the requests and are [talking to] the traders . . . to have greater confidence in what's going on so that the level of instruction they can give to the trader is more secure, is more accur-ate, and hence allows more opportunities.

Traders can, thus, emerge untarnished from the past as they are interested in the future and its material instantiations. They are seen to have been making the best of a bad job; of working with 'inappropriate' information through no fault of their own. The tasks of deciding 'what tank should be blended with what tank' and 'what demand levels were and . . . what stock levels should be', which is where 'problems' are now seen to reside, were, and are, undertaken by production schedulers at the refinery and by supply staff at Head Office, respectively. And a distribution of the problem between these two groups is exactly what is required for the BDU's *enrol-ment* of the actors essential for a successful OMS implementation.

Defining and coordination roles: the process of enrolment

As we noted above, the 'identities' and 'links' formed during the process of inter-essement are always contingent, and thus potentially temporary in their effects. The extended problematization and interessement process, the definition of actors and their putative links with each other, does not necessarily lead to firmer alliances between those entities. This subsequent effort to bond described/ascribed enti-ties together is termed by Callon the phase of *enrolment*. 'The issue here is to trans-form a question into a series of statements which are more certain' (Callon 1986: 211). Enrolment is the successful outcome of the problematization and interessement process. It entails a number of conflicts or battles between entities in a struggle to convince them to play the roles to which they are ascribed. As Munro and Kernan (1993) note, the process of enrolment entails the re-presentation of the interests of (potentially) interested others (see also Robson 1993). One hegemonic version of reality aligns disparate interests in such a way that the Machiavellian nature of the translation process is partially disguised for the entities ascribed roles by the enunciator. The reality they submit to belongs to the realm of necessity. It is not (easily) seen as the outcome of political choice. 'To establish a functioning network entails a *translation* of the interests of others into one's own interests. Translation, however, should be conducted in ways that make one indispensable to others and render *their* detour invisible to themselves' (Latour 1987: 108–21). 'The desired effects of translation are first, *control*, in that the work of others acts to propel one's own interest and, second, *invisibility*, in that one's own interests can successfully be re-presented in the name of others' (Munro and Kernan 1993: 2, emphasis in original).

Through the process of enrolment a number of entities and putative networks engage in trials of strength. If the enunciator's definitions are relatively victorious, other entities are successfully ascribed/described, or enrolled within the relational network set in motion by the problematization of the enunciator. And this is just what happened as OMS was materialized as a 'statement' addressing the 'questions' raised at Rotterdam.

Rotterdam refinery

Tensions between entrepreneurial marketing and the stability required for operations management were an increasing cause for concern during the early to mid-1980s. And, as we noted, at Rotterdam these tensions were particularly pronounced. A refinery-based OMS system came to be seen as providing the potential for a technological solution to the problem. One member of the BDU team who was deeply involved in the Rotterdam OMS strategy study described his 'personal view' of the situation as a 'resonance' problem.

> You've got variability at both ends with the plant in the middle and switching the plant activities was a slow process. If you did attempt to change inputs and requirements quickly a great deal of turbulence developed within the plant processes. Thus the plant was very difficult to manage . . . management were being run by the plant rather than running the plant.

Other managers noted the inadequacy of the SIS system in terms of its inability to look forward. But, in the representational tricks that enrolment entails, SIS's role in these arrangements does not render it part of the 'problem', for the computerization it represents is a major part of the emerging OMS solution. Rather, through its links to an inappropriate centralism of the past, SIS is rendered as partially misdirected and misplaced, or to put in another way, as an *insufficient* 'solution'.

It wasn't *enough* just to have what stocks are currently tested in tanks [at the refinery] today, what was really important in terms of committing the business of the next day and the day afterwards, which is what the traders were doing and had to do, is they had to have confidence in what was *going to be produced*. In other words they had to have confidence in a production plan. They didn't need so much to know the position now because they dealt in the future. They needed to know what the position was going to be tomorrow and the next day. Only then can you actually take control of the whole physical flow (emphasis added). (Interview with Systems Manager, Oiltown Refinery)

working stock levels for refineries are very limited, therefore you cannot work on a replacement stock basis because the variability, or 'noise' in requirements is greater than the stock balance. Hence *the need to control the future* (emphasis added). (Telephone Conversation with Systems Manager, Oiltown Refinery)

The production planning systems at Rotterdam are, thus, seen to have failed to move on to meet the changing world and were, as a result, lagging behind the rest of the group's empowered network organization. Their links with the 'old' organization's centralized network were blocking progress towards a future of reworked and *renewed* control. A small project team was set up at Rotterdam by the corporate centre's M&S BDU to try to address these issues. Their aim was apparently to conduct an examination of the systems in place in order to attempt to develop them to allow the site management to regain control (Interview with Senior Manager, Systems Development Unit, Mexaco Corporate Centre). They started off by asking the managers at Rotterdam what their principle objectives were within the refinery. According to the project team, the managers stated that their objectives were

1. 'Jump' for the corporate centre
2. Minimise stocks
3. Minimise costs. (Interview with Senior Manager, Systems Development Unit, Mexaco Corporate Centre)

Refinery management is thus seen to have been facing an endlessly defensive battle with an expanding logistical nightmare. Their network of attachments simply did not equip them to engage in communication with the centre and its representatives and they could not, therefore, take on the commercial role that the networks of the future demanded.

And, here, we witness the final bouts in the contest between the network of the old organization and the putative network organized around OMS and the 'refinery manager of the future' (Mexaco Oil Magazine). The Rotterdam study team tried to supplant the objectives of a loss reduction based operation with the idea of profit maximization. And, thus, the centre's renewed involvement is seen as the solution to the problematics of market trading. Mexaco's role in the creation of these markets and the centre's role in the exacerbation of their problematic effects must be strictly separated and rhetorically managed by our primary actor. Central control is now only seen to be appropriate for the definition of the boundaries of action, the overall 'strategic' direction. The details of activity are not seen to be amenable to corporate control in the emerging network of the future. However, intervention to improve the future capabilities of localized management to fulfil the detailed local work within strategic delimitations *is* seen to be appropriate. Managers at the Rotterdam refinery are represented as needing to regain control of processes before they could begin to direct the refinery's operations in a profit-seeking manner through engagement in 'commercial' communications with the wider group. And thus the study team can be represented as the vehicle of that *renewed* 'commercial' control through its creation of an 'integrated oil management system' (Oiltown Refinery Oil Management Systems Strategy Study, December 1987) or OMS.

The inadequacies of the SIS supply to manufacturing link as a solution to the problems of the emerging commercial scene are, thus, enrolled to demonstrate that the coordination problem itself could not be solved by merely making information on the refinery available to remote decision-makers. And such representational moves allow the OMS to appear as the logical solution to a set of external problems and opportunities.

> Therefore at Rotterdam they evolved from accessing operational data which was then shared . . . through to jointly planning. Then this whole OMS thing of single planning and control of refinery activity and the scheduling timetable arose . . . The operations of the plant were set on one set of assumptions which would be changed more rapidly than you could re-plan the effects of those changes. And it's actually speeding the whole process up to that degree of coherence which attempts to put you in control. (Interview with Systems Manager, Oiltown Refinery)

The systems at Rotterdam appear as a two-stage attempt to regain and renew effective control of the manufacturing and supply function(s) in the face of the new demands and opportunities presented by the emergence of intermediate markets. These markets necessitated the breakdown of long-standing practices that sought to integrate oil industry activities. Control is thus replaced by 'commercial' communication, enabling actors to draw on wider legitimatory network allies provided by contemporary management thinking. SIS was the first-stage response to the perceived need for a reworking of these internal linkages, providing a link between Rotterdam and the corporate centre. OMS is seen as the second-stage response to the realization SIS alone was not sufficient, that current stock data alone were not enough to solve the M&S coordination problem, indeed, that *alone* SIS might have represented little more than an inappropriate perpetuation of the logics of the past. And thus the Oil Management System is seen to fulfil the need for a coherent, wider, corporate production plan (Interview with Systems Manager, Oiltown Refinery) and a widely buttressed enrolment is successfully completed.

But our story is not finished. For this currently limited success goes on to be seen as offering potential for a wider integration, a larger associated network throughout Mexaco's world refining resources. And a key source of this (re)integration is the instantiation of similar OMSs at all of Mexaco's 'strategic' refineries. A progression of OMS with a strategically sanctioned common core could emerge as the source of a new *commercially* competent integration of activities. However, things are never so simple. For continued success and expansion, enrolled entities and the network they make up must be *mobilized* to act in the interests of the enunciator. In the following section we examine how Callon (1986) apprehends the notion of *mobilization*.

Mobilizing enrolled entities to act for the enunciator

The issue of representation, so far raised only obliquely and largely implicitly in our account of translation, takes centre stage in the phase of mobilization. For the 'power effects' (see Foucault 1975 trans. 1977, 1976 trans. 1979, 1991) of the enunciator's network to accrue, the entities enrolled in the network must not contradict their representation therein. To put it bluntly, if the entities present themselves in ways discordant with their representations in the emergent network, the programmatic ambitions of that network will remain unfulfilled. Or to use Latour/Callon's terminology, the network will be translated from its rendering by the enunciator.

> To speak for others is to first silence those in whose name we speak . . . [C]hains of intermediaries which result in a sole and ultimate spokesman can be described as the progressive mobilisation of actors who render . . . [certain] propositions credible and indisputable by forming alliances and acting as a unit of force. (Callon 1986: 216)

Mobilization, which we have already glimpsed in our account of refining, is the outcome of a successful and successive process of decontextualization from prior relations coupled with a concomitant recontextualization in the emergent network (see also Letiche 1993). Entities are represented through a process of description/ascription (Akrich 1992) that (temporarily) redefines their essence in terms of the demands and relations of the network in which they are to be mobilized. The (successful) result is a functioning network of acting entities mobilized in support of the enunciator.[14] And, for a while at least, this is what we see: 'The payback on a system like this is very difficult to calculate but Rotterdam suggested they saw a benefit of 17 cents per barrel' (Interview with Systems Manager, Oiltown Refinery).

Thus, entities throughout the network are enrolled and mobilized, screening their analysis through the commercial, profit-seeking discourse itself set in place as the network emerged. And so, here at least, for the moment, it appears that the ambitions of the network are realized. Yet, our story does not come to a complete stop here and in the following chapter we discuss the effects of stirring the issue of representation back into the mix. But before we do so, we may pause to consider just what *we* have said, so far.

Speak for yourself: Screening translation and appropriation

'To speak for others is to first silence those in whose name we speak' (Callon 1986: 216). Such a comment is just as applicable to those who attempt to 'use' accounts of systems to further their business and academic careers as it is to those involved entities that such authors seek to follow. In seeking to account for the transformation of a sociotechnical network, authors utilize accounts of change processes provided by organizational participants and their own accounts of the processes at work, culled by observation. But what is the 'truth' of that text and what is its context? Or to put it another way, what are the interests of the entity termed 'author'? Most superficially, these objectives entail a relatively easy passage through the rituals of examination (Foucault 1976 trans. 1979) or inspection (Meyer and Rowan 1977) of learned journals in order to (re)grant oneself access to the business/academic priesthood.

The repertoire of translation has not only provided us with a symmetrical and tolerant description of a complex process, which constantly mixes together a variety of social and natural entities. It has also allowed us to produce an explanation of how a few obtain the right to express and represent the many silent actors of the social and natural worlds they have mobilized (Callon 1986: 224). And what better way is there to explain the power of such phenomena and their seeming inevitability than to mobilize them in all their radiance? For as we hinted in our introduction, screens do not just serve the objects they frame. They also grant the subjects that mobilize them privileges, huge privileges including the illusion of an independent existence. For author and reader gain immensely from engagement with our account. Our distanced description of events, our 'efforts to fix things in place' (Weber 1996: 50), enable us to emerge above this world as its overseer. With the world spread out beneath us, our power to decide its direction appears secure.

▓ SUMMARY

It appears that there are various 'screens' by which we might 'observe' technology or society. We can start with technology, assuming it follows an untrammelled path, merely reflecting scientific progress, or with society and posit that technological progress is driven along specific trajectories by historical and social contingencies; or we can try and find a position that takes account of both. But even here we still find problems: the terms 'technological' and 'social' already come replete with structured meaning: to even attempt to explore systems with them drives us down pre-determined pathways. They cannot, in themselves, be used as the basis for analysis of sociotechnical systems. Actor Network Theory attempts to find a way through this impasse by using the notion of *translation*, in which the researcher seeks to account for the stability of a sociotechnical network through consideration of both the elements that make up that network and the relations that hold them in place, while ensuring that, as a researcher, they obviate all a priori distinctions between the 'natural' and the 'social', remain agnostic to competing claims, and maintain symmetry by explaining conflicting view points in the same terms.

The translation process requires attention to four 'moments': problematization, interessement, enrolment, and mobilization. In the first, a primary actor or 'enunciator' problematizes an issue, defining others and their situation in a network of relations, for which the enunciator is an 'obligatory passage point' through whom any solution must be constructed. The enunciator defines others and their situation in order to become indispensable to both. The network of relations, or solution to other actors' 'problems', can only be constructed through the enunciator. *Interessement* is, in essence, how different actors come to be connected within a putative network through the breaking of linkages with older networks and the simultaneous remaking of new linkages. Enrolment is the effort to bond described/ascribed entities together and to convince them to play their determined roles. Finally, for the network to achieve stability, the enrolled entities must be mobilized by the enunciator so that they are recontextualized in terms of the new network.

▨ DISCUSSION QUESTIONS

1. Why is the modern keyboard arranged in the QWERTY formation? Who does such an arrangement favour and who does it handicap? Is such a keyboard a 'neutral' technology?

2. Should we be more worried if all actors in a system are successfully enrolled, or if they are not?

3. Is there any evidence that deploying IT in the workplace actually increases efficiency and/or effectiveness?

4. How would you describe an information system that you know well using the different approaches discussed in this chapter?

5. Is any stability in a network as described merely a mirage?

▨ SUGGESTIONS FOR FURTHER READING

Other examples of organized arrangements described in the terms of Actor Network Theory include:

Latour, B. (1988). *The Pasteurization of France*. Cambridge, MA: Harvard University Press.

Law, J. (1987). 'Technology, Closure and Heterogeneous Engineering: The Case of The Portuguese Expansion', in W. E. Bijker, T. P. Hughes, and T. J. Pinch (eds.), *The Social Construction of Technological Systems: New Directions in the Sociology and History of Technology*. Cambridge, MA: MIT Press, pp. 111–34.

The following applies the approach directly to understand changes in the informational support available to health care providers and their managers:

Bloomfield, B. P. (1992). 'Machines and Manoeuvres: Responsibility Accounting and the Construction of Hospital Information Systems'. *Accounting, Management and Information Technologies*, 2/4: 197–219.

Although not explicitly adopting an ANT approach, the following is exemplary in its attention to the detail of technological development:

Kidder, T. (1981). *The Soul of a New Machine* (reprint 1982, 2nd edn.). London: Allen Lane.

5 | Representation 2: Representation and Simulation

KEY CONCEPTS

embodiment	simulation
hyperreality	simulcra
mobilization	symbolization
representation	technē
self-appropriation	the fold
separation	

KEY THEMES

At the end of this chapter, you should be able to explain those concepts in your own words and also to:

1. Understand the connection between technology and representation.
2. Discuss the importance of the body in representation.
3. Explain what is at stake when we talk about moving from representation to simulation and from simulation to hyperreality.
4. Explore the importance of representation in Actor Network Theory.

Introduction

In this chapter, we return to the theme of representation. In Chapter 2, we discussed how representational models simplify the complexities of the 'reality' that they purport to capture. This abbreviation allows action, for a world that can be expressed symbolically is a world that can be manipulated. But, as our example of the Body Shop in that chapter demonstrated, this cannot be seen as purely a local process—there are always connections to a wider representational network where some codings are more powerfully entrenched than others. And, again from that chapter, our tales from the city, of brokers and their designs upon the everyday world of mortgages, revealed how an existing network of relationships could be dismantled and reassembled into a new series of representative connections. A tale that mirrors our discussion of translation in the previous chapter and could, indeed, be told using the same tropes but which also points us to the necessity of considering the representational turn when considering translation. Thus, in this chapter, we revisit our story of the refinery so that we can expand upon the theme of representation and the progression into *simulation* and the *hyperreal*.

Re(-)presentation, mobility, and technology

At the end of the last chapter, we left our network surrounding the Rotterdam Oil Management System (OMS) seemingly successfully stabilized. But, unsurprisingly, there is no guarantee that the particular mobilizations of this stabilized arrangement will persist. Various entities may betray their network as they seek and achieve enrolment in counter networks. And this is just what we witness in the case of oil refining as the network surrounding the Rotterdam OMS seeks to extend itself over the whole Mexaco world. For, although initially seen to be a success, the logics of commercial progress instantiated by the Rotterdam system may also be seen to have subsequently 'betrayed' the system, at least at Rotterdam. The increasingly 'commercial' orientation towards refining and the value it could add had resulted in Rotterdam entering into a joint venture with another oil company's refinery in the area, making the Rotterdam OMS largely redundant. The refinery, thus, subverted the OMS as a more broadly defined commercialism overtook its relatively limited systemic instantiation. Rotterdam refinery, once decontextualized from its integrated past and thereby mobilized, had not submitted to the role OMS had sought to define for it. Rather, wider networks, of commercialism and 'the oil *industry*', had seduced the refinery and the Mexaco group. The benefits of a network built around OMS had not been allowed to accrue.

> I think you have to go through a learning curve, you have to implement the system first, settle it down, get confidence in it and get sufficient speed really to do such things [examine the commercial implications of various possible refinery operating options]. In the long term . . . that would be the goal. I don't think we've achieved it to date [at Rotterdam] *but that's not the system's fault.* That is . . . the circumstances surrounding the refinery . . . (Interview with European Refinery Analyst, Rotterdam Refinery, emphasis added).

The commercial properties of OMS had exceeded their limited materialization producing a curious mix of success and failure. Yet, the story does not end there: through some interesting *representational* moves the latter outcome is marginalized allowing the dispersed OM 'ideal' to remain untarnished by the redundancy of its initial materialized form. So, it is to the role of representation and its links to 'technology' that we now turn our attention.

According to Cooper, 'Technology and representation are immemorially connected' (1993: 279). However, while, following Heidegger, he notes that for the ancient Greeks *technē* described the process of realization, the art of making present, the modern conception of technology is seen to entail a 'curious twist' in meaning.

> Instead of the concern with making present, with the art of constructing something for the apprehension of the senses, the modern interest in technology puts the stress on immediacy of use, constant availability and the easing of effort. (Cooper 1993: 279)

Modern technology is seen as re-presenting 'actions in space and time according to an economics of mastery and control' (1993: 280).

> Ancient *technē* was directly dependent on the powers and contingencies of the natural world; it took advantage where it could. Modern technology, in contrast, is distinguished by its detachment from nature and this separation enables it to increase its advantage at will. (1993: 280)

Enter the body

Cooper is not questioning the 'truth' or 'adequacy' of representation. Rather, he asks more fundamental questions concerning the supposed primacy of objects and subjects over their mere representations. For from Cooper's perspective representations may be seen not only to describe, but also to *separate* and hence *create* the subjects and objects that they purport to display. Representations 'frame' their objects and subjects, severing them from the maelstrom of relational contingencies as they bring them into being as separate and separable entities. They are a key source of the decontextualization we have been considering. The human body, for example, is 'naturally' neither a machine to be repaired by physicians, an object, nor a centre of the discretion required of citizenship, a subject. Rather, it can be made into these forms through representation. And thus, following Foucault (1975, trans. 1977), Cooper conceives of the undifferentiated human body as a fragile, ongoing impediment to the realization of power.

> All representations originate in the instability of the body. All *technē*, all making, flows from this need of the body to re-present itself in terms of more durable external structures. (Cooper 1993: 280)

Cooper draws upon Scarry's (1985) insights into the 'counterfactual structure' of representation/technology, the ways in which it turns weaknesses into strengths. 'Inadequacies' of the body are apprehended in such a way that the process enables their turning to advantage—a glove mimics the hand but does so in such a way that its lack of insulation and protection are remedied—just as the 'questions' of problematization are materialized as the 'statements' and solutions of enrolment (see Chapter 4). 'Representation thus involves two complementary steps: (1) the separation and objectification of bodily attributes and (2) the recovery by the body of the objectified attributes in an act of self-appropriation' (Cooper 1993: 281).

These moves enable a detachability of bodily attributes, parts, and functions with the re-presented body consequently open to redesign and recombination. Yet there is, for our analysis, a particularly important further effect: 'A major consequence of the body being able to represent itself in external artefacts is that the human agent can more easily control and modify the latter than it can its own body' (1993: 281).

This revisits our discussion in Chapter 2. Representation is still that which enables control, manipulation, and modification, but here we are able to see the connections with Actor Network Theory emerge. For representation is both technical and social: accounts of representational moves not only talk about 'the social and the technical all-in-one-breath' (Law 1991*b*: 8) but reveal their interconnections. However, with the advent of industrial production the representational process seemingly moves further from its origination in the body and is accelerated and qualitatively altered. The world is represented as, and hence shaped into, a stock of parts that can be recombined at will. Objects, or re-presentations lose their 'essence' (see also, Kallinikos 1995), derived from the specifics of their bodily appropriation, and take on a mode of being that is metaphorically exemplified by Lego and Meccano.

> The detachability of bodily parts and functions enables an *ars combinatoria* to be applied to the act of representation . . . The whole object, formerly a creation of *technē*, 'now becomes a transient aggregate given to assembly, disassembly and reassembly' (Fisher 1978: 142). (Cooper 1993: 281–2)

Drawing on the work of Heidegger (1977) and Latour (1987), Cooper notes that the appearance of detached representations is productive of a new form of power. A power that enables a view of the world 'as a table top ruled by the human hand and eye' (Fisher 1978: 144). Without detached representation entities would not be mobile and hence mobilizable. And just as limited bodily re-presentation enables 'solutions' through the appropriation of 'problems', recursive chains of modern technologies of representation extend and enable power/knowledge effects through their appropriation of re-presented items on a grander scale.[1]

> Pressed to its extreme, this process tends towards finality through the construction of large-scale systems of certainty which seek to master what remains of uncertainty; a continuous chain of terms is forged which must reinforce each term's certainty. Heidegger calls this process 'the gigantic' (Cooper 1993: 288).

But such a process inevitably resembles nothing more than the proverbial dog chasing its tail. The attempt to trap all uncertainty tends towards an overarching and closed system. As a result everything is dragged closer together and made smaller, is displaced and abbreviated in order to facilitate remote control (see also Roszak 1986; Zuboff 1988; Cooper 1992). The diffusion of information technology and the creed of knowledge management may be seen as classic examples of this process at work. The deployment of IT holds out the dream of grasping the uncertainty created by its dispersal (see also Robb 1990, 1993; Lilley 1993*a*, *b*), as we witnessed in SIS's exacerbation of the problems that OMS went on to 'solve' at Rotterdam in the previous chapter. Similarly, the advocates of knowledge management (see Chapter 10, this volume) suggest that once knowledge is stripped down, packed, and stored, ready for redeployment, then organizations can finally begin to *learn*.

The fold

Cooper (1993) conceives of the reproduction of uncertainty in modern technology/ representation, following Heidegger (1977), Derrida (1972, trans. 1981*a*), Deleuze (1988, trans. 1993), and particularly Deleuze's reading of Foucault (1986), in terms of the spatial logic of the fold. For Derrida (1981*b*: 227) the fold is a gathering that is at the same time a dissemination, a joining that keeps apart, but never presents itself as such. And, for Deleuze (1988, trans. 1993), the fold is that which mediates between virtuality and actuality. It is not just a question of representation— organizing matter into visible form—but also the virtual relations of force that act to destabilize the determinable and bring forward what can be articulated. This logic is perhaps most clearly exemplified in the second OMS that was built at Mexaco's Cobber Creek refinery in Australia. Staff at Cobber had attempted to be 'technological innovators'. In the process, however, they 'ran into technical problems that were quite substantial' (Interview with Systems Manager, Oiltown Refinery). These 'problems' served to scupper the notion of a progression of systems that would allow reintegration of the refinery network through their possession of a common core, for in the belief that the second OMS implementation would 'overtake the Mexaco world' (Interview with Systems Manager, Oiltown Refinery), systems staff at that refinery had been allowed and, indeed, encouraged to 'destroy the core of the system' (Interview with European Refinery Analyst, Rotterdam Refinery).

> When we set out on the OMS project the idea was to make it as portable as possible and in fact 50% of the Rotterdam system was portable. The rest of it has to be tailored to the site and that's inevitable, but . . . the concept was that if you kept the core of the system portable then any enhancements at future implementations could be brought back into your other refineries. (Interview with European Refinery Analyst, Rotterdam Refinery)

The OMS solution to Rotterdam's scheduling problems,

> Rotterdam . . . is very volatile, things are changing incredibly rapidly there, great instability, variation of crude, you name it, . . . [with] essentially a large scheduling problem that dominates your production and control problem. (Interview with European Refinery Analyst, Rotterdam Refinery)

was seen to be transportable and applicable to different problems elsewhere, as we witnessed at Oiltown:

> You in fact ended up with a general tool for improvement which wasn't actually organisationally quite so dependent. (Interview with Systems Manager, Oiltown Refinery)

Indeed, at Cobber, the second OMS implementation by the Mexaco group, there was a very different set of concerns:

> Cobber is . . . a refinery, which serves a local market. Vessels are seen coming a month away, . . . so you don't have any volatility. However, they have a different sort of problem, which is in terms of competing plant, in terms of essentially a mass balance problem. And optimising the process operations was more critical than at Rotterdam. So you've got the emphasis one end on process modelling and at the other end, scheduling. (Interview with European Refinery Analyst, Rotterdam Refinery)

Nevertheless, the desire to maintain a portable, generic core for all OM type systems was inscribed in the introduction of Cobber's OMS Concept of Operation Document: 'Without strict adherence to the Rotterdam data model the relocation [of] any of the significant Rotterdam software models would prove costly, if not impossible'.

However, these noble intentions were soon repudiated. Indeed, this repudiation occurs later in the same document! Local contingencies which, in the emerging 'commercial' world, insisted upon a process modelling emphasis at Cobber, led to a decision to abandon the planning and scheduling system that had been developed at Rotterdam. And this had implications for the data model used in the Cobber system. As a result, there were

> a number of major departures from the Rotterdam data model in its implementation at Cobber Creek in order to accommodate the very different interface requirements of the Cobber Creek OMS system . . . Given the inevitability of these departures . . . and the consequent impossibility of 100% Rotterdam compatibility, it was seen as pragmatic, and desirable, to improve upon the Rotterdam model. (Cobber Creek OMS Concept of Operation Document)

The 'improvements' instigated at Cobber had far-reaching implications. Substantial changes were made to the database structure, architecture, and reporting. And most importantly for our discussion of 'the fold', radical changes were also made with regard to the way in which the process optimizer models were integrated into the site-wide linear programming model. One of the Oiltown system managers had this to say on the subject:

> The ambition with OMS was . . . to actually build systems which looked forward in time, predicted what we were going to do, and did it in sufficient detail to provide advice, to the operators at least, about how they should operate the plant . . . So you would have an LP . . . [and] that LP would drive in some way the optimisers which were responsible for providing the advice for the process control. Rotterdam did a little bit of that but still the systems were quite separate. Cobber tried to really integrate them and . . . they devised a system where [the process optimisers, for the example, the catalytic cracker optimizer] did multiple runs, hundreds of runs and produced lots of sets of data . . . by varying operating parameters. So then when the LP ran and decided at any stage of its solution what operating parameters it was going to use at that stage, it could go off to this database of the data from the optimiser and say 'That's the best fit at the moment, bring that back as the yield structure we're going to get if we run on those operating parameters'. Now as the LP went through its iterations it would continually go out and access this database and get a better fit.

However, 'They bit off more than they could chew' (Interview with Systems Manager, Oiltown Refinery). And in this inability to chew we can see Heidegger's 'gigantic' rear its ugly head. The fold enfolds upon itself, re-presenting the logistical nightmare that Rotterdam's OMS sought to conquer, in the very heart of the first-born offspring of that system:

> The technical problem really was in driving the optimisers to generate a database which you could actually understand and was suitable for solving the bigger problem and they never really cracked that problem. If you can imagine that those optimisers were filling up a sort of three-dimensional space with lots of data points and the LP was going in and finding the best point based on the sort of feed used, appropriate points on a blend, and interpolating between them. The theory of what they were trying to do was very complex and so was putting it into practice, just because of machine time restriction and so on. That planning part of it didn't work and because the target setting bit was integrated with some other systems, like reconciliation, two or three other systems sort of fell apart because they wouldn't work. So they had to fall back to the initial data capture system in one or two of the more straightforward systems . . . They overstretched themselves in terms of the production system design and because of that they basically failed to meet their goals and are still trying to implement the system. They were just trying to go too far with the technology available. (Systems Manager, Oiltown Refinery)

But is the problem merely one of 'trying to go too far', a problem that is cosily situated in the age-old tale of all-too-human attempts to surmount technical short-comings? Or is it something more fundamental that we see? For the system has now come to be seen as the source of uncertainty rather than the vehicle for its removal and the problem is now one of aligning different sets of representations, rather than matching any particular representation to some underlying 'reality'.

And so, without any anchor in some pre-representational reality, technology and its simulational objectives become the source of uncertainty rather than its solution.[2] The world functions as a gigantic simulacrum (Baudrillard 1983).

Gigantic simulation

The emergence of the 'gigantic'[3] here inaugurates a shift from representation to *simulation*. But what are the consequences of this shift? 'Simulation has gone beyond the stage of detachability . . . which enabled the world to be manipulated as "transient aggregates given to assembly, disassembly and reassembly", by abolishing the very notion of a substantive reference' (Cooper 1993: 302).

And once all reference points are lost, for Baudrillard, it inevitably becomes impossible to return to any underlying 'reality'.

> We are in a logic of simulation which has nothing to do with a logic of facts and an order of reasons. Simulation is defined by a *precession* of the model, of all models around the merest fact—the models come first, and their orbital constitutes the genuine magnetic field of events. (1983: 175, our emphasis)

With the emergence of simulation the 'system' becomes self-sustaining. 'Simulation folds back on itself again and again in . . . [a] process of dedifferentiation' (Cooper 1993: 303). The project has a self-collapsing characteristic of 'implosion' [4] (Baudrillard 1983) which inevitably leads to an undermining of the rigidities of categorical thought upon which representation depends. And so, in our simulatory world, what can we talk of once 'reality' is expunged from our critical lexicon? For Baudrillard:

> Abstraction today is no longer that of the map, the double, the mirror, or the concept. Simulation is no longer that of a territory, a referential being or a substance. It is the generation by models of a real without origin or reality: a *hyper real*. The territory no longer precedes the map. Nor survives it. (Baudrillard 1983: 2)

And technology is absolutely critical for this move:

> The real is produced from miniaturised units, from matrices, memory banks and command models—and with these it can be reproduced an indefinite number of times . . . In fact, it is no longer real at all. It is hyper real, the product of an irradiating synthesis of combinatory models in a hyperspace . . . (Baudrillard 1983: 3–4)

Which leads neatly back to our story. By the time of the implementation of the third such system, at Oiltown, the complete, or near complete, systematization of oil management that had been attempted with the Cobber system was no longer seen to be in the realm of current possibility. The Cobber system had sought to make oil management an automatic process in which a number of simulations of refinery plant processes would be run in order to ascertain the most profitable operating characteristics, given current product and crude prices, and current supply and demand. An overall simulation of the site then sought to draw these suggestions together and each of these levels of simulation would be rerun in the light of the output of other simulations until the overall 'value-added' of the system was optimized. However, practice did not replicate this theoretical utopia and the system had been prone to continual breakdown. While Cobber had looked like improving upon the original, it had not become the Mark II origin point of all future implementations, contradicting prior predictions made by visitors to Cobber from Oiltown. Rather, Cobber's system was now seen as something of a technological blind alley, a mistake in systems design from which future designers could learn important lessons. The complete, or near complete, systematization of oil management that had been attempted with the Cobber system was no longer a realistic goal. Rather, a new conception of the support of refining activities was emerging in which appropriate solutions to 'business problems' had to be congruent with the 'technological' capabilities of implementable systems. A conception that firmly and explicitly inscribes a place for the human body as overseer of the simulations it sets in train (an important point that we return to in our discussion of accountability in Chapter 7). This inscription is reflected in choices concerning the level of resolution to be used when recording and modelling the refinery within the OMS, choices predicated upon knowledge of the 'performance' implications of the more complex refinery representation that had been employed at Cobber Creek.

There was a compromise made as to the number of operational data collection points out of that mass of ironwork out there on the refinery that would be collated for production planning purposes. The design is for relevance in the overview level of production control, not in terms of the technical control or operations control of the plant. (Interview with Systems Manager, Oiltown Refinery)

Control, of the 'real', is to remain distributed and local whilst a simulated overview advertises its epistemological and ontological status through an explicit openness regarding the 'veracity' of its representations. It is an unabashed simulation, an 'overview' to assist in commercial direction. It is definitely not to be mistaken for a 'real', or even a 'realistic' picture of, intervenable refinery hardware. Simulation is revealed as simulation, and kept away from the action whilst the tacit knowledge of situated bodies manages reality at those places where matter *matters*. Yet even here, there can be no certainty. For Baudrillard, there can only ever be access to an *image* of the real, its pretence of being. (Baudrillard 1989: 45)

▓ SUMMARY AND CONCLUSION

Our somewhat meandering story has taken us a long way. We have seen how tensions between the general and the specific in software and organizational arrangements play themselves out (Boland, personal communication) in our story of refining 'realities'. More fundamentally, our adoption of the translation approach has allowed us to juxtapose representations provided by a number of entities to ascertain their convergence. We have been able to glimpse the construction of reality at work as certain power effects and relations are established, to challenge the necessity of these arrangements and demonstrate the contingent nature of their perpetuation, and to witness the ways in which representation and eventually simulation continually inveigle themselves in this never-ending oscillation. We have seen how the instability and frailty of the human body is both cause and consequence of these processes. And we have also seen that however we approach these moves we inevitably *instantiate* a chimerical sense of identity and purpose for our own good 'selves' in the process, establishing ourselves as one more 'user' of 'the system'.

But what was it all for? Well, 'Strictly speaking, nothing remains for us to base anything on. All that remains for us is theoretical violence—speculation to the death, whose only method is the radicalisation of hypotheses' (Baudrillard 1983: 5). We do not cloak ourselves in such revolutionary garb: our aims are more modest. But one thing that we would wish to claim is that by glimpsing the forces that lie behind the seemingly 'natural' entities of our world, we may begin to discern what other arrangements of forces have to offer in terms of alternative forms. This notion, however, seems a little abstract and we therefore close with a rather lengthy quotation from Kurt Vonnegut, Jr. (1969, reprint 1991) who gives us a practical demonstration of what is at stake here in terms that are much more eloquent and convincing than anything that we can produce alone. The story comes from *Slaughterhouse 5*, in which Vonnegut's (anti)hero, Billy, witnesses a 'movie about American bombers and the gallant men who flew them' (1991: 53) in a rather unusual way:

Seen backwards by Billy, the story went like this:
    American planes, full of holes and wounded men and corpses took off backwards from an airfield in England. Over France, a few German fighter planes flew at them backwards, sucked bullets and

shell fragments from some of the planes and crewmen. They did the same for wrecked American bombers on the ground, and those planes flew up backwards to join the formation.

The formation flew backwards over a German city that was in flames. The bombers opened their bomb bay doors, exerted a miraculous magnetism which shrunk the fires, gathered them into cylindrical steel containers, and lifted the containers into the bellies of the planes. The containers were stored neatly in racks. The Germans below had miraculous devices of their own, which were long steel tubes. They used them to suck more fragments from the crewmen and planes. But there were still a few wounded Americans, though, and some of the bombers were in bad repair. Over France, though, German fighters came up again, made everything and everybody as good as new. When the bombers got back to their base, the steel cylinders were taken from the racks and shipped back to the United States of America, where factories were operating night and day, dismantling the cylinders, separating the dangerous contents into minerals. Touchingly, it was mainly women who did this work. The minerals were then shipped to specialists in remote areas. It was their business to put them into the ground, to hide them cleverly, so they would never hurt anybody again. (1991: 53–4)

▓ DISCUSSION QUESTIONS

1. Does the representational shift enhance or diminish the separation of subject and object?

2. Would you expect our OMS to continue to be viewed as a simulation? Or are managers likely to attempt to turn back the representational clock?

3. Is the hyperreal world such a bad place to live in?

4. Billy's view allows him to see that technologies of war can, potentially, be removed and made safe if enough care is taken, but does this view, in itself, enable such a change to take place?

▓ SUGGESTIONS FOR FURTHER READING

Jean Baudrillard's *Simulcra and Simulation* (1994) is the obvious place for a more detailed examination of the ideas presented in this chapter. *America* (1989) and *The Gulf War Never Took Place* (1995) offer Baudrillard's intriguing take on what 'reality' has come to mean in other areas of contemporary life. Reading of the latter should, perhaps, only be undertaken alongside a reading of Christopher Norris's timely response to the original publication of these ideas, *Uncritical Theory: Postmodernism, Intellectuals, and the Gulf War*. A simpler introduction to the ideas and dangers of simulation can be found in Theodore Roszak's (1986) *The Cult of Information: The Folklore of Computers and the True Art of Thinking*. For an application of poststructural thinking to a range of matters informational, see Mark Poster's (1990) *The Mode of Information*. Paul Virilio's (2000) *The Information Bomb*, an 'exploration of the relationship between technology, speed, war, and the new information sciences' (back cover) also repays careful consideration.

As well as Cooper's own writings, Robert Chia's (1996) edited collection, *In the Realm of Organization: Essays for Robert Cooper*, demonstrates how pervasive Cooper's writing on technology, representation, and organization have become.

6 New Management Practices: Empowerment, Information, and Control

KEY THEMES

When you have read this chapter, you should be able to define those key concepts in your own words, and you should also be able to:

1. Understand the emergence of the so-called 'new organization' and the 'new managerial work' that populates it.

2. Explain the role played by information systems in the delivery of the self-discipline seemingly necessitated by the increased demands for accountability within this 'new organization'.

3. Explore the interrelationships between Bentham's panopticon or inspection tower and contemporary information systems.

4. Understand, through examples, power as both repressive and productive.

Introduction

During the last two decades of the twentieth century something of a sea change was ascribed to the practice of management. Managers were exhorted, by a number of extraordinarily vociferous 'gurus',[1] to adopt new ways of thinking about, and practices of, organization and its management. At the heart of much of this advocacy of the 'new wave' (Wood 1989) was a proclaimed need to shift from a 'command-and-control' mode of management to one that can perhaps best be captured as that of 'facilitate-and-empower'.

In this chapter we examine the role played by information systems in this putative change, for it is not an insignificant one. In practice, 'empowerment' seems only to be seen to work and is thus 'granted' only when mechanisms are in place to ensure that the empowered continue to perform as the empowerer would wish them to: mechanisms that, in the main, turn around knowledge of the production and dissemination of information on that performance.

To explore the role of these mechanisms in the realization of new management practices we draw extensively on two main sources: a paper on 'The "New Organization" and the "New Managerial Work" ' by Ezzamel, Lilley, and Willmott (1994, but see also 1993, 1996a, b; and Ezzamel et al. 1996) and some ethnographic work conducted at one of Safeway's superstores, investigating the organizational practices surrounding the introduction of the ability to *self-scan* the bar codes of one's own groceries. We examine the latter, since this transformation in the practices of consumption, particularly the ways in which 'free' consumers are 'controlled' as they conduct their 'normal' shop, mirrors and exaggerates the issues we explore in relation to the role of information systems in empowering modes of management. For if we can understand how 'discipline' can be produced where there is no employment contract, no mutually signed up to basis for cooperation, we may also be able to understand the role that similar arrangements play in the realization of empowered discipline 'inside' organizations. What we seek to explicate are the contributions of information systems to modes of control through which employees are disciplined in ways that leave their potential initiative 'intact'.

Why new now?

The changes in management practice seen to be required since the 1980s can be at least partially tied to a series of fuelling factors. These would include the rapid globalization of markets, the volatility of currency movements, the diffusion of information and communication technologies, government policies in support privatization, deregulation, and a widespread emphasis upon improvements in quality, attentiveness to added-value, and the pursuit of value-for-money. Together, these factors have combined to intensify competition and stimulate pressures for a major transformation in organization and management. Setting this transformation in its historical context, Peter Drucker (1988) has suggested that management is now entering a third phase of development. The first phase occurred with the separation of ownership and control, when shareholders appointed a separate cadre of experts to manage their interests. The second phase involved the introduction of administrative techniques and systems to plan corporate development, manage complexity, and monitor the operational achievement of policy objectives; and it culminated in the restructuring of large companies into multidivisional forms. The third, contemporary phase is characterized by Drucker as the shift from a command-and-control approach to management towards an *information-based* organization in which reliance upon the vertical and horizontal partitioning of hierarchical levels, departments, and divisions is weakened by the development of cross-functional teams and task forces to tackle problems and exploit opportunities. This latest phase in the development of management is seen to demand greater self-discipline and individual responsibility for managing relationships and communications.

How the way forward in the new situation is seen is, to considerable degree, the result of characterizations of that new situation and its consequences by a growing body of international management superstars. Wherever uncertainties and anxieties arise, an opportunity exists for 'experts' to provide lucrative counselling and direction. In response to the unprecedented pressures for change that now face corporate managers, 'gurus' have emerged and multiplied to provide managers with advice on how to meet and beat the challenge. These experts have produced a chorus of prescriptions that, among others, urge the development of more flexible forms of organization, the strengthening of corporate culture, and the determination to make continuous improvements in the quality of products and services. At the heart of such prescriptions is the recommendation that reliance upon 'hard', rational, mechanical techniques of management and organization should be moderated by a greater use of 'soft', intuitive, organic methods of management.

Of course, such exhortations by management pundits and gurus are invariably met with a degree of scepticism from managers: practising managers are not slow to identify weaknesses in their assertions, especially when the changes urged unsettle or directly threaten their job security or career prospects. *Middle* managers, in particular, find themselves in a precarious position here. For although, as Drucker (1988: 50) notes, it is 'the middle aged people in middle management who tend to be the least mobile', it is precisely those occupying the middle layers of management who are expected to implement 'the new organization'.

However, the intensity of pressure on *senior* managers to survive in a hostile marketplace has rendered them more amenable (or vulnerable) to the diagnoses and prescriptions of the 'experts'. Under pressure to demonstrate their concern and capacity to be proactive, managers have sought the advice of consultants who, in response to this demand, have absorbed or adapted the teachings of the gurus. Alternatively, they have at least flirted with the recipes of the new management theory in an effort to adapt their organizations to rapidly changing and unpredictable market conditions, or at least dress those adaptations up in fashionable rhetorical garb.

What's new?

The emerging new managerial rhetoric of the last decades of the twentieth century questioned much of the received wisdom about how to organize and manage effectively. In particular, the merits of bureaucratic structure and hierarchical control were severely challenged. Such structure and control were and are criticized for their cost, lack of responsiveness, and perhaps most importantly in terms of the rhetorical appeal of the alternatives, for their deadening effect upon employee initiative and productivity. Horizontal divisions between departments as well as layers of hierarchy came to be seen as inhibitors of effective communication and creators of unnecessary managerial overhead. Most crucially, established practices apparently constrained the speed and quality of responsiveness to changing conditions and a leaner, more creative, and adaptive form of organization was commended in order to ensure that one is not left behind by similarly dynamic competitors.

Instead of a mechanistic reliance upon rules and procedures, the new organization is built, and depends, upon the commitment of all staff to shared values. The organic network, rather than rigid hierarchy, is the central organizing principle. The expense and cumbersomeness of hierarchy can be avoided once employees have absorbed, and become committed to, the core values of the organization. These values, rather than inflexible and quickly outdated regulations, guide employees to form and reform the collaborative intra- and inter-departmental teams and networks through which the mission of the organization is realized.

With the new form of organization comes a new kind of management, performing 'the new managerial work' (Kanter 1989). Managers are no longer required to develop and enforce the rules, which control a recalcitrant workforce. When employees are self-disciplined, and no longer require a narrow 'span of control' to ensure their compliance with company requirements, levels in the hierarchy can be substantially reduced, if not entirely abandoned. Thus, the responsibility of those managers who remain employed is to act as 'facilitators' who ensure that the staff are fully equipped, materially and educationally, to work organically—for example by developing new project teams that exploit emergent opportunities—to both develop new synergies in activities and deliver their full commitment to the organization. Managers with responsibility for these new deliverables are rewarded accordingly, and not just on the basis of their formal position.

The new organization demands new forms of managerial work. Reliance upon formal position within the hierarchy is supplanted by demonstrated ability to facilitate collaborative activity and innovation that is cross-functional and interdepartmental. Command is replaced by consent, as the key to corporate success is the development of employees capable of constantly responding, with the minimum of managerial direction, to emergent opportunities and threats. Complying with established practice and conforming to established codes of conduct are no longer a low risk strategy for achieving recognition and promotion. Instead, advancement comes to depend upon the demonstration of skills that empower, energize, and support staff in continuously producing and refining quality products and services.

This is a potentially bewildering world in which old certainties associated with the prerogative of rank and the authority of expertise no longer provide a reliable basis for action (or compliance). In the effort to eliminate rigidities and improve responsiveness, it would seem that almost everything has now become flexible and negotiable. People are increasingly valued for their contribution in unsettling conventions and rigidities that are deemed to be counterproductive for stimulating innovation and enhancing competitiveness. Managers and employees are no longer urged to strive for 'excellence' (Peters and Waterman 1982). Increasingly, they are exhorted to 'cherish impermanence' and 'thrive on chaos' (Peters 1988), or so the revolutionary rhetoric goes.

Rhetorics of empowerment

Rhetorically, empowerment and the range of other human resource management (HRM)-type practices (Keenoy 1990; Noon 1992; Sisson 1994; and in particular, Legge 1995) with which it is associated are very attractive to both managed and managers, but for both practice is often a little more prosaic and problematic. For example, in one of the companies studied by Ezzamel, Lilley, and Willmott (1994) the superior use of financial and management information by major competitors had led to the implementation of a productivity and effectiveness programme designed to increase the extent of management by information. In this example, the installation of 'fundamentally a very simple work measurement system' was said to 'empower' managers by requiring them to quantify the contribution of their staff against planned improvements in performance. In such cases, the rhetoric of new management theory is deployed to describe what might otherwise be interpreted as a typical case of 'command-and-control' in which bureaucratic systems are introduced to direct effort and raise productivity.

That the idea of 'empowerment' is used to justify tighter management control is not surprising, given the anxieties among managers that any other form of empowerment can fuel. 'Empowering' employees is all very well so long as they act in ways that are acceptable to management—a concern that becomes more critical for managers when their rewards become more closely linked to the performance of their staff. This anxiety was voiced by a number of the interviewees, and was summed up by the view that

> I have no problem with the idea of empowerment, it's just the practical application I'm worried about. I don't mind empowering people so long as we actually train them to get a better answer before they're let loose. (Customer Services Manager, Financial Services)

This comment also draws attention to the complex conditions and consequences of implementing 'the new organization'. For while many might accept the need to change and the necessity of developing a new approach or 'paradigm' and adopting it throughout the organization, such a shift might also be seen to endanger positive qualities—such as pride and loyalty—without effectively engendering new ones. In such circumstances the push for 'empowerment' and 'commitment' might actually weaken established expressions of loyalty without replacing them with a more robust and effective alternative. The key term used by managers to fill this potentially worrying gap is *accountability*, the subject of our next chapter. But accountability alone is no solution to the problem here. That space must be filled by a self-discipline that accepts and enacts the demands accountability places upon it, a self-discipline that is in large part the result of particular arrangements of information systems.

Systems for self-discipline

The work of the historian, social theorist, and philosopher Michel Foucault has provided a major impetus to consideration and theorization of control in organizations. Particularly important has been work building upon the book, *Discipline and Punish: the Birth of the Prison* (1975, trans. 1977). Here, Foucault provides not only an account of the emergence of the modern prison, he also delineates a historical shift in the form of control employed in European societies. Through this shift the spectacular exercise of power by the sovereign, exemplified in acts of public torture, is replaced by the more detailed and continuous disciplining of the body throughout society, exemplified in its most extreme form by the total institution of the reformatory prison. At the centre of Foucault's argument is an account of the English philosopher Jeremy Bentham's (1787) putative model for an ideal prison: the panopticon. The panopticon design featured a central tower, occupied by the prison warders into which, through careful usage of lighting and blinds, it was impossible for prisoners to see. The prisoners themselves were to occupy largely open cells, organized in a concentric ring around the tower, in which they would always be potentially visible to those who occupied the tower. (See Figure 2.)

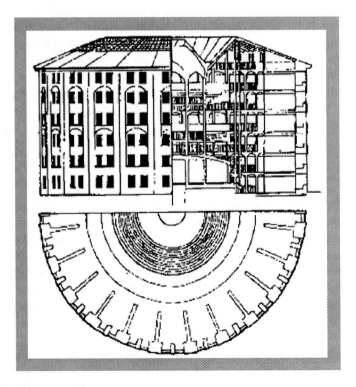

Figure 2 Bentham's panopticon

Foucault builds upon Bentham's understanding of the functioning of this architectural arrangement to delineate how self-control, of, by, and through the individual is constructed through the action of an intermittent, but potentially omnipresent, surveillance acting upon that individual. According to Barry Smart (Smart 1985: 88), the panopticon constitutes a method for 'the efficient exercise of power'. This efficiency is achieved through arranging those subject to power in such a way that at any moment they may be exposed to 'invisible' observation. In Smart's words (Smart 1985: 88):

> Bentham's conception of the Panopticon has been described as a machine which 'produces homogenous effects of power', as an 'architectural figure', and as a 'laboratory' . . . The Panopticon was to function as an apparatus of power by virtue of the field of visibility in which individuals were to be located, each in their respective places (e.g. cells, positions, rooms, beds, etc.), for a centralized and unseen observer. In this schema subjects were to be individualized in their own spaces, to be visible, and to be conscious of their potentially constant and continuous visibility. Given that those illuminated by power were unable to see their observer(s) the latter condition, a consciousness of being in a visible space, of being watched, effectively ensured an automatic functioning of power. As a result individuals became entangled in an impersonal power relation, one which automatized and disindividualized power as it individualized those subject to it.

Power works here through the distribution of knowledge that the architectural arrangements determine. Prisoners 'know' they may be watched, but they do not know when. They know that if they transgress the rules, that they will probably be caught (as a result of their visibility). But they must also know that the power that views them has at its disposal certain unpleasant sanctions that can be applied to punish and correct their behaviour, that misbehaviour will be apprehended and disciplined. The application of sanctions is only likely to be required in the early stages of the adoption of the panoptical mechanism and in the socialization of new members/inmates, because of the efficient functioning of the relationship between power and knowledge that is established within the set-up. It should become increasingly unnecessary

> to use force to constrain the convict to good behaviour, the madman to calm, the worker to work, the schoolboy to application, the patient to the observation of the regulations . . . He who is subjected to a field of visibility, and who knows it, assumes responsibility for the constraints of power; he makes them play spontaneously upon himself; he inscribes in himself the power relation in which he simultaneously plays both roles; he becomes the principle of his own subjection. (Foucault 1982: 221–2)

Foucault uses the image of the panopticon to describe the forms of control increasingly adopted throughout modern society, forms of control in which direct confrontation with brute force seemingly becomes rarer and rarer. Instead, subjects assume responsibility for their own control: they control themselves in the knowledge that if they do not, their inappropriate conduct will immediately be seen and corrected. They accept and enact discipline on and of themselves. Such an account of control differs from the notion of 'negative conditioning' offered by a Pavlovian or Skinnerian behaviourism (see, for example, Brown 1982). This is because it does not see compliance on the part of the subject as an automatic response, as a simple conditioned reflex to avoid pain. Rather it conceives of control as operating through the consciousness of the subject. For this is control *of the self by the self* that results from the combination of reasoning and knowledge of the situation. The self, on the basis of the knowledge available to it, calculates the action most likely to result in reward, and least likely to result in punishment (see, for example, Barnes 1988; Rose 1990; Miller and O'Leary 1987).

These ideas have been deployed to account for control in organizations in two key ways. In attempts to make sense of contemporary HRM (see, for example, Townley 1993) decisions concerning the appropriate modes and methods of recruitment, selection, appraisal, development, and compensation—to deliver the right sort of employee working in the right sort of way—are seen as exercises in the construction of appropriate 'selves'. The relationship of the employee to the organization is increasingly individualized, in the employment and the so-called 'psychological contract'. And the individual employee, by 'reading' HRM systems, learns what is important to the organization, and thus how to garner the best rewards that are available.

Of much greater interest to us is the role of information systems in the maintenance of organizational control in conditions of 'empowerment' in the face of the stripping away of the of the preceding 'command-and-control' structures (see, for example, Sewell and Wilkinson 1992; Zuboff 1988). Here, the knowledge that information systems allow the tracking both of work flows and of individual contributions to those work flows is seen to lead individuals to ensure that they are always working according to, or exceeding, the norms of 'best practice' that apply in the organization. For they know that if they do not, their deviance from this ideal will immediately be identified and unpleasant consequences are likely to follow. It is obvious, however, that information systems also play a key record keeping and managing role that is essential to HRM's realization of panoptical control, illustrating the interconnectedness of the collection and management of information on the individual with management of the individual. Such processes work through the fact that the individual knows that information on their conduct is being collected and assessed (see, for example, the various contributions to McKinlay and Starkey 1998).

Graham Sewell and Barry Wilkinson build upon Shoshana Zuboff's work to suggest that the use of computer technologies can allow the construction of a panoptical mechanism that exceeds the limitations of visibility associated with the architectural version of the arrangement. That what they term the electronic panopticon can enable control through the collection, storage, and instantaneous display of data on individual performance on a scale that would be impossible if one were to rely on the extent of vision of a single human eye and the storage capacity of a single human memory, for, as long as information on each individual's performance can be delineated as an account of that individual's performance, then that individual will discipline his or her own conduct to avoid being called to account.

It is crucial to note, however, that the applicability of Foucault's ideas is in no way limited to understanding the ways in which control operates within organizations. For it also enables us to understand the operation of control in liberal-democratic societies more generally, as the work of writers such as Nikolas Rose (1988; 1990), Peter Miller and Ted O'Leary (1987), and, indeed, Foucault himself suggest. To illustrate this point and the role of computers in realizing the electronic panopticon, we bring the chapter to an end using an illustrative case of panoptical control derived from Safeway stores in the United Kingdom and its decision to introduce a customer operated bar-coded scanning device to its shoppers (see Bateson 1989: 40; and Kanter, Schiffman, and Faye Horn 1990, for accounts of the origins of this innovation). A recent example of changes within employment relations that reeks of potential for the application of a Foucaultian analysis is the attempted introduction of a swipe-card system for check-in staff at British Airways. Indeed for some, the case may represent 'an incipient revolt against the close control and monitoring of our lives and movements that modern information technology enables' ('How BA clipped its own wings', Will Hutton, *Observer*, 27 July 2003; see also Rosen and Baroudi 1992). Here, we choose to monitor the monitoring of shopping.

Self-scanning?

Shopping has never been so easy!
The revolutionary *Self*Scan™ system, putting you in control

. . .

What is ***Self*Scan™**?
Self Scan™ is a unique hand held bar code scanner that you operate yourself. It allows you to scan your purchases as you shop. It tells you the price of every item, enabling you to monitor your total spend. It is a totally flexible system, that allows you to add or delete any item at any time during your shop . . . (Safeway promotional leaflet).

This device was piloted, among other places, in the Safeway Megastore at Newcastle-under-Lyme, Staffordshire. It comes as part of a package. The customer receives an Added Bonus Card (ABC) on completion of a relatively detailed 'joining form'. This card is used to store an accumulated discount and/or entitlements to 'free gifts' based upon prior spending, a practice increasingly common in the United Kingdom's major supermarket chains. More importantly for our present purposes, it is also the key that allows the shopper access to 'the revolutionary *Self*Scan™ system'. The ensemble is completed with the addition of the 'Safeway Green Box', 'a unique new packaging system that will revolutionize the way you shop' (Safeway promotional leaflet). Four 'Green Boxes' (currently purchasable at a fraction of their 'normal' price) sit snugly in the shopping trolley, allowing a quick and easy exit once one's shopping 'encounter' (Gutek 1995*a, b*) is complete. As Safeway's promotional leaflet reminds us: 'Shopping has never been so easy!'

Helping oneself with a handset 1

After parking (Newcastle's Safeway, despite its in-townness, is not exactly pedestrian friendly), you approach the automatic electronic gateway to the store, selecting one of a number of different types of trolleys as you go. Personal choice is ubiquitous in the 'shopping experience' offered here. Behind the doors brilliant white light mingles with the smell of freshly baked bread. Openness is apparent, with nothing allowed to hide in the shadows. The tall ceilings add to the impression of space, with separate departments contributing to a supermarket feel. The expanse of goods on offer suggests that all tastes can be accommodated. Only the inconvenience of the elements is excluded.

The latest 'revolution' is apparent from the moment one enters: just inside the door a stack of the 'unique' Green Boxes is displayed. Leaflets describing their advantages are also available, giving the customer everything that is required for an informed choice. A desk at which one can join the revolution, by acquiring an ABC, foregrounds the array of perfected fruits and vegetables. For the experienced scanner, however, this is easily bypassed as you head straight for the 'selfscan handset dispenser unit', located just to the left of this administrative gatepost. A slot to the right of the unit invites the insertion of the ABC card and, on acceptance of this invitation, a digital display responds by indicating the bay from which one's handset should be taken. To make things easier your allocated device illustrates its availability by helpfully flashing its light at you. And the flashing stops once the handset is removed from its housing, as if to remind you that its functioning is now entirely under *your* control.

The handset itself is somewhat reminiscent of a sci-fi phaser. It is made of textured, shaped plastic in three complementary, muted shades. It is smoothly curved, cut away to the rear to allow the fingers of the user to sit comfortably in a pre-figured moulding. The sides and back of the unit are the pale grey of personal computer housings. The top half of the central section is black and surrounds a small liquid crystal display panel. The bottom half is corporate green, with a disc at the base to lend an air of substance to the unit. This hilt sits conveniently in a housing provided on each of the different trolleys, allowing the head of your scanner to face the array of products from which *you* will select *your* personal choice. Embedded within the green plastic are three buttons: a plus, a minus, and an equals. In the centre of the boundary between the green and black sections is the light that helped us earlier. When you scan your groceries with the head of the device, holding down the plus button as you trace the parallel lines of the bar code, this light shines red, changing briefly to green to show that the information has been successfully recorded. The price of the item is simultaneously displayed on the LCD panel. If you decide to return an item to the shelves its trace can be eliminated by repeating the above procedure while holding down the minus key. A press of the equals reveals a current subtotal and a count of the items scanned so far. At the end of your shop you simply return the handset to any available housing in the dispenser unit and a summary of your activities emerges, in the form of a bar-coded 'total' slip, to be read at the checkout and translated into a standard supermarket till receipt. Here, your accumulated discount on your ABC card is updated while payment is made. And, all being well, you leave the store unhindered by any rechecking, ready to deposit your Green Boxes straight into the boot of your waiting car. *Shopping has never been so easy!*

Most items seem to scan relatively successfully. Bent barcodes and shiny packaging create the odd problem, but the devices seem at least as effective as their larger scale cousins that are installed at the checkout. Fruits and vegetables are brought into the self-scannable regime through the provision of electronic scales in these sections of the store. Having selected your fruits and/or vegetables and placed each variety in a separate bag, you put each in turn on the scales and press the appropriate button on a panel above them (words and pictures are provided to aid identification here). A bar-coded price label is generated by the machine, which you then apply to the bag before scanning it as you would any other barcode. If problems are encountered when scanning any items they should be reported to the checkout staff who will attempt to scan them for you using their less mobile devices.

Instructions on how to use the device are provided as '*Six easy steps . . .*' in the promotional leaflet on the self-scanning system. And its advantages are reinforced by photographic images of an attractive young woman breezing her way through near deserted aisles as she completes her technologically mediated shop. A final picture in the sequence exemplifies this impression. Our happy shopper's grin reaches from ear to ear and her perfect teeth gleam as she hands over her bar-coded total slip and her ABC card to an equally happy checkout assistant. In this representation the dynamism of the new experience is particularly emphasized. Our shopper looks as if she is not even going to stop as she glides through the checkout, such is the efficiency of this new 'shopping experience'.

The sardonic tone adopted up to now is perhaps a little disingenuous, for according to those who have taken up the hand-held challenge, it is a thoroughly enjoyable experience; at least the first time. It adds a spark of difference to an eminently tedious activity. A deep-seated technophilia can be allowed to run riot as one zaps and unzaps aisles overflowing with Klingons and Romulans, a.k.a. groceries. (Scanners with children beware—the temptation to subject every item in the store to the electronic memory is apparently irresistible to younger shoppers). The speed with which the checkout barrier can be breached is also more than welcome (self-scanners have the additional advantage of dedicated tills, the use of which is prohibited for more technologically reticent shoppers). And it is, apparently, also nice to know by how much one has overspent at a time when one can still correct the problem without the embarrassment attendant upon standing in front of a queue of impatient fellow shoppers when doing so. Yes, all in all, it does appear to be an eminently preferable 'shopping experience'. Such a reaction seems, on the basis of conversation with a number of scanners, to be typical. Most who try it thoroughly enjoy it. And once one has invested in the Green Boxes . . . well, then there's no turning back. If the opportunities for less than honest behaviour that the system provides can be kept in check, it looks as if self-scanning will be here to stay. And it is, of course, these opportunities, and particularly the checks placed upon them, that are our key interest here in our attempts to illuminate the panopticon and self-discipline at work.

Maintaining control

According to Safeway's promotional literature, under the neutral sounding title of 'Accuracy':

> For both your benefit and ours, the computer system will randomly select shopping to be re-checked for accuracy. The procedure is as follows. The first few times you self scan, you may have your shopping re-scanned at the *checkout to ensure you have fully understood how to use the system.* Further random checks will then occur on future shopping trips—determined solely by the computer system. No-one decides when to check you or knows the result of the check, however, the more accurate you are the less frequently you are likely to be checked. Equally, if you are inaccurate every time, your shopping is likely to be checked every time. Customer Service Staff can help you find out why if you ask them. After an accuracy check you will always be asked to pay the total shown by the till (our emphasis).

Furthermore, under the small-print 'terms and conditions' on the same piece of literature: 'Safeway reserves the right to prosecute any person when they consider theft or other mis-use of the card may have taken place'. 'The decision of Safeway in all matters shall be final and binding'.

This possibility of theft, only obliquely acknowledged in the promotional literature, is the first one raised by everyone spoken to about this 'exciting new innovation'. Indeed, the possibility that others might assume that a deliberate act of theft has taken place in following accidental misuse is the reason given by many older shoppers for not even trying the innovation. And it is also this possibility that highlights the applicability of Foucault's use of Bentham's panopticon for understanding these arrangements. Safeway's 'random checks . . . determined solely by the computer system' plead for the analogy to be made. Furthermore, the tying of this future so-called 'randomness' to past observation, 'the more accurate you are, the less frequently you are likely to be checked', is just the sort of auxiliary mechanism required for the 'internalization' of control in the enterprising subject. And Safeway's preferred subjects are enterprisers (see, for example, du Gay 1994, 1996) par excellence. Witness merely the way in which their stores are situated to enable maximal access for the bourgeoisie.

As we have noted, rhetoric of revolution pervades the company literature introducing SelfScanning. This is to be sure a technologically mediated revolution but one in which an atomic 'self' takes centre stage. The impersonality of the computerized monitoring system seems to facilitate the sustenance of the self-contained individual by keeping the supposed caprice of social relations at bay,[2] by providing an 'objective', level playing field upon which personal preferences can be expressed. This self-oriented sell is exemplified in sections of the promotional literature provided on the new system:

How does *Self*Scan™ help me?
You are totally in control of **your** shopping (original emphasis).

As Hoskin (1995), among innumerable others, has noted, this self-viewing and monitoring self has a long pedigree. He, *pace* Foucault, ties a primary turn in its realization to the emergence and diffusion of the examination. Technologies of examination are seen to provide the material basis for the emergence of self as manager of the body. Performance is examined both by the self and by a 'higher' authority, an impersonal authority that contributes to the prescription and proscription of texts of the self. As Paul Theroux renders this power in his novel, *Milroy the Magician*: 'That's what God does. He doesn't punish us. He watches us—and there is something terrible in the brilliance of his steady gaze, like a light searching our hearts. That's how he lets us punish our own selves' (1993: 129).

Forms of selfhood are 'chosen' within this disciplinary matrix through the discursive resources produced by, and available to, individualized human actors, in particular places at particular times. In the contemporary occidental context the self as enterprise is a particularly favoured trope (du Gay 1994, 1996; and Keat and Abercrombie 1991; but also Armstrong, forthcoming; and Fournier and Grey 1999). And, as we have noted, the maintenance of such a construction seems entirely consonant with the enterprising strategy of the Safeway corporation. The self-scanning prosthetic incorporates body and self in an individualizing technological nexus, with this construction being buttressed through the surveying ramifications of a computerized electronic panopticon (Sewell and Wilkinson 1992).

Within these processes the shopper's 'relationship' with the Safeway corporation is (re)constituted as a series of technologically mediated 'encounters' (Gutek 1995*a,b*; see also Kanter, Schiffman, and Faye Horn 1990). A system is constructed in which appropriately prosthetized, individualized, consuming bodies appear as 'interchangeable parts', a 'stock' (Heidegger 1977; Fisher 1978) of difference with a consistently enterprising core that can be drawn into manageable economic relations by the tracking and management that is enabled through the self-serving action of those selfsame bodies. A calculative and calculable automated consumer (Miller 1992).

The self-development we have been tracing thus far is deeply ambivalent. As Foucault (Foucault 1980: 119) has noted, the power associated with its construction is a 'productive' achievement that induces pleasure in its outcomes. But as the foregoing analysis reveals, it is simultaneously a bleak and tragic achievement, a seemingly impoverished and dissimulating shadow of what 'we' could be. The supposed pessimism of Foucault's analyses of power, and their concomitant lack of an adequate conceptualization of resistance, have been frequent objects of critique (see, for example, Fine 1979; Neimark 1990). And it is, thus, to the role of resistance in the self-scanning regime that we now turn our attention to conclude our account.

Helping oneself with a handset 2

Just as the automation of production provided both opportunities and threats for those whose skills were its object (see Chapter 1), so too does the automation of consumption described above. In particular, the invitation to increase one's participation in the monitoring of economic transactions creates a space in which the 'freedom' of the individual can be expressed to further interests that are not shared by the other party to those transactions. In short, one can try to exploit the system to pinch stuff. This space seems essential for realization of the pleasurable aspects of self-construction. The pleasures of a break in monotony and convenience discussed above are largely instrumental in orientation. But the 'true' pleasures of selfhood, upon which the former depend, may be seen to belong to another, more fundamental order, for by 'complying with' or 'resisting' Safeway's desired ends one is able to further realize the construction of self with which existential satisfaction is associated. As one of the managers interviewed by Ezzamel, Lilley, and Willmott pointed out, 'people enjoy having a bit more control over their own destiny' (1994: 458), however chimerical that 'control' may be. And, indeed, however it is exercised. It is the 'freedom' associated with this exercise of 'choice' that both exacerbates and assuages the existential concerns of self. One can 'do the right thing', pursue the course of action preferred by the impersonal authority, but equally one can do precisely the opposite. Of course, intentions are materialized that seek to ensure that the former is the more likely outcome, but the latter is by no means impossible. The social relations surrounding and sustaining the 'free individual' can be many things. But they cannot be determinate. Given these circumstances, how are we to conceptualize a decision to misbehave? It may certainly be recognized as resistance. But is this resistance to be seen as 'outside' and against the power relations of obedience, 'beyond' the panopticon, in some sense? Or would we be better advised to conceive of such 'aberrant' behaviour as an essential and constitutive component of such relations? A brief foray into shoppers' experiences of stealing from Safeway[3] may provide us with some purchase here.

One shopping couple that we spoke to reported that they had, on about their seventh self-scanning excursion, become increasingly frustrated at their device's lack of ability to play its proper part in their new shopping experience. A number of items, worth about £10 in total, had refused to provide the scanning unit with the bar-coded information it required. The couple told us that they had frequently discussed the possibility of deliberately not scanning the odd expensive item once their 'accuracy' was such that they could pass the checkout unharrassed, as trusted and appropriately disciplined consumers. They had even tried to work out the pattern behind the computer's 'randomness' in order to minimize the chance of getting caught if and when they eventually embarked upon our dishonest enterprise. They had apparently been checked on their first scanning mission, on their third and on their sixth[4] and felt that the aforementioned pattern was starting to emerge. So, reportedly, they took their chance. The sense of annoyance induced by the 'failing' technology coupled with both a calculation of reduced risk and a desire to 'rebel' against the self-disciplining regime led them to take their first steps on the road to criminality. When asked whether they had had any problems scanning any of the products they had selected they 'fibbed', albeit carefully, saying that they had not 'noticed' any such problems. With their hearts reportedly racing they had waited while the computer 'decided' whether their shopping needed checking. And it was apparently very hard for them to suppress their grins and maintain normal shopperly deportment when it decided they did not. They paid and skipped gaily out, laughing all the way to their car. They knew it was bad, but also described the experience as a lot of fun. It apparently felt good to resist the demands of the system, to exploit the new gaps it provided. But to what extent can we sensibly see such resistance as 'outside' of the power regime that surrounds self-scanning?

At a most basic level we may suggest that Safeway's drive for capitalist accumulation was minimally subverted. Their attempts to reduce 'headcount' and hence costs through the automation of compliant consumers had created the conditions of possibility for a minor bypassing of monetary/commodity exchange. Our shoppers had seemingly beaten the system. But even cast in these somewhat simplistic terms we can see that their victory was a hollow one. Safeway had lost, at most, £10. The goods purloined by our shoppers were patently of less 'value' than this figure and the accumulated 'staff savings' they had contributed to enabling may have more than compensated. Moreover, it is this latent possibility for theft that gives the system a large part of its appeal (at least to those of dubious moral character like our shoppers). And £10 may be a small price to pay for their ongoing custom and concomitant disregard of less technological, and hence less 'connable', competitors. One can spend a great deal of money on seven trips to the supermarket!

More fundamentally, however, we can see such behaviour and its possibility as an essential constituent of the disciplinary regime surrounding self-scanning. Foucault has suggested that 'power is "always already there", that one is never outside it, and there are no margins for those who break with the system to gambol in' (1980: 141). Resistance in this rendering appears as productive of and for 'power' (and indeed, vice versa), not as something outside, standing against it. As Knights and Vurdubakis (1994: 180) note 'Resistance . . . plays the role of continuously provoking extensions, revisions and refinements of those same practices it confronts'.

They provide the pertinent example of IT consultants who utilize the notion of sites of ' "resistance to change" . . . as [a] crucial vehicle . . . through which the services and expertise of consultants are sold, and spaces of intervention carved out in client organizations' (1994: 180; see also Bloomfield and Vurdubakis 1994). The existence of 'resistance' serves here to legitimate the instigation and extension of practices that seek to combat it. And this extension of practices will likely provoke further resistance, providing further grounds for further 'extensions, revisions and refinements'. This gaming is endless:

> there are no relations of power without resistances: the latter are all the more real and effective because they are formed right at the point where relations of power are exercised; resistance to power does not have to come from somewhere else to be real, nor is it inexorably frustrated through being the compatriot of power. (Foucault 1980: 142)

And a similar case may be made about the power relations surrounding the self-scanning regime and 'resistance' thereof. It is the possibility for resistance through theft, provided by the system, that necessitates the computerized 'accuracy' checks. And it is this electronic surveillance that provides a mechanism for the (re)instantiation of an atomized, individualized, enterprising self. 'Free' will is both condition and consequence of these relations: 'power is only exercised over free subjects and only insofar as they are free . . . for where the determining factors saturate the whole there is no relationship of power' (Foucault 1982: 225; reproduced in Knights and Vurdubakis 1994: 179).

As if to emphasize the point about freedom, we came across a posting to the Critical Management Workshop discussion list by Sheen S. Levine of the Wharton School, University of Pennsylvannia (C-M-WORKSHOP@JISCMAIL.AC.UK), while carrying out our final revisions to this chapter. The posting claimed that a Ph.D. student working at MIT had developed a 'Corporate Fallout Detector' that 'reads barcodes off of consumer products, and makes a noise similar to a Gieger counter of varying intensity based on the social or environmental record of the company that produces the product' (http://web.media.mit.edu/~jpatten/cfd/, consulted on 1 July 2003).

Similarly, but from a very different traditional moral base, the subject who steals from Safeway by exploiting the potential gaps in the new system is in every sense a free, individualized, enterprising self. She or he calculatingly spots the opportunities for a bit of enterprising self-advancement and exploits them. She or he cares not that others will be inconvenienced by the more frequent checking that may result from Safeway's calculations about the effectiveness of the current level of intermittent monitoring and appropriates the commodities stolen as individually owned. She or he is, in short, a carbon copy of the obedient self-scanning subject, in all but one respect. And that (dis)respect is just what the system needs to legitimate its perpetuation.

▨ SUMMARY

In this chapter we have briefly described the emergence, since the 1980s, of a new conception of organization. A shift that is perhaps best captured in terms of a proclaimed move from a 'command-and-control' mode of management to one putatively characterized more by the 'facilitation' of the work of 'empowered' others. We illustrated how in practice such a shift may often be more rhetorical than real, with 'empowerment' only being realized when the empowered can be relied upon to act as the empowerer would deem appropriate if they were present, even when they are not present. We noted briefly how inculcation of appropriate values was seen to contribute to such an outcome but considered as more significant the roles of information technologies in enabling systematic monitoring of performance. Although utilized throughout the practices of the rather literally named HRM, we noted that information systems seem best to promote the self-discipline required of empowerment when deployed to capture conduct within panoptical modes of inspection. We examined how Foucault's mobilization of Bentham's imagery of the panopticon provided considerable purchase on many aspects of contemporary life, particularly through an examination of the use of a computer system in an attempt to ensure compliance in consumers utilizing Safeway's self-scanning system. We delineated the essential space created for freedom within such arrangements and concluded by considering briefly the status of resistance in regimes that turn around disciplining of the self, by the self.

▓ DISCUSSION QUESTIONS

1. Who is 'the user' of a panoptical system?

2. What distinguishes panoptical surveillance or inspection from hierarchical forms?

3. Why might intermittent surveillance be more powerful than constant?

4. How can the surveyed utilize their freedom to turn power back upon the surveyors?

5. Is a distinction between surveyors and surveyed tenable in contemporary circumstances?

6. How might a Foucaultian analysis illuminate recent industrial disputes over working practices involving the use of swipe-cards?

▓ SUGGESTIONS FOR FURTHER READING

Obviously the work of Foucault himself is an excellent place to start exploring the ideas raised in this chapter, particularly and perhaps most accessibly, *Discipline and Punish: The birth of the prison* (1975; trans. 1977). The classic attempts to apply Foucaultian analysis to understand the electronic or information panopticon are Shoshana Zuboff's (1988) text, *In the Age of the Smart Machine: The Future of Power and Work,* and Graham Sewell and Barry Wilkinson's (1992) article in *Sociology, ' "*Someone to Watch Over Me*": Surveillance, Discipline and the Just-in-Time Labour Process'. The recently inaugurated on-line journal, *Surveillance and Society* may also provide an interesting way into work in this area covering a range of arenas, particularly issue 1/3. The journal can be found at www.surveillance-and-society.org.

More on new management practices can be found at any airport bookstore! Attempts to theorize these changes and place them into a historical context can however be found in recent books by Dave Collins (2000), *Management Fads and Buzzwords: Critical-Practical Perspectives,* and Brad Jackson (2001), *Management Gurus and Management Fashions: A Dramatistic Perspective,* and also in Roy Jacques' masterful and eminently readable (1996) book, *Manufacturing the Employee.*

7 | Accountability and Systems Success

Introduction

As we noted in the previous chapter, *accountability* is one of the key linking themes in the plethora of 'new' management practices that has emerged since the end of the 1970s. In this chapter, we explore the linkages between accountability and information systems, returning to our example of oil management systems in refineries.

Being accountable

To be held 'accountable', according to the *Concise Oxford Dictionary* (1982), is to be 'bound to give account, responsible, (*for* things, *to* persons, or absolutely); [to make one's actions] explicable'. In this view the world is seemingly reducible to a series of relationships through which predictability is maintained through the careful distribution and delegation of responsibility for the future (Hoskin 1996). But the notion of delegation is far from straightforward and thus accountability *for* the success of 'technical' systems to the generalized 'others' who hold stakes in the contemporary corporate world is unsurprisingly also labyrinthine and indistinct in practice. Evidence for such a view abounds in the endless arguments over where the fault for systems' failures lie.[1]

One way to unpick this muddle is to accept that accountability is a process as much as an outcome, and a complex social process at that. The attribution of accountability to various actors re-presents and solidifies, or *translates* (Callon 1986; see Chapter 4, this volume), various conceptions about various entities and their capabilities and interests. But when appraisers seek to apportion credit for the accrual of 'benefits' from such systems or blame for the lack thereof, the contingent, social nature of this preceding attribution process is often forgotten. Rather, the inscribed accountabilities that resulted from the process are typically seen as uncontroversial resources that can serve as models against which 'reality' can be measured, to judge whether it matches, exceeds, or falls short of that which was planned. When 'fixed' or stabilized in this manner, these model accountabilities are rendered 'natural', 'ordinary', and beneath the purview of all but the most critical challenge. The accountability attribution processes of the past become occluded in the present, allowing tidy stories of victories and villains to emerge. But the authors of the script in which such plots make sense are often forgotten, merged into the background of the truisms that lionize accountability in contemporary corporate life. To illuminate what we have in mind here we tell a story in which both the designers and users of systems and the designers and users of the accountability measures intended to secure the success of the former are all present. We thus attempt to open up the 'black box' of inscribed accountabilities by exploring the ways in which accountability is defined and *realized* in practice. And the practice in this case is once again derived from an examination of the development and implementation of a major management system in the refining sector of the oil industry.

Central to this story are negotiations between developers of the system and those that came to be seen as its 'users' over where their respective responsibilities began and ended, or to put it another way, over where 'the buck' started and stopped. Developers attempt to 'pass the buck' as they dramatize where their responsibility stops, while users attempt to suggest that they cannot be blamed for 'non-use' since the system fails to completely capture the problems that they face in their day-to-day engagement with refining reality. During these negotiations views concerning the 'nature' of the final system and its relations to various other refining entities are seen to change, emphasizing the active nature of the accountability 'attribution' process. For accountability is not merely ascribed on the basis of the shape of a final system; processes of accountability ascription themselves affect the shape of that system. Accountability does more than just *reflect* the positioning of independently formed centres of calculation and action in aligned chains of people and resources. Processes of accountability ascription are active in both the shaping of the form of alignment achieved and in the selection and shaping of the peoples and resources that constitute that alignment.

As we noted in Chapter 2, Cooper (1993: 279) suggests that 'the modern interest in technology puts the stress on immediacy of use, constant availability and the easing of effort'. Modern technology 're-presents actions in space and time according to an economics of mastery and control' (1993: 279). Such a conception of technology is just the one required as a firm basis for accountability. For when a system is seen to present opportunities for 'mastery and control' and such mastery and control is not achieved, then, clearly, it is the master of the system, its *user*, who should be held accountable.

This possibility of mastery and control therefore appears as the objective behind systems introduction, if anyone is to be held accountable for the success of the system. And thus we have two accountabilities: an accountability for establishing the *potential* for mastery and control; and an accountability for the *realization* of that potential. Conventional systems and managerial wisdom suggests that the former is the province of the system builder while the latter is that of the system user.

In re-viewing this distinction there are two key questions which emerge:

1. How is the 'potential' of the system inscribed as the system comes into being?
2. How is accountability for the actualization of this potential attached to those actors who come to be seen as 'users'?

Answering these questions may allow us to understand how builders of systems can absolve *themselves* of accountability for systems success, through their deployment of a number of techniques that inscribed and prescribed *user* accountability for the accrual of systems benefits. For users to be rendered accountable, they must be 'configured' (Woolgar 1991) by designers as the 'natural' site in which accountability should reside. The chapter suggests that by laying the commercial accountability for returns on systems investment at the door of prospective *users*, system *builders* may insulate themselves from a questioning of *their* worth. Given the seemingly endless litany of prior system failures, such insulation may be seen to be of paramount importance for continued systems deployment.

The system builders

The Oil Management System (OMS) to be built at 'Oiltown' was designed and implemented by a diverse team of individuals including consultants from a specialist systems design company ('ITCo.') and 'Mexaco Oil' employees.[2] The System Design Team who undertook the Feasibility Study consisted of four people, but the team grew to include up to thirty (Interview, Systems Manager). Over this period, the proportion of Mexaco staff declined from around half as progressively more ITCo. Consultants joined to carry out programming work. Non-programming members were mainly Mexaco secondees, providing systems analysis, specification, and administration.[3] ITCo. come along with the technical skills, the actual information systems skills, and also with the experience of what they have done with implementing OMSs in other refineries. And Oiltown is providing primarily the user expertise, the local expertise, but also the people to support the system in the longer term (Interview, Systems Manager).

We have then a number of different groups with differing relations to the system that was coming into being. We have the programmers, some of whom are 'inside' Mexaco and some of whom are 'outside' in ITCo. (which was owned by Mexaco up until just before the implementation). And we have the non-programmers, all of whom are 'inside' Mexaco, but some of whom are 'outside' Oiltown.

Central focus

The Mexaco staff, unsurprisingly, sought a system that would deliver a commercial advantage to the refinery. The group as a whole sought to replace a centralized and directive commercialism with one more dispersed and dynamic, one in which, reflecting the corporate Zeitgeist, 'Capital must be made to circulate, no longer around a fixed point, but as an endless chain of investments and reinvestments, just as value must be made to radiate in all directions' (Baudrillard 1990: 153).

A new, commercial orientation across the organization was explicitly linked with the desire for mastery and control to which we have already alluded. It is important to note, however, that a large technological system such as a refinery demands, and always has demanded, control (Kallinikos 1995; see also Harvey 1989). The precise nature of control was however clearly subject to translation as a result of this shifting emphasis. The objectives of the system are to take operational information and hold it centrally, and then to analyse that information in terms of commercial rather than operational criteria. 'It's part of a wider project to alter the focus of the plant to emphasise commercial, financial issues' (Interview, Systems Manager).

Through an intriguing sleight of hand, the lack of commercial information prior to OMS was seen to be one of the key reasons behind the lack of demand for OMS from the site. The 'need' for information to improve the refinery's performance could not be articulated without information on the refinery's performance!

> The measures on refinery performance were a lot cruder than they really are today, and they're pretty crude today. The refinery had measures of value added type profitability, but they're rather imprecise and aren't given quite as much credence as they would be if it were a solely operated company . . . Since the refinery wasn't really operating in a plc mode and since it's bottom line wasn't all that visible with credibility, that's why I think it wasn't pulling this into being beforehand. In a sense it's the management environment which sets the expectations and the criteria of success, for what [the refinery] is actually a division within Manufacturing and Supplies. It's an organisational issue really. (Interview, Systems Manager)

Managers at Oiltown were apparently not keen on information systems 'in general', partially as a result of 'overselling in the past' (Interview, Systems Manager). However, the introduction of OMS seemed, for most of the individuals interviewed, to be virtually a foregone conclusion. Sceptical managers may have been able to ignore OMS or partially divert its developmental trajectory, but they seemed to believe that they had little alternative but to accept the implementation of some sort of OM type system. This perceived inevitability coupled with a lack of demand brought issues of the management of accountability to the fore. In the absence of local 'pull', issues of accountability become even more problematic: if no one 'asks' for the system it is difficult to see who should be accountable for the exploitation of the 'benefits' it supposedly provides.

The database

The cornerstone of the system at Oiltown was to be a central database that would organize the production of commercially oriented information, apparently to ensure 'common rather than distributed information' (Interview, Systems Manager). A solution that could conveniently also be presented as integral to the sharing of information that emerging views on management both within and beyond Mexaco saw as so important. 'Hopefully, the sharing of information in a common database will result in a better understanding and working relationship between departments' (Interview, Systems Manager).

We have seen such claims for organizational improvement through technological change before, and we shall see them again. However, these are not the only forces at work here. The 'choice' of a central database as the key organizing principle behind the system in part reflected prior design choices taken at the first two OMS implementations. As we noted in Chapters 4 and 5, the original OMS, at Mexaco's Rotterdam refinery, had emerged from a peculiar set of local contingencies but the system so developed was subsequently seen to have much wider applicability. However, at the second OMS implementation at the group's Cobber Creek refinery in Australia, changes were made to this common core that were seen, at the time of the Oiltown implementation, to represent significant improvements upon the supposed 'original'. Consequently, there had been some debate during the early stages of planning and implementing the Oiltown system as to whether database precedent should be imported from Cobber Creek or from Rotterdam. The Oiltown team plumped for the 'improved' system as their keystone and guide. It was clear however that this 'guide' would not be seen as an immutable template. 'Cobber tables [are used] as a starting point, but we don't implement any columns we don't require, and we've implemented columns of our own as needed. The basic philosophy is to use the Cobber model until we cannot' (Interview, Systems Manager).

However, one of the designers said that 'we've had to make more changes to the Cobber Creek model than I would've expected use of the Rotterdam model to involve' (Interview, Systems Manager), a view buttressed by performance problems with the Cobber Creek system that emerged during the implementation at Oiltown. Programming staff were keen to ensure that they did not transfer these along with its central database, for these 'systemic' errors were something for which they would have been held accountable. Indigenous Oiltown staff were also happier to adopt tried and tested solutions. 'Riskiness' and 'newness' were seen by indigenous staff to be largely synonymous:

> Our general policy has been not to take technical risks. Yesterday's blue sky is quite good enough I think and no nasty surprises has been a policy I've been very happy with. And I do have a say because although the OMS project is separately managed, separately funded, and separately staffed, I still end up with the responsibility of running it once it's been developed, which of course is its benefits stage. (Interview, Systems Manager)

Such views perhaps present nascent realization on the part of refinery staff of a possible future in which they would be held accountable for the accrual of benefits from an unworkable system. And, as the quotation suggests, they were keen to intervene, and to intervene early, to prevent such an outcome. Aiding them in this endeavour was wider group dissatisfaction, with Cobber Creek losing some of its attractive gloss as the system's performance problems became apparent, as we saw in Chapter 5. Oiltown's attempts to ameliorate these problems were not altogether successful and the choice of this 'technologically sophisticated' starting point was, on balance, seen as a retardant on the development of a usable system at the refinery (and hence as a basis for accountability for the site's performance).

The core application: modelling accountability

The key application of OMS at Oiltown was to be the production planning and scheduling system. And given the problems alluded to above, the system builders recognized that they could not automate all the decisions that staff were required to make: 'so instead we're aiming to provide the information to make those decisions and provide facilities for him (sic) to use that to allow "What if?" analyses' (Interview, Systems Manager). OMS was seen, as it had been at Rotterdam, as a tool for, not a replacement of, refinery personnel. Staff savings were expected in some areas but the increased computer support that OMS required meant that there was little expectation of a net reduction of staff as a direct result of the implementation. The OMS development was to be kept distinctly separate from improvements to the process *control* systems and this in turn affected the type of accountabilities for system success envisaged for OMS (Interview, Systems Manager). 'The object is to give people as much information as they need to do their job, *without trying to do their job for them*' (emphasis added—Interview, Systems Manager).

Such views on the relations between refinery operatives and the technology, both new and old, with which they are provided offers the system builders a particularly seductive 'let out clause' in the face of future failures to realize promised benefits. For such failures could clearly be seen to be the fault of users since the system designers were explicitly not 'trying to do their job for them'. By leaving users nominally 'in charge' of *their* systems, builders can also appear sensitive to the needs of users, reflecting precisely the prescriptions of human-centred design.[4] Crucially, however, this 'sensitivity' may be seen to be predicated upon a view of users as *remainder*, as oil for the wheels of a currently imperfectable system. In other words, users' needs and capabilities would be taken into account because they *had to be*. It would seem as if there would be no hesitation in trying to do the user's job for them *if such a solution was seen to lie in the realm of 'technical' possibility*. 'Real' technological control is necessarily deferred but luckily the presumed flexibility of human users is available for configuration as the crux of a successful implementation.

This system with enhanced space for human agency, albeit somewhat forced, is thus clearly only a *simulated* overview of the underlying refinery. And as we stressed earlier, such simulations are themselves 'predictable'; a function of the linear nature of their programming and the basis for their support for prediction of the wider world. But, although the system was 'predictable', the plant it simulated was not seen to be amenable to such a description. Simulations will 'always be by-passed, confounded and exceeded by practical experience' (Baudrillard 1990: 155). Indeed, at an old site with built in 'unpredictability' and concerns about the consequences of the automation of control, the importance of accurate and timely management information was, somewhat ironically, seen to increase. 'Better' information was seen to be required due to the lack of immediacy in the exercise of direct process control, and in turn this lack of immediacy was seen to introduce a constraint on the benefits derivable from OMS information. Not only was an automated control loop for refinery processes rejected, simple automation to allow remote human control of valves was also 'impossible' for economic reasons—the relatively unskilled humans fulfilling these roles were simply too cheap (Interview, Systems Manager).

More space for more accountability for users was consequently created, leading to fundamental questions being asked about the functions of the refinery operators. Accountability in the context of the new system required *translation* of extant refinery roles. Given that the control and planning systems were not to converge, effort was devoted to improving the interface between them, that is, the operators' role. The operator is thus seen to represent an appropriate site of accountability, a site of decision-making that could exploit the opportunities and avoid the threats that multiple simulations provided.

> 'I think the challenge in the future and the interface that is going to be concentrated on is actually the human interface. What is the operator's job? What are his (sic) tools? What information is he being given and what responsibilities has he got?' (Interview, Systems Manager).

But at this point it is important that the OMS system is not seen to be merely a system for achieving operational control.

> 'I think we have to be careful . . . that we don't kid ourselves that an OMS project is in real time and is associated with activating control valves'. (Interview, Systems Manager)

Control was thus not seen as lying in the simulational realm, but was only possible in that of tangible 'reality', a place where the turning of actual valves could alter actual oil flows. Such control could only be achieved through a system that represented, and could intervene in, 'reality' at this level of resolution. The process control system mentioned above had been in existence for some time and operators were seen to have developed the tacit knowledge required to challenge its representations about their 'truth'. OMS had no such history and was therefore seen to require a different level of respect, a level that entailed a deeper scepticism with regard to its more avowedly simulational output. This disjuncture between the real world of production and the seductions of simulations is not restricted to oil refineries. The order and consequent control of productive mechanisms is always predicated upon a *model* of the process of production (Armstrong, 2000; see also Armstrong and Tomes 2002). Now, as we discussed in Chapter 3, as a model, it must always be a simplification, a reductive simulation which in practice is taken to be real by those who utilize it to maintain (the appearance of) control.

The perpetuation of any such impression of complete order is tendentious to say the least (Chia 1998). For there is always 'irruption of that minimum of reversibility which exists in every irreversible process' (Baudrillard 1990: 161), requiring our endless human intervention to keep it running and to maintain the illusion that we were not required. Our islands of automation and information which we continually defend against entropy are, according to Baudrillard, only made interesting to us by this interminable maintenance requirement. The attractiveness of ordered production is thus ironically provided by its potential to fall back into disorder, which 'secretly' ruins and dismantles it 'while simultaneously ensuring that a minimal continuity of pleasure traverses it, without which it would be nothing' (Baudrillard 1990: 161). And for Baudrillard this means that the seduction through which all our attempts to stabilize the real world are undone 'doesn't belong to the order of the real' but rather surrounds it, providing the background against which our small victories over chaos are able to shine. '[S]eduction envelops the whole *real* process of power, as well as the whole real order of production, with endless reversibility and disaccumulation—*without which neither power nor production would exist*' (Baudrillard 1990: 159, original emphases). This continual disintegration of order and manufactured form is the very ground that production and power require for their perpetuation. It is what makes *these* processes seductive.

These 'problems' (or opportunities) of the irruption of reversibility within representations and simulations were seen to be particularly acute for operators who were simultaneously receiving both information from OMS and directions and information from the process control system. Given that these systems did not look likely to converge in the near future, there was seen to be a 'need to adjust human resources to technical capabilities' (Interview, Systems Manager). Differences in the 'reality' of the system's outputs and their implications needed to be made crystal clear to the operators.

Look at it from the process operator's perspective: at the moment he's going to see two different screens, very different things, and he's probably going to be slightly confused. He's getting some information out of his [process] control screen, which is real, and some of it's calculated. And he's got plans which are there and targets to meet. (Interview, Systems Manager)

It was thus important for operators to be able to divine the 'real' from a variety of sources of differing ontological status[5] and work out how to act upon it. For them to do so, these differences in the status of information, the extent to which it should be believed, had to be made immediately apparent. And this is no simple matter. For despite the claims in the quote above, none of the information provided to operators can be seen as 'really' real. Even the direct output of a tank gauge provides only a mediated account of the contents of that tank. For it alone cannot distinguish between an empty tank and a malfunctioning gauge that defaults to zero. Resolution of this problem relies upon a congruence between appropriately marked information and appropriately configured users (Woolgar 1991), with the latter as 'designed' as the significations of the former. And while it is perhaps more 'correct' to see the accountability that results as attendant upon the nexus of user and machine, humanist[6] doctrine ensures that the former normally gets more than their fair share.

Simultaneous simulation, understanding, and the translation of accountability

The new LP system (the planning and scheduling modules of OMS) was seen as a success by the system builders: 'The Production Department seem to be very happy with it' (Interview, Systems Manager). And some wider 'unintended' benefits were also seen to have accrued as a result of the introduction of a new simulation of refinery processes. Staff in the Production Department had 'had a lot of work in terms of understanding why they're getting particular results' due to the fact that they 'had to go through and test [the new LP] against [the old]' (Interview, Systems Manager). As a result Production staff were seen to 'understand the results they're getting a lot better' (Interview, Systems Manager).

Other applications that were deemed to be 'more important perhaps in that they are the more commercially orientated, rather than the more technically orientated activities', such as Performance Monitoring, were however 'much less clearly defined' (Interview, Systems Manager). There was seen to be no problem with the availability of data for the support of these applications, rather the problem was seen to be in terms of 'identify[ing] what you are actually monitoring, what does it mean, performance monitoring?' In short, although enhanced accountability was seen to be an inevitable part of the drive behind the system, the specific *nature* of that accountability was severely problematized by the shift to new systems. Are you measuring against your LP targets? Are you measuring against your process model targets? Are you measuring against both, I suppose? And what sort of sensitivities and how do you want to see it? How do you want it grouped?

Some of these problems were seen to be soluble through the use of more flexible reporting formats. Standard reports may not reflect and accommodate particular concerns. But fixed formats were seen to be required for accountability to *others* and we go on to consider mechanisms that were designed to fulfil this need in the following section. Before doing so, however, we will briefly examine these flexible reporting tools as they illuminate some of the myriad ways in which users were configured by the builders. Configuration of users was envisaged to be most successful when the users were themselves involved in the process. The 'parameters' within which users could produce their own reports were a key source of direction in the enrolment of the self in these configurational moves.

The existence of a central core database from which flexible reports could potentially be derived provided both opportunities and risks for self-enrolment on the part of users, and requirements for database reporting were defined relatively late in the implementation of OMS. Each of the Mexaco programmers working on the project, and each of the systems staff in the wider Mexaco Group with an interest in Oiltown's OMS, had their own 'intuitive' views of what should be provided. There was however little agreement between these views and the diversity of reporting tastes within the wider Mexaco group was reflected at different OMS implementations. And not only was there no general agreement within the Mexaco group over how database reporting facilities should be provided, there was also little consensus on, or even consideration of, this matter by those more senior organizational participants employed to oversee the development as a whole. According to one of the system builders, 'The [Oiltown OMS] Management Steering Group either doesn't have a view on this, or if they have, I haven't found it yet'.

Given this fairly limited 'external' colonization of a key area of their endeavours, the system builders within the Oiltown refinery settled on a number of different approaches to satisfying users' reporting needs. The different approaches to reporting on the part of the system builders were accommodated through the provision of a number of different reporting routes. The 'potential' of the technology employed was seen to interact with the competencies and wider context of refinery management. For example, a member of the BDU Systems Group who had been intimately involved with the development of the Rotterdam system and the early stages of the Oiltown implementation, believed that while relational database technology provided a simpler and neater way of conveying information between subsystems than a conventional hierarchical structure would allow, complications re-arose when the database was to be queried (Interview, Systems Group Manufacturing and Supply BDU, Senior Manager).

This individual felt that managers would be 'too busy' to learn the skills required for sophisticated interrogation of the database, but they nevertheless were seen to want access to the sort of information that such queries would provide. While staff and some managers could, and did, use spreadsheets (e.g. at Eurofine and later at

Oiltown) to manipulate data extracted from the database, they were not seen to be capable enough, or willing, to use fourth generation 'natural' language tools to manipulate, and indeed extract, the information they required.

End-users cannot use fourth generation languages. They need professional support both for security reasons and in terms of data definitions. There is no problem with simple systems but with larger scale systems the complexity of table linkages precludes their use by the non-expert (Interview, Systems Group Manufacturing and Supply BDU, Senior Manager).

Similar views were expressed by one of the system managers at Oiltown with responsibility for OMS and the view was solidified in the database reporting made available at the refinery. Although predicting future demands for non standardized information, he saw little evidence of current expression of these demands.

> I always expected that the computer department would have to provide a facility where they would respond very quickly to particular queries. Nevertheless, I don't see any evidence of that sort of thing happening. I still expect it to happen. Once we've got all our data in the database I think managers are going to have need for *ad hoc* queries and they're not going to set these things up themselves. (Interview, Systems Manager)

> Whilst the manager quoted above was 'keen on *ad hoc*' facilities, they were seen to be 'dangerous'. He thought that they could be provided to 'more sophisticated users' but that such users would still require a user support team to set up appropriate access to the database for them (Interview, Systems Manager).

Cross referenced information emanating from more than one OM subsystem, and from other systems communicating with OMS, was provided, but this sort of information was not seen as 'important' for refinery managers; its production was not seen to be 'justified'. OMS was seen as 'just' an oil production planning system, access to, and combination with, other sources of information was not seen as important.

Higher management were not seen to be aware of what cross referenced information they required. The 'activity based' nature of the site meant that such information was seen to be required only in certain circumstances, for example comparing relative performance against budgets, and standard reports were already available for such purposes. More general information to assist in understanding wider, more fundamental questions was not seen by management as appropriate to their roles and was, perhaps more importantly, explicitly outside the scope of the OMS. And the system builders were keen to retain this restricted scope: 'we've avoided looking for expansion' (Interview, Systems Manager). This restricted view of on-site managerial responsibility meant that aggregated, cross referenced information on wider issues was seen to be irrelevant to managers at Oiltown (Interview, Systems Manager).

Another concern was that users at the refinery were generally of 'limited' computer experience but the possibility of allowing users to make such queries was not precluded by all. Unknown 'experts' were thought to exist in certain departments, their expertise having been acquired through 'hobby usage'. As a result, one of the system managers with responsibility for OMS was, from his programming perspective, keen to allow such users access to enable them to structure their own queries.

It makes things easier and allows them to do possible little odds and sods not anticipated in the programmes (Interview, Systems Manager).

'Hobby users' were seen by this builder as a potential resource that should be exploited. He did however note that there were quite big differences between users 'levels of imagination and realisation of the potential of the system' (Interview, Systems Manager). In his opinion, user imagination was the limiting factor; users seemed to 'want to be told what the system would deliver' (Interview, Systems Manager).

Unsurprisingly, perhaps, ultimately the refinery opted instead for a fast response (in the order of half an hour) to complex queries from the Computer Services Committee (CSC). Users had not previously approached the CSC with information requests 'because of the slowness of response' (Interview, Systems Manager). And as part of the general aim to encourage a more commercial orientation within the refinery, the CSC charged user departments for the time involved in answering such queries (Interview, Systems Manager).

The facilities provided were seen to represent a balance between provision of pre-defined reporting formats to reflect and embody 'business needs' deduced and constructed by the system builders in their discussions with users, and predicted and current user demands for ease of access to novel information. The forward-looking orientation of OMS at Oiltown was recognized to require some flexibility in the design of future reports. Lessons learnt from previous and ongoing OMS implementations were built into the system's reporting structures. And system builders were, on the whole, happy with their response to these demands. 'You can't afford to go to either extreme. And I think we've got the right balance here' (laughter) (Interview, Systems Manager).

In the next section, we examine how the realization of the benefits that OMS was expected to provide was managed at Oiltown.

Managing the benefits of OMS: the buck stops here

The views of the system builders concerning reporting facilities are illustrative of the views that they held of the OMS's potential users and the ways in which such users were thereby 'configured'. This configuration is an essential part of the translation procedures that seek to render *users* rather than *builders* accountable for the accrual of systems 'benefits'. The view of users as 'needing to be told', as 'lacking in imagination', as 'unaware of business needs' provides ideal grounds for the builders' specification of what the system would do. All they then had to do was to make the users, rather than themselves, accountable for doing it. The importance of these moves was heightened by an increase in the demands for systems' accountability coming from the wider group.

Obtaining ratification and funding for OM type systems within the Mexaco Group became 'more difficult' in the period preceding and during the Oiltown implementation as a result of the emergent 'perception of failure' surrounding the first two implementations at Rotterdam and Cobber Creek (Interview, European Refinery Analyst). While these 'failures' were primarily attributed to changes in 'environmental' circumstances and technical difficulties, respectively, the resulting increased reluctance on the part of *some* senior managers to support large scale IS projects at refineries led to increased demands for the provision of *systematic* 'benefits management' procedures on concurrent and subsequent projects of a similar nature. The key to successful benefits management was seen to lie in an early, *systematic* enrolment of the system's prospective users. One of the senior managers involved in the Rotterdam project, who was also a member of the Oiltown Management Steering Committee, had this to say on the subject:

> I think the key thing is having solved the technical problems with putting the systems in, you then have a secondary problem in that if you don't use the system and . . . the users, aren't committed to it, then you don't get the benefits. And that is one of the key problems that we're facing really . . . bringing the users along with the implementation of the system and ensuring that they use it after the event. (Interview, European Refinery Analyst)

The benefits management procedures employed at the Oiltown implementation were seen to be exemplary in this respect. Although 'a bit bureaucratic . . . having seen the lack of enthusiasm, certainly in the Rotterdam refinery', it was seen as 'important that' an attempt be made to 'boost' enthusiasm early in the project (Interview, European Refinery Analyst).

> [One of the system managers] at Oiltown has picked up on this point . . . and he's actually generated some ideas on management of the benefits. And the way he approaches that is he actually allocates responsibility for recovering benefits to people who claimed for individual components of the system. He's aiming to delegate the responsibility and what he proposed is that as bits of the system are implemented they will be audited and what I've recommended is that twelve months after the completion of the whole system we audit it again, just to make sure. (Interview, European Refinery Analyst)

Accountability for various aspects of the 'claimed' benefits here were thus formally inscribed against individuals and groups of claimants. Through this process an indelible record of 'user involvement' could also function as a basis for a formal segregation of builders from this accountability, once the system had been 'signed off' to the satisfaction of both parties. An ongoing process of auditing against these claims further ensures that it is to be the users rather than the builders who are to be held accountable. A seductive approach to user involvement and participation is translated into a set of accountabilities that are expected to function as 'real' demands upon a set of users in a future in which system builders are notable only by their absence. Not surprisingly it was the system builders rather than the users who were most enamoured with such an approach.

Concerns were, however, expressed by the senior manager on the Oiltown Management Steering Committee about the manageability of such an approach, perhaps reflecting some awareness that what was being created was merely a translation system between different sites of simulation: 'Now whether, at the end of the day, that's actually a manageable thing, I don't know . . . it's a step in the right direction' (Interview, European Refinery Analyst).

Other organizational changes underway at the time of the implementation increased the visibility of these issues, and problems were exacerbated by the ephemeral nature of some of the benefits thought to accrue from the system and made particularly acute by the emerging commercial orientation that OMS was expected to play a role in delivering.

> Many of the benefits are cultural and although lots of them are measurable, they are very difficult to cost justify (Interview, Systems Manager).

Nevertheless, despite the potential problems with the approach's application, benefits management at the refinery was seen to have furthered its cause. The uncertainty and impreciseness of the procedures were not perceived to undermine their effectiveness. Certainty could be achieved within the simulational realm (of course); it was stepping outside to a supposedly 'real' world that presented problems. Still, this did not effect the principle being enacted and systems managers are, after all, professionals, so they could not go back on their principles.

> The principle of using Benefits Management in order to make people think ahead about how they're going to use the system and what the implications are for their department has been really useful. Clear accountability is one part of it and can help. If you can get to the point where a person is responsible for producing a million dollars worth of benefit then it certainly helps to concentrate their mind a bit! (laughter) (Interview, Systems Manager)

We return to consider further the implications of these moves in our concluding remarks. Before doing so, we briefly examine users' attempts to resist and subvert some of the demands that the system and its associated accountability regime placed upon them.

Precedent, practice, and practicalities

Oil Management System was seen to be an information system, not an automation of refinery processes, and in such circumstances precedentially sanctioned understandings and methods of working could conspire to circumvent the use of OMS, at least to a certain extent. OMS data and information were recognized as being partially remote from refining 'reality', as it was defined by Oiltown staff, and human involvement was deemed to be essential for the prevention of reification of the system's somewhat dubious representations. Acting blinkeredly on the recommendations of reified computer-based models of reality was seen to be potentially disastrous, and contextualized user expertise provided some defence against these dangers.

> I think the perception is that at a certain level of detail process plants like this are a bit like weather systems. There is a degree of unpredictability built into them and to retain responsibility for that continuous operation you probably need to put some human being in charge of it. Somebody who, if you like, can put up the umbrella when it's actually raining rather than when the weather forecast says it should be. (Interview, Systems Manager)

Obviously such moves played right into the builders hands. These claims necessitated an accountability that resided with the system's users. But some users appeared still to resist full enrolment in the emerging system's arrangements. Staff in the production programming department still had 'a lot of faith in paper systems' since they were 'often simpler and quicker to use' (Interview, Systems Manager). And in many cases the largely informal, personal contacts with operators, lab staff, and Head Office personnel continued to be seen as the route through which novel problems and queries would be solved and answered. 'When you just want a small piece of information it's quicker to telephone the lab rather than exit the system you're using, enter OMS, get the information, exit OMS, and go back into your original system' (Interview, Production Programmer).

This continuing importance of social contracts throughout the refinery presented an interesting tension around the emerging OM system. On one level it served to further configure the users as the 'natural' site of accountability for the accrual of benefits, while at another it enabled those users to bypass the system in their fulfilment of the demands such accountability placed upon them (a theme that is apparent in more than one system, as we shall see in the following chapter). And given the characterization of production programming presented in the quotations above, it is easy to understand how the email system whose introduction was contemporaneous with OMS's was seen to be the most important change in computer support for production programming activities. Users seemed to be keener on exploiting the opportunities provided by computer-mediated communication than on the use of computer-generated information. 'The email system has provided some really big benefits. That's definitely the change that's helped the most' (Interview, Production Programmer).

Moreover, the refinery's attempts to gain BS5750 Quality Assurance accreditation meant that email gained some precedence over previously widely used telephone contacts. BS5750 accreditation necessitated some formalization of these previously 'informal' contacts. 'If we note problems with a unit's performance we 'phone the unit supervisor to find out what's wrong with it and then inform the blenders. . . . When BS5750 comes in we'll have to contact them via email as well so that the contact is documented'. (Interview, Production Programmer)

Our discussion of the precise shifts in accountability that are made possible by this shift to textual media is explored in more detail in the following chapter. But for now, it is enough to note that such documentation allows users some personal freedom in negotiating their accountability outside the larger system. Other changes in working practices predicated upon the introduction of enhanced computerized support were seen to be less welcome. Previously developed successful applications of simple computer tools were partially displaced by OMS and concerns were raised about the consequences of such actions. For users in the production programming department, OMS was seen by some to be too much of a move towards automation. Existing practices interacted here with notions of the importance of contextualized expertise and knowledge. Prior to the introduction of OMS, production plans and schedules had been constructed by production programming staff on Lotus spreadsheets, using information from the ITCo. LP models. Rather than being seen as a tedious rekeying of information and a waste of time, processing of information and plans using spreadsheets was seen to have distinct advantages. Not least of which was a (more) human 'check' on the reasonableness of the plans produced, although the precise nature of this check seems open to question, given our earlier discussion about modelling. 'We use spreadsheets to make up the blending requirements. *We take the original qualities in the tanks, what we want to end up with, and then mess about with the components on the spreadsheet until we get what's required.* That's then printed out and goes down as instructions to the blenders' (emphasis added) (Interview, Production Programmer).

Use of spreadsheets made information and plans 'checkable' and this was seen to be 'the most important function of spreadsheet analysis' (Interview, Production Programmer). Attempts to increase the automation in the production of plans and schedules were seen to be inappropriate by production programmers as it required 'contextual knowledge not held on the information systems' (Interview, Production Programmer). Indeed, complaints were made about OMS's inability to accommodate and reconcile freestyle commentaries providing explanations of deviations from the routine operation of plans and pieces of plant with OMS information on the 'technical' status of those plans and pieces of plant (Interview, Production Programmer).

So again we see users wanting a computer-based storage and communication system rather than a 'technical' information system. These characterizations of 'users' tasks, provided by users themselves, are perhaps the clearest indications of the seductive power of the accountabilities that had been established during their 'involvement' with the development of the emerging OMS. For although they point out that the system did not resolve all the problematic issues surrounding the planning, programming, and scheduling of refinery production, and indeed that in some cases it exacerbated them, they also clearly articulate a belief on the part of the users that *they* would eventually be the ones held to account for both failure and success. 'Involvement' with the development had heightened accountability, but not for the developers. There were new tools for, and increased expectations of, users at the site. And whether those tools helped or not, expectations would have to be fulfilled or explained away by the users in the absence of the makers of those tools.

In large part, these increased expectations upon users at the site were reified by other users who sought to act at a distance upon refinery activities. Staff at Mexaco

Oil's National Head Office wanted *certain* plans about future refinery production produced and distributed by the OMS. They wanted to treat the refinery as something of a modularized 'black box'. Given inputs, they wanted to know outputs, and vice versa. Only with such certain and deterministic information could they provide the traders with opportunities to 'generate value'.

> Oiltown produces their production plans with [the linear programmes] for the next week to two weeks, at the most. And we [want the system designers to] somehow get an interface that takes the production rates out of [the LP] into OMS and extrapolates forward, quantity and quality. I mean we're working to this plan and we believe this plan is right and it's the correct model. It's the best data we have on the future. We shouldn't be allowing people to say, 'No, I don't think it's quite like that, if I were you I'd allow for this'. In this day and age we shouldn't be doing that. Those things should already be accounted for and embodied in the model. If it isn't, if somebody does now and again say, 'Look!', which they're going to do, then the model should be improved. (Interview, Refinery Programming Manager)

The Head Office users' relative distance from the practicalities of refining on an imperfect site are made clear. Traders needed to believe in the certainty of the information they were provided with internally in order to be able to manage and make money out of the external uncertainty with which they were confronted. But refinery production programming staff were no more able to provide a definitive plan with the system than traders were able to provide a definitive figure for the oil price in two weeks time. Users recognized the importance of *their* expertise to do *their* job but the tasks of others were seen to be relatively programmatic and routinized. And such processes of attribution may be seen to enable both heightened accountability and self-acceptance of that accountability by system users.

▓ SUMMARY AND CONCLUSION

This chapter began by elucidating a distinction between two types of accountability for the promised benefits of information systems. An accountability for producing a system that potentially enables a user to exercise mastery and control; an accountability that is traditionally seen to lie with the system developer; and an accountability for the realization of that potential that is traditionally seen to lie with the user. But what if the attempt to establish the potential for mastery and control can itself destabilize and hence recede the possibility of the realization of this potential? What if the desire for mastery and control harbours a *reversible imminence* (Baudrillard 1983; Cooper 1993) at its core? That is, when the search for control eliminates the possibility of *real* control: when control of the 'denatured' is all that can be attained since the denatured has replaced the *real* during the struggle for control. When it is only a simulation that one controls?

Some nascent awareness of the simulational potential of systems is perhaps reflected in the insistence that users are the ones to be held accountable for systems success (or its lack thereof). 'Users' who will be left to 'carry the can' are almost inevitably seduced by the reversible linkages between the simulational and 'the real'. For it is they who will have to move between these two realms to make the system and the refinery work.

If the 'technical' system was truly systemic, if it were 'closed', then it would need no enrolled users and its builders would be accountable for its functioning. But we 'know' the system cannot do this, because as we have noted, accountability *in action* must live in the realm of the social, not the technical. 'Free' humans may be accountable because they can exercise *choice*, and systems cannot, or so the theory, supported and instantiated by humanist doctrine, goes. But other forces are at work here in this attribution. Reality is too 'hard', too recalcitrant to submit *directly* to mastery and control. Symbols are 'softer', more malleable, and so we seek to bring the real into the symbolic through *representation* (as discussed in Chapters 2 and 5). Thus, the 'problem' of accountability becomes one of *translation* within the simulational realm, primarily between simulations of processes and acts of intervention upon those processes, and simulations of 'value added' (or removed!). Such are the costs of life in a culture obsessed 'with the instantiation and instrumentalisation of all things' (Baudrillard 1990: 152).

Users have to work with and through seduction, a seduction that leaves them caught in an accountability trap. This seduction, whereby creative work between the simulational and the 'real' is performed, is perhaps most apparent in the attempts of users to resist complete compliance with the demands of an overarching system. User resistance to the demands being placed upon them by the emergent system is revealed as being largely pre-figured and organized around the notion of accountability. A recognition of the emerging system as simulational leads users to reject some of its injunctions and modes of organization to ensure that they retain contact with 'reality'. They had come to see themselves as accountable for results and benefits, indeed their accounts glorify their own roles as entrepreneurial and skilled, as the source of added value. They were not to be seduced by simulations but ironically one may see that as precisely what happened as their actions brought about ongoing and interminably unstable mergers and divisions between the simulational and the 'real'.

At the point where accountability and responsibility for a 'real' figure, such as 'a million dollars worth of benefit', can be inscribed to an individual, it no longer matters whether he or she has been provided with the tools that can enable a meeting of this promise. For the promise is already made and it is seen to be made by that 'individual', by the prospective user of the tool and not its developer. Indeed, it is unlikely that the developer will even be present when the promise is to be called in. And the laughter on the part of the informant that accompanied this comment perhaps reflects some awareness of this situation. The user, through 'involvement' with the system, is configured *as* accountable for the delivery of such benefits because of (and in spite of) the system's (lack of) potential to support such achievement. In many ways, the developer's task is successfully accomplished once the accountability is in place, regardless of whether the tool he or she has developed provides any direct support for the user. For the developer has indeed delivered a 'commercial orientation' on the part of refinery users. It is for the configured user to actualize that orientation in a newly 'commercial' future.

▓ DISCUSSION QUESTIONS

1. Does technology merely make more visible pre-existing patterns of accountability?

2. Can our systems builders ever escape accountability when, as we saw in Chapter 1, we are all too ready to blame the system?

3. Which users are most able to avoid being held accountable for their actions? Why?

4. What are the processes of accountability that are enacted upon you?

5. How does the idea of accountability connect with Labour Process Theory?

▓ SUGGESTIONS FOR FURTHER READING

Perhaps the best collection of work on this theme is gathered together in Rolland Munro and Jan Mouritsen's (1996) edited collection, *Accountability: Power, Ethos and the Technologies of Managing*. However, much recent writing on accountability is informed by Foucault's concept of *governmentality* and Graham Burchell, Colin Gordon, and Peter Miller's (1991) edited text, *The Foucault Effect*, provides an excellent introduction to these ideas.

8 | The Virtual Organization?

KEY THEMES

When you have read this chapter, you should be able to define those key concepts in your own words, and you should also be able to:

1. Discuss the concepts that inform groupware.

2. Identify some of the problems of implementing new technologies.

3. Understand how accountability is played out in specific media.

4. Have a deeper understanding of how management, organization, and technology interrelate.

Introduction

Although, as we have argued earlier, there has been breathless talk since the 1940s of the utopian futures that information systems might bring, a powerful new vision of how modern organizations could be radically reshaped has been widely disseminated since the late 1970s, based upon the bringing together of *information* and *communication* technologies (ICTs). In their influential thesis, *The Network Nation*, Hiltz and Turoff (1978) argued that over the next two decades, computer *mediated* communication would come to have a profoundly democratizing effect on organizational structures, resulting in decentralized, flatter, or 'virtual' organizations built around open exchanges between dispersed groups of individuals with common interests. Geographical and hierarchical barriers would be overcome in this organization of the future through widespread use of computerized conferencing and electronic messaging facilities. Such media would, it was claimed, not only supersede much routine face-to-face interaction, but would also come to replace a whole range of communication tools, like postal services, fax, and voice telephony. In the organizational heartlands of the networked nation, computer mediated communication would be the norm.

Perhaps unsurprisingly, the reality of the contemporary 'virtual organization' is somewhat different. There is, for example, little evidence to suggest that computerized conferencing is as yet allowing organizations to dispense with more traditional face-to-face meetings. Despite its ubiquitous presence, email also seems to have expanded upon rather than dominated the range of potential communications tools available to modern organizations (Sproull and Kiesler 1998). The crucial questions to be posed around the impact of computerized communication technologies are then not around what is *gained* or *lost* in the shift towards the virtual, but instead how electronic and traditional media mutually shape one another in the context of what might be called 'semi' or 'partly' virtual organizations. In particular, we want to draw this out through a focus upon the impact of a particular set of communication technologies collectively known as 'groupware', which typically lie at the heart of what is seen as the 'virtual organization'.

Groupware: a new hope for organizational sociality

Groupware is a term that broadly refers to a range of office organization software based on local and wide area computer networks. Such networks typically consist of a large number of personal computers or workstations distributed throughout the organization (clients), which are all connected to a smaller number of server systems. Users are then able to use these clients to access information stored on central servers as well as pass information by way of these servers to other clients. Common groupware activities include supporting workflow (e.g. receiving and processing customer orders), allowing access to common databases, facilitating computerized conferencing, and offering email or document sharing protocols.

Proponents of groupware emphasize the ability it affords to integrate the storage and retrieval of information with computer mediated communication occurring across different places and times (Kirkpatrick 1993). Meetings may, for example, be held between participants dispersed across a number of sites using either video or text based services. Alternatively, much of the work which was previously routinely achieved at meetings (e.g. communicating schedules, consultation, assigning tasks) can be performed either through emails sent to specific groups of individuals (i.e. members of a department) or through specific centralized agenda and project management tools.

One particular advantage that is often claimed for such technologies is that electronic communication can generate a continuous record of any exchange, providing a far more detailed (if not complete) account of what transpires than the seemingly etiolated traditional minutes of meetings. In this way groupware can more effectively support a more substantial 'organizational memory' (Khoshafian and Buckiewicz 1995), that is, the ability of an organization to retain and archive its own history. And, indeed, as we shall see in Chapter 10, once we find 'knowledge' can be organized in this way, then we find that we can talk about the 'learning organization'.

Much research into the introduction of groupware systems has concentrated on their impact on interpersonal relations between users (Rice and Love 1987; Schmitz and Fulk 1991) or directly upon organizational efficiency. Vogel and Nunamaker (1990), for example, list a whole range of benefits, including improved meeting *efficiency*, increased *quality* of input by participants, and the creation of more *complete* records. These studies tend, however, to assume that the availability of and access to increased amounts of information is, de facto, an unalloyed good. They do not explore, for example, the uses that might be made of these more complete records by managers and others, nor the *content* of computer mediated interactions between users. There is also an idealized view contained in these studies, of how meetings should operate. Meetings are treated as though they were purposively created sites for the exchange of information so that decisions can be duly generated. Similarly, participants in meetings are assumed to be equally determined to act rationally, at all times, in the organization's best interests.

Yet it is also possible to take a very different view of meetings. They are exchanges where participants struggle to establish their own version of past events, while simultaneously guarding their own *accountability* (see Chapter 7). Although decisions are often retrospectively attributed to meetings, they often occur outside the area bounded by the formal agenda—with decisions made in more informal areas between key executives and the meeting more formally ratifying predetermined events. And why not? After all, surely only the most inept strategist would risk having their authority and power substantially undermined by unnecessarily allowing decisions over their work area to be made in a volatile and uncertain arena. Thus, the relationship between the formal record of a meeting and what actually happened is often ambiguous and can sometimes be subject to multiple interpretations by participants. Meetings can thus be highly strategic affairs, with participants engaged in skilled rhetorical performances to secure their own objectives.

This approach to meetings is informed by ethnographic and discourse analytic studies of organizational life (Drew and Heritage 1992; Law 1994; Watson 1994). One of the major concerns here then becomes how participants in meetings formulate matters-at-hand in rhetorically persuasive ways. In this sense recollections of past events by participants are treated as accounts, which are structured in accord with the speaker's current interests and objectives. Groupware thoroughly impacts upon the ability of participants to generate accounts in this way. The potential to provide a more complete record of the meeting, for example, makes it increasingly difficult for participants to provide alternative interpretations of what actually happened (or, at least, interpretations that can be presented and accepted as a valid account of what happened). It would seem that participants cannot refer, in general terms, to 'the main thrust of the argument' presented in a meeting, or the 'underlying tone of the discussion' (and thereby make the meeting's decisions more fluid and amenable to their own ends), when anyone can call up the full record of what was 'said' and reinterpret it themselves.

Thus, it becomes clear that the content of meetings may be substantially affected by participants' prior concerns with how the meeting will be subsequently recorded. Furthermore, when the work previously done at meetings is performed instead through exchange of emails or other computer media, an entirely different range of rhetorical skills are required to manage the interaction. Participants in such exchanges are faced with a new set of problems. Dialogues are less ephemeral, less forgettable, and less easily contested when memories of them are brought back into play. Instead, dialogues may be edited or archived by either participant, ready to be summoned forth when necessary. And the new communication systems allow these dialogues, in their entirety or in a truncated form, to be forwarded throughout the organization and even beyond. Participants in this arena must rapidly acquire skills for the strategic use of the medium.

Two interlinked sets of issues then become pertinent. First, the ways in which groupware systems affect the organization of meetings. This includes the choice of the medium through which meetings are held and the degree of formality which is accorded to a particular meeting, along with a consideration of how the content of meetings, both 'face-to-face' and electronic, are shaped by the availability of groupware facilities in an organization. It also includes the willingness of participants to retrospectively attribute decisions to meetings. Second, the rhetorical and self-presentational strategies that are adopted by participants to manage public and semi-public interactions occurring over email. Concerns here centre upon how participants negotiate issues of recordability and the management of their own accountability in situations where multiple participants are electronically present.

Groupware in an organizational context

We explore these concerns in three sites. The first, to which we return later in more detail, is that of a conferencing system. Arguably, such systems are the forerunners of modern articulations of groupware in that many of the literate and democratic ideals of these ad hoc developments of bulletin boards have spilt over into the revolutionary claims ascribed to more recent developments. Yet such systems are still used by a variety of organizations to achieve many of the goals of latter-day systems. The other two sites are organizations at different stages in the introduction of groupware systems, studied by Steve Brown and Geoff Lightfoot.[1] The first was a commercial newspaper publisher moving towards web based electronic commerce, who employed intranet and email communication across multiple regional sites and had been testing a number of additional systems to facilitate intergroup communications. The second was a major United States and Japanese owned infrastructure builder to the oil industry that has a wide variety of groupware and video-conferencing systems. However, neither company was making anywhere near full use of the groupware systems that they had installed.

In this, these two organizations reflected the typically erratic take-up of groupware systems. As Brown and Lightfoot (2002) make clear, a number of organizations approached to take part in their study reported that they had either only partly implemented or had abandoned altogether the use of common groupware products such as Lotus Notes or GroupSystem. The reasons varied considerably: some users found certain groupware facilities, such as electronic conferencing, a poor substitute for face-to-face interaction because of the degraded quality of the images. Some managers felt that the continuous effort to spark sufficient interest among staff to use these systems was repaid by scant benefits, and remarked upon the excessive logistics required in arranging computer mediated meetings or electronic conferencing. And, in a related point, many users felt that groupware was being implemented by Information Technology (IT) managers in a 'me too' fashion, without proper consideration of the actual needs and demands of the organization concerned. Thus, for example, the democratic ambitions of system designers to allow all participants a voice and an equal say in the outcome of meetings was felt, by managers who might otherwise have directed the meetings more forcefully, to have created problems both of a lack of accountability in the 'meeting' itself, particularly where users were anonymized, and an excessive and unwieldy accountability in the weighty transcripts that were circulated after the meeting.

So, with the more radical groupware systems apparently dismissed out of hand by users at all levels, what then was left? In both of the organizations under discussion here, electronic communication and email, in particular, were widely used. However, users reported that they experienced these technologies as a highly formal medium—very different to the utopian vision of electronic communication as a means of informalizing working relations and democratizing organizations. Underpinning this experience was a high level of awareness of the potential damage to one's professional standing that could result from sending either badly formulated or ill-tempered messages across the system. Most users expected that their messages would be routinely archived by the recipient (indeed some managers specifically copied in particular users renowned for 'keeping everything' as a means of creating distributed stores of messages). Other users reported on the strictures imposed to ensure that they remained within this formal space: for example, if they didn't constantly contribute to text based discussions staged on the system's messaging or text based electronic conferencing facilities, they faced the risk of being negatively judged as being 'out of the loop'.

Yet users were able to describe a range of informal strategies that they were able to deploy in this formal space, designed for both avoiding such demerits and accruing merits to their own personal standing in the organizations. These included subverting the required 'flow' of documents by delaying their replies, or simply moving outside the system by printing out difficult or offending messages and using these to seek advice from co-workers and friends. More highly visible tactics might include copying messages or parts of dialogues to superiors or a selected range of potentially interested parties.

Indeed, users display considerable attention to matters of accountability and routinely attempt to forestall possible counter-arguments. Of course, one might expect to find similar features in face-to-face conversation, but this attention is particularly acute in email exchanges because of ambiguities surrounding the footing on which the exchange takes place. Senders are often uncertain about who may actually read their message, since in both organizations messages are routinely forwarded to others, and recipients are likewise wary of who else may have been copied (cc) or blind-copied (bcc) into the exchange. And, with text available to be flourished in any subsequent argument, the possibilities of claiming mishearing or misunderstanding are much reduced. Unsurprisingly, this anxiety over personal accountability routinely results in communication problems, such as excessive attention to detail in messages or the distribution of yet further copies of any emails (in an attempt at 'ass-covering'), helping spark the much-remarked email overload.

Similarly, other consequences of the formal nature of the space realized by this technology can be seen as contributing to this deluge of email, even as other claims for the emancipatory powers of the technology fail to materialize. There is little evidence to suggest that groupware packages reduced the number of face-to-face meetings attended by managers, simplifying the decision-making process. Indeed, rather the reverse seemed to have happened: one of the most common complaints was of the heavy traffic of emails generated around the setting up of traditional meetings, and of the need to hold additional meetings in order to resolve issues raised across electronic communication media. And a substantial number of email exchanges are brought to conclusion with the resolution to 'hold a proper meeting about this'. Thus, even though many users felt that they were forced to participate in text-based discussions by their managers, those same managers later felt that excessive participation added to their own time-management problems.

There are signs, however, that electronic communication is having some impact on the formal nature of meetings. Managers reported that less of their meetings are now formally minuted. This is particularly the case with higher level meetings. In place of minutes, it is now common for action points to be electronically distributed as the formal record of the meeting. It seems therefore that much of the rhetorical work which managers previously engaged in at formal meetings—ensuring that particular versions of the past or statements designed to shore up their own accountability are 'on record'—can be more readily achieved on electronic media, which managers are able to directly archive themselves.

On this latter point, it appears that many users are routinely storing colossal numbers of email messages, sometimes stretching back over five years or more.

Take, for example, this senior director of the publisher:

> I am the worst I am afraid I am probably the last person you should ask because I am probably the most hated in IT because my email, my email erm file is bigger than probably the rest of the company.
>
> [Laughter]
>
> I wish I was joking it is huge I never delete anything I am afraid I keep, I get regularly erm nice messages from [the IT manager] saying can you please take your file to less than ten gigabytes [laughter] which is just obscene and I go through trying to rifle out crap but I do find that my housekeeping is very poor with email and that is part of the problem and the other side of it is that I like to keep prompts for myself because we are actually talking about *minutes* at the end of the day that is what we are talking about erm I do keep prompts of the discussions that have taken place so that I can go back to them and refresh erm you know my memory as to what I said or what action points were agreed and *follow them up*. I do tend to keep, I mean the sent mail is the ones that I keep forever [laughter—as we all do yes] yes, in boxes so it is a little more erm tidy in terms of its housekeeping I do delete quite a bit erm but I also as I will show you I mean if I show you my email trees erm there is my basic list of email folders (laughter) okay, and then I can show you each element just for the purpose of the tape recorder erm Geoffrey is now looking at a tree which is about erm shall we say you can see (laughter) we are looking at a tree of emails of maybe fifty folders deep.
>
> Sure, sure, so how far back do some of those emails go just out of interest?
>
> I actually purged my storage, erm, last week because they really did have a whinge at me erm and if I.
>
> Because you had [emails going back to before] ninety-six?
>
> Yes, they are down to ninety-five (laughter). (Interview with Director, publishing company. Emphasis added.)

Organizational memory or organizing memory

The common reason given for this meticulous archiving of emails is that of preserving the organization's history for future strategic benefit. It may indeed do so (and indeed has a powerful resonance with some of the claims for knowledge management that we shall come to in Chapter 10). But what is clear is that such archives also serve to the benefit of individual managers, who are then able to rapidly offer evidence in support of their own credibility when their actions are questioned and also to assemble persuasive accounts questioning rival's actions by reintroducing potentially damaging prior exchanges. Groupware then serves as an important material resource for the production of *memory*. But the practices of remembering which it supports are creative acts that establish credible looking but nevertheless partial accounts of times past. In particular, the ability to put back into circulation subtly edited versions of exchanges is a powerful argumentative tool.

And here a little detail may be appropriate. We turn, then, to a first extract from an email sent to one of the authors of this volume (as well as many other interested observers) after a brief dispute that had led to a member (S^2) of a conferencing system (TCS[3]) being excluded from that system. Already, then, we see some of the tactical uses of email as the managers of TCS, one party to the dispute, were excluded from this 'blind copying-in' of potential allies.

> From: [S's personal e-mail account.]
> [...]
> Just so that the situation[4] is clear, I'll give you a frank account of what happened. Let me say here and now though, I apologise for nothing that I have done or said; the weeklong outage at TCS was unacceptable from an ISP positioning itself as a business supplier. The fact that TCS chose to manage it's communication with subscribers by misleading them over recovery times is indefensible, and highlighted that TCS has no effective disaster management or recovery plan. After this, I'm sure that TCS would find it difficult to keep existing business customers on anything other than conferencing, which in turn they have failed to recognise as a value product.
> OK, it became apparent early last week that the TCS WWW and FTP capability was broken. TCS started to give out projected resumption of service times, which came, went and were replaced by new ones. Like others users of the system, I was contacted by /my/ users to ask for resumption times. As the times given by TCS were not too far ahead, I passed those on and asked for patience rather than implementing another strategy. Thus, TCSs lies became my lies.

S has purposefully deployed a number of accounts here to establish his personal standing. First, and most obvious, is that he depicts himself as entrepreneurial, as running a business—always a powerful rhetorical move—but particularly on this conferencing system where many users are contract IT professionals and frequently identify themselves as self-employed entrepreneurs. But being in business also implies adherence to a set of contractual relations. S draws this out by emphasizing his contract with his users before twisting the knife by pointing out that TCS 'position[s] itself as a business supplier' and, by implication, must be subject to the same rules as he adheres to. And so, we can see how accountability is starting to be constructed. S's accountability has been rendered in terms of his obligations to his customers; TCS's in terms of their own contractual obligations. But S is not finished: he enrols others to his cause by pointing out he merely faced problems '[l]ike others users of the system'. And a final flourish is worthy of note: 'TCSs lies became my lies' introduces a moral dimension, with clear positions both for S and TCS. A dimension reinforced with the suggestion that S is being 'frank'.

These attempts to establish standing are particularly important on TCS for most users do not know one another except through 'conversations' on the system. For when it comes to taking sides in the dispute, we need to know for whom, and why, we might take up cudgels. So now, having given us a brief 'whom', S begins to produce a narrative of 'why' by producing more of the exchange that led to his exclusion.

> As the hours turned into days, it began to become apparent that TCS were, IMO deliberately, giving PR (as opposed to concrete) estimates, I posted this query on Wednesday at 09.42 in TCS:TCS.support/5internet:4745

Any chance of offering a service?
Is there any chance at all of FTP being restored within the forseeable future? Your post-
ings so far seem to indicate nothing more than a moveable feast. Forget the time, would
it be today, tomorrow, this week, next?

at 13.38, I had this response TCS:TCS.support/5internet:4756;

> The ftp service on the unix webserver should be live by around 15:00 hours this
> afternoon—a confirmation message will be posted in TCS:TCSnews/information
> Apologies for this downtime.

S is starting to indicate the dangers inherent in text-based systems. Here, he has been
able to retrieve two mails from his archive and represent them in *his* narrative
which, at the moment, is the only one that stands. A narrative that continues to
develop an accountability for TCS and S himself based upon market relations and
customer contracts. Establishing this narrative is critical, as we shall see, first as S
further develops the context before escalating the dispute:

> I waited patiently, as I had some online learning materials waiting to FTP, for which
> people had alreday been waiting long enough. I tried FTP at 15.54, and it was still down.
> I'd seen enough, as this was the umpteenth missed deadline which I'd been foolish
> enough to pass on myself to others. They clearly had major problems which they were not
> coming clean about. I posted this TCS:TCS.support/5internet:4775

>> Still no service.
>> Essentially, you haven't got a fucking clue have you?

Unsurprisingly, such words moved the dispute on to a different level. And without the
context so helpfully supplied, S might easily be seen as the unjustified aggressor. Hence
so much effort to establish the lines of accountability. Yet S recognizes that accountability is still not settled, and such a message posted in an open conference (where
anyone might see it) can be (and indeed was) seen as provocative. He then moves to
forestall such problems by placing any such criticism in a different context, separating
it from what he seeks to establish as the main issue: that of contractual accountability.

> Hmm. Some people were annoyed by that. That's their right. These same people however
> can't grasp that I find TCS brown-nosing and holier-than-thou outrage equally annoying.
> Someone called A posted this;

>> Personally, I don't think there was a need for that kind of rudeness.
>> A.
>> (Totally disgusted by the attitude of *some* users).

> I responded robustly with;

>> get stuffed you pompous halfwit

> No apologies for this. He could have kept his disgust to hisself. He had a go at me, I had a
> go back.

And as things start to get a little vicious, we see a different rendering of accountability. This time, A is held accountable for, and through, his text, which has been

incorporated into a different narrative than perhaps the one that A expected. A's standing is now weak in this story, for his entry is shown as being calculating and unnecessary, and gets the response it 'deserves'. But things are only now starting to hot up:

At 22.29, I had the following e-mail from K;

> Dear S
> This type of conduct is neither helpful nor constructive.
> I understand your frustrations—but being abusive doesn't help the situation and can demotivate the staff working long hours, doing their utmost to ensure we provide the high quality of service our customers expect.
> I've also appended the most recent TCS:TCSnews/information posting, which I hope you will find informative and re-assuring.
> If you have urgent changes you wish to make to your website—please let me know, it may be possible to arrange this for you.
> Kind regards
> K

Now, it's always my policy to go public with these kind of things, particualrly as there was nothing in it that couldn't have been said in open conf. I replied to the e-mail, but also copied the original and my reply into the support conf, thus;

> Please spare me the sanctimonious claptrap. Just get someone in who can provide the service for which we pay, complete with effective disaster management and planning. I was responding to a clear statement you had made. You clearly had no basis on which to make it. Had you been working for me you would now be looking for another job.

> A little brusque you may think. Let's be frank though; I'm not interested in having K as a friend, and I'm not keen on being bullshitted or patronised. My reply was honest and non-abusive and, for me, restrained after days of no-service for which I'm paying. Sometimes these people forget who pay their wages. [. . .]

There are two points of note here. First is the attempt by TCS management to try and take this dispute out of the public forum. Once private, and established on a private footing, any public accountability of TCS is much diminished (effectively for good, as TCS etiquette is strongly against the publication of email exchanges in open conference) for once private, any attempts to enrol others or mobilize groups of users can swiftly be discounted. S is alert to this possibility and so immediately moves back from the private into the public by reposting the email back into a public conference. Second, there is the question of where accountability can move. K draws upon the discourse of business, but attempts to move to a wider one that includes staff relations and would thereby make S accountable for his ill-mannered outbursts. But S is well aware of this and continues to ensure that accountability lies only along one dimension—task-oriented business management. But back to our debate:

> Then R really lit the blue touchpaper with TCS:TCS.support/5internet:4792
> I'm sorry but that kind of rudeness will not help any of us.
> We do have a clue.

I can only apologise for the lack of information posting today.
This is primarily because I have been off ill (having working a 35–40 hour shift with a cold, along with another 3 staff, without colds), people were expecting me to carry on my role of ensuing smooth communications between the Operations Team and the Customer services Team.
Now I'm back, I'll ensure K is kept up to date and of course we'll also keep you up to date.
R
TCS

Far from coming clean about the continuing outage, this fool was claiming personal 'illness' as a cover for their inability to tell the truth, or fix it. No mention of recovery time you'll note. That strategy now abandoned in favour of saying nothing at all. Don't forget though, me and plenty of others are still awaitng resumption. 09.20 on Thursday, I reply to that post with TCS:TCS.support/5internet:4806

Once again, accountability is the principal question. R 'volunteers' acceptance of a certain level of accountability, but this definition would also render S partially accountable, thus S attempts to refute such shifts:

Still no service.
Essentially, you don't have a clue do you. Although illness is always worth a try.

Note that I dropped the expletive, but included my opinion of his tactics.
R then admonished me for [another] message. I decided to give him a taste of his own medicine with a parody as TCS:TCS.support/5internet:4841

I can only apologise for the lack of courtesy today.
This is primarily because I have been in work, ill, (having working a 35–40 hour shift with a cold, along with another 3 staff, without colds), people were expecting me to carry on my role of ensuing smooth communications between paying clients, their legal teams, and their inability to use services for which they pay.
I'm sure you'd agree that this excuses everything. Ever.

Which I though was rather good, actually. No prizes for guessing that they didn't

So, once again, messages are resources of remembering to be pulled in and out of play. S trawls through the entire archive to present a particular screen for us to view what has happened—one that makes a reasonably convincing case. And S displays a fine knowledge of the ironies of his play by referring to his 'opinion of [R's] tactics'. But such rhetorical skills may not always be enough—after all, when discussing accountability, we are always turned to an examination of power effects. And surely power is never so open to shifts by 'mere talk'.

Friday morning, another e-mail from K;

Dear Mr S
I am writing to inform you that after discussion with our directors, your account with TCS will be terminated in 7 days from todays date (Friday 8th December).
This is in accordance with our terms and conditions, a copy of which is enclosed for your reference.

> We also reserve the right to suspend your account, without further notice.
> This will also be confirmed to you in writing shortly.
> Kind regards
> K
> Customer Services Manager

Deary me. Have they nothing better to do? Like fixing fucking broken systems, and formulating a competent disaster management plan and strategy? Obviously not. If they were expecting a grovel, they'd come to the wrong boy. I replied;

> Oh dear,
> of course it's your privelege to sulk and take your ball home. Are you really sure you can afford to voluntarily lose subscribers after the TCS performance this week?
> We look forward with anticipation to receiving the T&C's.
> Thank you.

[. . .]

So there you have it. One F word, a couple of mild slapdowns of TCS users who came looking for trouble when they could have stayed quiet, and giving as good as I got to a couple of below-par performers in the TCS hierarchy when I robustly asked that they came clean about delivering what I, and you, are paying for. Jizzus, Eminem would openly laugh at me in the street for being a pussy. Am I bitter? Am I fuck. it's their garden, their game and their ball. Do you think I'd let some of these bozos join any club of mine? Course I would, but then I'm a big lad. Is there a wider issue for TCS and its users here? Indeed so. However, at the moment that's a debate I can't join. Knowing TCS as I do, I'd be surprised if even those who hate me and EVERYTHING YOU STAND FOR, YOU. . . . . YOU . . . . (sorry) didn't also recognise the wider issues here.

> Feel free to post this in its entirety to whatever place you see fit.
> A Spineless-Twat

S was duly evicted from TCS.

Just talk?

So was this all in vain? Is the rhetorical turn, even when backed by textual media, still *just* rhetoric? Is accountability ever malleable by those *made* accountable? Well, for once, our tale does have what seems to be a happy ending (for some at least): S was reinstated on the system a week or so later. The care that he took to place the different exchanges in a coherent narrative, a narrative which excused and explained his actions and worked to continually refocus attention upon TCS and their actions, was successful in enrolling and mobilizing enough other users, through his strategic use of the system itself, that his account came to be established as the accepted history. TCS, configured as an implacable, under-performing bureaucracy, not playing by the rules of business, would confirm that representation by maintaining his exclusion. And so, revealing that they were well aware of their accountability to the 'community' of users, TCS backed down.

But this example was from an organization (at least initially) evolved from a democratic vision, where the whole point of the network was to allow open debate and the majority of the users who subscribed entered on that basis. In most companies, despite the siren calls of the developers of groupware systems, the ability to use those systems as a resource for practices of remembering is rarely found across the entire organization. Senior members are not only able to decide what might be entered in electronic archives, they are also less likely to be challenged for taking up large amounts of server space. Moreover, senior members are able to switch mediums more easily than subordinates. They are able to exercise the authority to put an end to email exchanges, call face-to-face meetings, or book video-conferencing time. More junior members of both organizations are often limited to electronic communication as the prime means of managing their personal standing beyond their immediate workgroup. They may be summoned on to the system to respond to enquiries, or seek allies to support their own position amongst other users currently logged into the system.

This imbalance between the positions of junior and senior staff also shows how conflicts between inherently flexible and potentially democratizing technologies and control of the labour process are (partially) resolved. As senior managers can withdraw, while junior staff cannot, and while senior staff potentially have access to *all* email conversations (via access to the store of emails maintained on the central systems), the virtual space becomes one that is a powerful resource for ensuring compliance, and one which junior staff are obliged to subscribe to.

However, although this resonates with our discussion in Chapter 1, it would be facile to depict email *merely* as a tool that managers employ in a struggle to control the labour process. In order to manage electronically mediated interactions, junior members have developed a range of strategies to serve their own interests. The most common are techniques for prolonging discussion and for copying in other participants. Prolonging discussion is achieved by tactics such as sending innocuous sounding enquiries about prior events (e.g. past departmental protocols)—this almost inevitably provokes lengthy accounts—or by referring back to early comments using cut and paste facilities. This latter strategy usually results in a rhetorical struggle between participants to reconstruct the proper sequence of the exchange (as we have seen so eloquently performed in our email extract). Copying in of other participants is routinely done in situations where personal accountability is threatened. Superiors are an obvious choice here, but participants also copy in a range of potentially interested parties or even copy the exchange to internal discussion lists. Casting about for allies in this way can be an effective strategy, but it also generates substantial volumes of messages. Managers in both organizations were sensitive to these practices and tended to monitor and archive exchanges where they were strategically copied in, only intervening at the point where their own external accountability appeared to be threatened.

SUMMARY

Overall, the picture that emerges is of electronic communication as a thoroughly formal medium where participants experience considerable anxiety over their own personal accountability and interact in highly strategic ways. Groupware systems do play a key role in the preservation of organizational memory, but these memories are strategic constructions, which are most commonly assembled by senior managers from the resources contained in extensive archives that they are able to maintain. Only when freed from the economic and power relationships that characterize business does 'freedom' emerge. And even then, it is a bitter freedom, laying bare the disputatious nature of such textual transactions.

This is a description of a virtual world completely different to that envisaged by system designers. The incorporation of system features such as blind copying, continuous voting, and auto-copying, seen as innocuous tools in providing the grail of greater, *better* information for everyone, become ambiguous and contestable weapons when put in a management setting. Revealing the strategic or 'political' dimension to groupware use also helps put our knowledge of different kinds of information communication technologies on a new footing. Previously many theorists have used a distinction between 'task oriented' and 'relationship oriented' activities to focus on the impacts of communication technologies and the development of the virtual organization. Yet it seems more likely that running between this distinction is a whole series of strategic activities aimed at sustaining accountability and reconstructing the past. These activities lead to the creation of formal and informal communication networks based not on common interests, but rather around common *antagonisms*. The impact, then, of the virtual organization has been to provide a new set of resources in which managers can re-enact the work of managing, as they define it, rather than a democratization of the workplace.

And this gives us little hope for our own text. For we know that in a few years time, even the title of our book will look hopelessly outdated and any reader who has opened this book for a learned disposition on the Internet, dotcoms, texting, or any of the more recent technological shockwaves will be disappointed. A retreat into the certainties of management, though unlikely to impress many of our colleagues, may ensure that we still retain some timeousness. For we certainly will not win awards for our advice: following an ill-tempered argument on TCS, one of the authors of this text received the following email.

> A point you make [in a paper on Groupware] is that no one sensible should wash their professional linen electronically as they have no idea who else may be watching.
>
> Incidentally, it may be an idea to expunge 'Geoff Lightfoot' from your TCS resume. Many users keep quiet about their full names, so it's not unusual. Knowing your surname made it easy—far too easy, in fact—to find out about you.
>
> Thus anonymised, you can continue with your erm acerbic wit, safe from the risk of antagonising someone who later turns out to be a commissioning editor . . .
> (personal email)

DISCUSSION QUESTIONS

1. What constitutes organizational memory, if such a thing can be said to exist? And in talking about remembering, what is being forgotten?

2. Can community exist online?

3. Does text always have more status than talk?

4. Is the nature of organization more important than changes in technology?

▧ SUGGESTIONS FOR FURTHER READING

Other works from the ESRC's initiative is gathered together in Steve Woolgar's (2002) edited
  collection, *Virtual Society: Technology, Cyberbole, Reality*, Oxford: Oxford University Press.
There have been many forays into virtual communities. Favourites include Sherry Turkle's (1997)
  Life on the Screen, New York: Simon & Schuster and Sandy (Allucquère Rosanne) Stone's
  (1995) *The War of Desire and Technology at the Close of the Mechanical Age*, Boston MA:
  IT Press.

9 | Representation 3: Risk, Control, and the Escape of Uncertainty

---

KEY CONCEPTS

codification	representation
contextual knowledge	rules
control	semiotics
experiential knowledge	signification
objectification	spectaction
reconstruction	symbolic representation

KEY THEMES

When you have read this chapter, you should be able to define those key concepts in your own words, and you should also be able to:

1. Discuss different ways of representing the relationship between 'the user' and technology.

2. Explain how symbolic representation works.

3. Discuss the *principle* of selective objectification.

4. Evaluate the importance of contextualization.

5. Explain the relationships between *sense, reference*, and *meaning*, and explore their relevance for 'information systems'.

6. Appreciate the technological and instrumental representative orientation of the modern world.

Introduction

The elimination of risk and uncertainty seems to be one of the key objectives underlying systematization. In this chapter we return to themes introduced earlier in the book and we consider those risks that are entailed by attempts to completely eliminate risk itself, primarily through tying these themes to the problems associated with large-scale systems. We will be seeking to examine the ways in which information technologies can exacerbate the problems identified, but it is important to realize that these issues have a somewhat longer pedigree. They result from the nature of *representation* and the ever-expanding scale of its processes and purview.

Representation and the accomplishment of organization

Organizing in the modern world relies upon 'the ability of . . . institutions to transcend the limited spatio-temporal coordinates of immediate contexts and to act on signs or cues that represent absent states of the world, i.e. states extending beyond the here and now' (Kallinikos 1995: 118). The ability to act is increasingly dependent upon making the absent present, through abbreviated and ordered codification, or *representation*. As we discovered in Chapter 2, representation requires and allows

> the interlocking of actions and things separated in time and space and their insertion into extended regulative frameworks. The numerical representations of the market, for instance, are able to unite actors separated by spatial and cultural barriers. Similarly a map, a population census, a balance sheet, a database are all codified versions that recapture the diversity and extension of the world in forms that enable immediate visibility and inspection. (Cooper 1992; Kallinikos 1993). (Kallinikos 1995: 118)

Kallinikos draws upon the work of the philosopher Heidegger (1977) and particularly his essay, *The question concerning technology,* to explore how representation is tied up with both the technological and instrumental orientation of the modern world and the problems that come along with such an orientation. According to Kallinikos, representation

> differs from any other prior mode of knowing in that it is not simply concerned with the duplication or symbolic coding of the world in all its detail and diversity, but rather with the selective *objectification* of things, states and processes. Representation is selective in the sense of objectifying properties or facets of the world: for instance, when human beings are considered as labouring bodies, consumers or role incumbents, nature as raw material, objects and actions as products or services, etc. It abstracts from the totality of things and events which it reduces in order to survey and master them. (1995: 118)

The world is not simply miniaturized and moved for consideration, it is selectively captured. And this selection is instrumental in orientation. It only seeks to capture that which is necessary for mastery and control. The modern project of enhancing human control or rule entails a process in which thinking about the world is substituted by representing of the world (Heidegger 1977). The world is (re)written and (re)constructed 'from the horizon of human intention' (Kallinikos 1995: 119).

> This does not ... mean that representation produces ... [a] fictional world. Nothing is more alien to representation than hallucinatory fiction. [But it does mean that]

[r]epresentation is concerned with society and nature only insofar as they can become the objects of its reconstructing capacity. Utility and functionality are notions intrinsic to a way of thinking that has become represenational. (Kallinikos 1995: 119)

At first sight then, it appears that we enter a realm in which the ubiquitous 'user' takes the sovereign, centre position. But first sights can be deceiving. For as the quote above about the ways in which 'human beings are considered' by representation makes clear, this is a world in which 'the user'—as that which naively we might believe the system is intended to serve—becomes, instead, an entity that is perhaps best captured not by the imagery of a human body assisted in its activities by the technology that surrounds it, but rather as merely a part of the 'technology' itself. Our commonsensical understanding of the relationship between technology and its 'users' is inverted, with the latter appearing as simply another category or 'gap' which representation seeks to fill out according to its own demands. As Lisanne Bainbridge's *Ironies of automation* (1983, reprint 1987; see also Reason 1994) alerts us, in our contemporary circumstances we tend to automate the 'middling' jobs in our productive processes, the so-called 'semi-skilled'. We do not, in the main, bother to automate either unskilled jobs—there is simply no economic imperative to do so (see Chapter 1)—or highly skilled tasks—they are often simply too difficult to mimic technologically. The outcome, for large-scale critical control systems, such as those employed at nuclear refineries with their so-called 'defence in depth', is that we construct largely self-sufficient systems which, nevertheless, require highly skilled 'minders' engaged in a curious form of activity that Richard de Sotto (1990) captures with the notion of 'spectaction'. Operators must be highly skilled, for they have to cope with the situations which the system builders found too complex to cost effectively automate, at the same time as working with a system which tends to have automated away the need on their part for routine interaction with the system. Ironically, this results in our critical systems being minded by those who have no experience of 'ordinary' usage, but who are, nevertheless, expected to be able to regain control when the 'extraordinary' happens. However one chooses to see such a scenario in terms of its implications for safety, it is clear that both types of remaining human bodies in the mix are 'users' only in the most bizarre sense. They seem much better conceptualized as biological remainder, the remnants of 'flesh' that the system needs to oil its functioning in a world both driven by economic imperative and apparently stalked by uncertainty. In the next section we examine the genesis of this seemingly parlous state.

Symbols and materials

More easily movable and observable symbols have long been employed to stand for other material things, for they bring immense benefits for their 'users'. Clay tokens—utilized to 'stand' for absent goods—along with lists and tables, seem to have been present at, and necessary for, the dawn of civilization (Goody 1986; Schmandt-Besserat, 1992). But the intensification and recursion[1] of these practices in our so-called information age does seem to require us to pay more attention to the consequences of these simple facts of (modern) life. And this intensification itself has a somewhat longer history than our contemporary information fever would tend to suggest.

Techniques of representation are a requirement of the above examples, and thus seem to date back to pre-history. But such techniques inhabited a world not yet 'disenchanted' by the rise of Weber's technocracy (1968) and the orientation with which they are associated was not able to dominate 'other forms of conceiving and acting upon the world' (Kallinikos 1995: 121). However, with the advent of industrialism and the view of the world as a stock of parts to be drawn upon to both control and refabricate that world, representation ascends to dominance (Heidegger 1977). Humans initially appear here as separated from the world, standing over it— in the ultimate 'user' position—but also intimately involved with it, as they bend it to their will. In this Heideggarian view, representation '. . . proceeds by (re)constructing the world from particular standpoints' on the basis of 'sets of initial assumptions that define and single out particular facets of [that] world' (Kallinikos 1995: 121) for investigation and subsequent action.

> Desire, for instance, is differently conceived by economics and psychoanalysis. Similarly, nature is not the same for geology, biology or physics. Different disciplines posit the world in accordance with their initial set of assumptions, but common to all of them is exactly the *principle* of selective objectification. (Kallinikos 1995: 121–2)

When this view extends to become an all-encompassing orientation to the world (which is arguably the case in the West at least):

> the world—mankind included—exists only insofar as it can be reinscribed with the texture of the intentions, purposes and artifacts of modern man ... [It] must always be conceived in terms which render it calculable and masterable, and allow for intervention and change. (Kallinikos 1995: 122)

Representing objectification in the information age

This world-view is most obvious in the field of science but it is not limited to this domain; for science is a field and way of knowing that increasingly dominates all others. 'Modern science is the example *par excellence* of representing objectification and its mastering ambitions. This is the overall context within which *thinking* and world *engagement* become *science* and *technology*' (Kallinikos 1995: 122).

This substitution, or colonization, by science whereby selective objectification and self-referentiality are escalated and accompanied by a 'growing and successive removal from immediate contexts and the concrete and tangible world' (Kallinikos 1995: 123), is the hallmark of the modern world. A hallmark which brings new and potentially subversive meaning to the notion of 'defence in depth' we encountered earlier. It is also made all the more apparent by the advent of electronic information technologies.

The result is a world made up of *objects* that must be regulated and transformed by separated *subjects* who stand and rule over them.[2] And these subjects require centres within which representations of diverse aspects of the world can be gathered together and compared before this knowledge is applied back on the world to regulate and transform it.

According to Kallinikos:

> The enormous growth of writing and of verbal and numerical techniques that catalogue and write down the world must be understood in this context. It is by means of these techniques and the institutional settings that carry and are carried by them that representation becomes an *ongoing activity* (Heidegger 1977). (1995: 123)

And this is increasingly what (working) life entails for the 'symbolic analysts' and 'knowledge workers' of the 'information age', the contemporary equivalents of the bureaucrats and administrators of the pre-computer age. Industry and administration of all sorts are thus seen as coincident with representation as 'the dominant way of conceiving and acting on the world' (Kallinikos 1995: 124). But this is no *mere* coincidence. To take but one example, as Weber (1968) points out, the modern capitalistic enterprise is inconceivable in the absence of rational bookkeeping and accounting. Such techniques enable not only the separation of industry from home, but also the appearance of the former as a wealth-producing machine. The rise of Information Technology (IT) merely accelerates and escalates a process already in place, and it is perhaps no accident that again accounting is at the forefront of these changes. Accounting not only offers its pre-electronic computations as prototypical site of application, it also enables the capture of the financial impact of similar interventions elsewhere in the organization (see Ezzamel, Lilley, and Willmott 1997, in press). This is what we are witnessing in the computerization of the management of business and medicine. As Kallinikos suggests

> If work or *health*, for instance, are to become regulated, they need first to be conceived as separable parts of human life that can be singled out and studied, and then further reduced by the invention of aspects and dimensions along which they can be recorded, counted, compared, inspected, in short managed. (1995: 123)[3]

These dimensions are currently experiencing an ongoing effort to translate them into electronic impulses to further enhance the mastery and control they enable. It is in this sense that digital technology is to be seen as just the latest stage in this representational project. Here, representation's world orientation is embodied in the very nature of the technology that is constituted by little more than an organization of codified symbols. But the world of materials and bodies is not dispensed with here. Rather, it is further subordinated to the organizing power of symbols as we increase our distance from the world of handicraft and active and direct engagement. As we move from crafts, through industrialism, to the so-called 'knowledge' work, our power to act in the world ironically recedes as the tools that we construct to allow us to do so become more powerful, for it is frequently no longer 'us' that does the acting. In some senses we cease to be actors and become spectators (cf. Reason 1994; Sotto 1990). And as spectators in the information age we do not even get to watch directly!

> Thus understood, digital technology implies the further dissociation of working knowledge from concrete labouring bodies and its formalization into abstract relationships and principles of operation. The tacit knowledge that was previously lodged in sentience, in living, labouring bodies confronting a tangible, albeit preconceived and prearranged, world of objects becomes either articulate and formalized in the products of conceptual engineering or abandoned (Sotto 1990; Zuboff 1988). (Kallinikos 1995: 125)

With the advent of digital technologies our mastery is not assured. For new problems arise from the 'extra' dissociation they bring:

> Quite generally, digital technology confronts human beings with two interrelated sets of problem, i.e. those of *sense* and *reference*, the meaning and the *ars combinatoria* of the abstract symbolic cues that make up the electronic text, and the things, states and processes represented by the abstract symbolic cues. (Kallinikos 1995: 126)

When the symbols that stand for 'things' increasingly derive at least some of their meaning for us from the other symbols with which they are surrounded in our representations, it becomes increasingly difficult to make the journey from symbol back to symbolized. For the connections, 'distorted' by the order of the symbolic level, no longer travel directly to the 'thing' in the world for which the symbol apparently stands. And as a result, mistakes can and do happen (cf. Reason 1994). We are, however, implicitly aware of this risk and try to ensure that mistakes do not occur. If we say to a friend, perhaps a currency trader who seeks to blind us with his science, that 'I know money', the auditor is able to distinguish between the otherwise identical sounds of 'no' and 'know' primarily through the context of other sounds within which the 'know' sound is rendered. The meaning of 'know' is indicated not only by direct connection to a concept, but also and in the process by the closing off of another, in isolation, equally plausible connection. But it is not hard to imagine a situation in which this confusion would be harder to resolve. Various forms of colloquial, ethnic, and 'pidgin' English allow the usage of 'no' within verbal arrangements which the grammatical rules of 'standard' English would preclude. In such cases the auditory signal 'I know money' could entirely conceivably be read not as 'I understand how money works', but rather as 'I have no money'.

This is what Zuboff (1988) is referring to when she explores the problems of *informating*. Reconstructing meaning out of symbols is very different to playing with the materially grounded reality of processes and things, although control is the required outcome of both sets of practices. Problems of meaning (re)construction are present in all representations (think of how hard it is to 'interpret' a work of art or a set of accounts) but they are amplified and altered by digitization. Information systems seem to have a tendency to try and inform on everything, pulling many symbols from extremely diverse sources into a similar place. In the process, they blur distinctions between production and administration, confronting the latter with the problems of the former, leading to the subsequent calls for 'hybrids' highlighted in our previous note. But distance from the world not only presents problems for control in a simple, functional sense (cf. Reason 1994). The desire for control tends to result in us losing contact with the world. The only world that counts is the world that we can control, and in many ways the world 'as is' is lost. 'In a straightforward fashion, digital technology creates a context where work literally becomes an ensemble of readings, inferences, and interpretations (Zuboff 1988)' (Kallinikos 1995: 128).

The represented world is at a somewhat frightening level of remove from the material world with which we, as terrestrial beings, engage. Indeed, the grounded materialities of our existence may even be entirely absent in the idealizations of representation. In the search for control we soon become lost in attempting to control our controls and their effects.[4] In representation the world remains always and inevitably beyond our reach.

A representational communication

To try and make these somewhat arcane notions a little easier to grasp, Kallinikos (1995) draws upon Italo Calvino's novel (1972, trans. 1979), *Invisible Cities*. He focuses on the parts of the novel that deal with the problems of sense and reference which, as we have already hinted, are exacerbated by our move to digitized representations.[5] Calvino's narrative concerns an imaginary relationship between the Chinese emperor Kublai Khan and the Italian merchant Marco Polo in the late thirteenth century. The latter acts as an agent of Khan, who travels throughout the vast territory of Khan's empire, returning periodically to the palace to report what he has seen. The two protagonists initially lack a common language, through which to communicate and, thus, the desire to exchange information that their symbiotic roles entail, 'must pass through the immediate signifying capacity of things and gestures' (Kallinikos 1995: 129).

> From the foot of the Great Khan's throne a majolica pavement extended. Marco Polo, mute informant, spread out on it the samples of the wares he had brought back from his journeys to the ends of the empire: a helmet, a seashell, a coconut, a fan. Arranging the objects in a certain order on the black and white tiles, and occasionally shifting them with studied moves, the ambassador tried to depict for the monarch's eyes the vicissitudes of his travels, the conditions of the empire, the prerogatives of the distant provincial seats. (Calvino 1979, mobilized in Kallinikos 1995: 129)

Here, objects signify in ways that are tied to their immediacy. For example 'A coconut may exemplify agriculture and the helmet an army, but not the other way round.' (Kallinikos 1995: 130) But it is not simply individual objects that express something here. It is also their arrangement into certain patterns, their *ars combinatoria*. We are dealing not only with reference but also with sense.

> Kublai Khan was a keen chess-player; following Marco's movements he observed that certain pieces implied or excluded the vicinity of other pieces and were shifted along certain lines. Ignoring the object's variety of form, he could grasp the system of arranging one with respect to others on the majolica floor. He thought 'if each city is like a game of chess, the day when I have learned the rules, I shall finally possess my empire, even if I shall never succeed in knowing all the cities it contains'. (Calvino 1979, mobilized in Kallinikos 1995: 130)

As with the syntax and grammar of sentences, it is the structure 'that joins the elements of a work, which opens up the space of meaning and reveals what it conveys' (Kallinikos 1995: 130). Thus, the great Khan downplays the significance of individual objects, focusing instead upon the greater system formed by their combinations. In particular, he seeks to understand the generative rules (i.e. the *ars combinatoria*) which lead to the relationships, the object combinations that are manifest in each specific arrangement. Objects and their combinations are of use to Khan only as examples which can be interrogated to enable him to ascertain the underlying rules which are themselves rendered as the essential knowledge of the empire. However, as Kallinikos (1995: 131) notes, 'The very image of the empire that results from the knowledge and application of the generative rules gains precedence over what such an image is supposed to refer to.'

This is a special kind of knowledge. It relates to mastery and control, the *possession* of the empire. It embodies the 'economy' of representation (think back to Chapter 2) in which as much as is needed is carried in as little as is necessary. Such an orientation in our contemporary world is, perhaps, best exemplified by the activities of those specialists of computerized language who have been inspired by Noam Chomsky's (1972) depth theory of language (see also Pinker 1994). It is an orientation that seeks the underlying generative rules of an overarching system, parameterized by the speaker/hearer's particular culture, through which suitably downplayed units (words) are combined to produce meaning.

> [T]he human mind is in some way 'pre-wired' for language, . . . we are born with a special sensitivity to certain universal features of human grammar. We are programmed to be able to learn to speak, but the actual language we learn (English, Chinese or whatever) depends on the environment in which we are raised. (Gribbin and Gribbin 1995: 43–4)

From context-embedded signification to abstract signification

Returning to our story, we discover the pre-eminence of rules over units has potentially profound consequences. For Khan, pondering the arrangements of his agent's objects, begins to consider the possibility of replacing Polo's idiosyncratic system of representation with one with which he is more familiar, 'the ready-made and standardized world of chess' (Kallinikos 1995: 131):

> Actually, it was useless for Marco's speeches to employ all this bric-a-brac: a chessboard would have sufficed, with its specific pieces. To each piece, in turn, they could give an appropriate meaning: a knight could stand for a real horseman, or for a procession of coaches, an army on the march, an equestrian monument: a queen could be a lady looking down from her balcony, a foundation, a church with a pointed dome, a quince tree. (Calvino 1979, mobilized in Kalllinikos 1995: 131–2).

Here, we start to move from context-embedded signification (the objects that in some senses carry context with them) to abstract signification, from 'the concrete and particular' to 'the general and universal' (Kallinkos 1995: 132). And we can see this clearly in the particular slide of significations with which Calvino confronts us. For despite not being a 'real' horseman, the knight resembles its appearance sufficiently to 'seem' to stand naturally for them. This resembling function may also be perceived in relation to the army (or more particularly the units which may make up such a force), and indeed, in the equestrian monument. But how are we to distinguish between these possible significations? What does *this* knight in *this* position stand for? The potential confusion becomes even more apparent as the arbitrariness of the link between signifier and signified (Saussure 1974; Barthes 1964) comes more clearly into view. A queen is necessarily a lady (although, interestingly enough, not in more contemporary, colloquial renderings!) but the link to 'foundation' is tenuous to say the least. And Calvino continues to play with us, showing the multiform meanders that any linkage might take. The shape of a queen piece may resemble that of a church with a pointed dome, while quince and queen begin with the same letter! The routes between symbols and that for which they stand are thus shown as anything but 'natural' in the emerging system, the infinite nature of the range of possible connections precluding such a possibility.

For Khan, far removed from the action contexts of the empire, the representational form derived from context embedded signification is 'useless bric-a-brac' (Kallinikos 1995: 132). The order and limited (there are still very many) possibilities of the standardized game of chess are more to his liking; they offer more potential for control. Only through a central notion of order, however complex, can the leader avoid the problems of information overload attendant upon an empire of vast scale. Just as the British Civil Service could govern India with a manpower that today seems tiny, through various summary acts, and just as our managers are enjoined to exploit the benefits of 'exception and variance reporting and analysis', so too can Khan maintain control only through the initial establishment of a 'standard' which is subsequently utilized to note deviations of potential import. And although there are similarities between chess and Polo's initial game, it is important to realize that it is through the former that Khan understands the latter, *not* the other way around.

Experiential knowledge is not simply transcribed or translated into another system, but replaced and disregarded. Overall, the transition to the game of chess implies that the initial objects that bear the traces of the merchants' adventures, and have literally been involved in the contexts and sequences they attempt to reconstruct, are abandoned and replaced by the standardized appearance of chessmen, and their combinations dictated by an equally well delineated and standardized repertoire of rules. (Kallinikos 1995: 132)

These passages capture something of 'the transition from an immediate system of signification still tied to sensations to an abstract and disembodied language'. But in order to work such a system must 'demonstrate its ability to capture and reconstitute the empire' (Kallinikos 1995: 133):

Returning from his last mission, Marco Polo found the Khan awaiting him, seated at a chessboard. With a gesture he invited the Venetian to sit opposite him and describe, with the help only of the chessmen, the cities he had visited. Marco did not lose heart. The Great Khan's chessmen were huge pieces of polished ivory: arranging on the board looming rocks and sulky knights, assembling swarms of pawns, drawing straight or oblique avenues like a queen's progress, Marco recreated the perspectives and the spaces of black and white cities on moonlit nights. (Calvino 1979, mobilized in Kallinikos 1995: 133)

Marco has to give up his ways of showing and knowing, and use those of the leader Khan. It is a difficult task, but he does not 'lose heart'. Khan is in control and what he 'says' goes. Khan's standardized system is appropriate for position of detachment and controlling preoccupations. And thus, Polo, as agent, must conform his knowledge and modes of expression to it.[6] For Khan to stay in control, to manage at a distance, he needs a primary order with which to note disorder that is ripe for corrective action. Khan's order is superior for control *but it is not necessarily a superior way of knowing*. It does, however, seem that he can only seek to control the diversity and scale of his empire by reinscribing it in ordered terms.

Contemplating these essential landscapes, Kublai reflected on the invisible order that sustains cities, on the rules that decreed how they arise, take shape and prosper, adapting themselves to the season, and then how they sadden and fall into ruin. At times he thought he was on the verge of discovering a coherent, harmonious system underlying the infinite deformities and discords, but no model could stand up to comparison with the game of chess. Perhaps, instead of racking one's brain to suggest with the ivory pieces scant help visions which were destined anyway to oblivion, it would suffice to play a game according to the rules and to consider each successive state of the board as one of the countless forms that the system of forms assembles and destroys. (Calvino 1979, mobilized in Kallinikos 1995: 134).

The rules here are not a model, a static picture of the world. They are 'constitutive but not determinative of the game'. Like representational systems, rules have a 'resilient character', an 'almost unlimited capacity . . . to produce versions or recapture the shifting state of the world'. But they do not make direct contact with the world, 'they are about the game, they concern the game itself' (Kallinikos 1995: 134–5). And although they can construct versions of the world, as rules they are seductive in themselves, distracting attention from the world that they purport to capture and control.[7]

Now Kublai Khan no longer had to send Marco Polo on distant expeditions: he kept him playing endless games of chess. Knowledge of the empire was hidden in the pattern drawn by the angular shifts of the knight, by the diagonal passages opened by the bishop's incursions, by the lumbering, cautious tread of the king and the humble pawn, by the inexorable ups and downs of every game. (Calvino 1979, mobilized in Kallinikos 1995: 135).

In some ways 'representation cannot exist except by negating the concrete and tangible world'. The world will not play the game, unless it can be made like the game and/or kept away from it. 'Such a radical shift is, however, not without problems' (Kallinikos 1995: 135):

The Great Khan tried to concentrate on the game: but now it was the game's reason that eluded him. The end of every game is a gain or a loss: but of what? What were the real stakes? At checkmate beneath the foot of the king, knocked aside by the winner's hand, nothingness remains: a black square, or a white one. By disembodying his conquest to reduce them to the essential, Kublai had arrived at the extreme operation: the definitive conquest, of which the empire's multiform treasures were illusory envelopes; it was reduced to a square of plane wood. (Calvino 1979, as mobilized in Kallinikos 1995: 136)

Connections, contextual knowledge, and oral language

Representation when it achieves its mastery appears empty. 'Sense and meaning cannot totally dispense with reference' (Kallinikos 1995: 136). This would not be a problem if the path back to the world were a direct one, but as we have noted, representational symbols do not just stand for aspects of the world. They *selectively objectify* them. Signs do not coincide with what they signify or refer to. Their 'sense' comes not only from that to which they refer but also from the complex (rule governed) network of relationships in which they are placed. Rules are as (more?) important as (than?) individual relationships, creating an ongoing tension that precludes a direct and unambiguous back translation. So Khan becomes a victim of the rules he requires to control his world in the absence of direct engagement with it (see also Hesse 1943/1969). In coming to possess his world he realizes that he possesses nothing. The only route back is through the reintroduction of contextual knowledge, knowledge that only Marco Polo, with his direct engagement with the empire, can provide, 'breathing life back into the disembodied world of representation' (Kallinikos 1995: 137):

Then Marco Polo spoke: 'Your chessboard, sire, is inlaid with two woods: ebony and maple. The square on which your enlightened gaze is fixed was cut from the ring of a trunk that grew in a year of drought: you see how its fibres are arranged? Here a barely hinted knot can be made out: a bud tried to burgeon on a premature spring day, but the night's frost forced it to desist'

Until then the Great Khan had not realized that the foreigner knew how to express himself fluently in his language, but it was not this fluency that amazed him.

'Here is a thicker pore: perhaps it was a larvum's nest: not a woodworm, because, once born, it would have begun to dig, but a caterpillar than gnawed the leaves and was the cause of the tree's being chosen for chopping down ... This edge was scored by the wood-carver with his gouge so that it would adhere to the next square, more portruding ... ' (Calvino 1979, mobilized in Kallinikos 137)

What is amazing here is the ability to reconstruct a living world starting from what initially appear to be inconsequential details. These details are particularly inconsequential if we too adopt Khan's representational orientation to the exclusion of all others. But to the trained and experienced eye, this smorgasbord of seemingly disparate signs can enable a 'semantic journey' (Kallinikos 1995: 137) through which the previously subsumed and ignored terrestrial world can reappear. Of course, this reimagined world may not be totally 'true' but within the richness of its rendering truths will certainly reside. A rather delightful contemporary example of this move, and one that is increasingly sacrilegious in a world dominated by hegemonic quality discourses, is the describing of an endlessly defective vehicle as a 'Friday Afternoon Model'. This moniker captures hidden truths, truths that give the lie to accounts of manufacturing of high-tech products in which human operators function with the same slickness as the machines which they mind. A world of 'real' humanity, driven not only by working pride, but by avarice, greed, laziness, and lunch-time drinking is conjured up to take a rightful place next to that of the 'black boxed' corporation.

> *The quantity of things that could be read in a little piece of smooth and empty wood overwhelmed Kublai; Polo was already talking about ebony forests, about rafts laden with logs that come down the rivers, of docks, of women at windows . . .* (Calvino 1979, mobilized in Kallinikos 1995: 138).

Thus, it is not the techniques of representation per se that 'cause' the problems we have encountered, but rather a world-view in which representation and disembodied knowledge are allowed to dominate all other forms of knowing. The signifying medium of natural, oral language can remake connections as it 'seems to be able to embrace and translate any other system of signification into its own terms (Barthes 1964; Eco 1975). The road back to the world is *verbal* one' (Kallinikos 1995: 138, original emphasis). A road on which representations and experience can combine.

▓ SUMMARY

Representation is a process through which the absent is made present, a process with resulting products that can potentially allow the transcendence of spatial and cultural barriers. However, because representation seeks to represent economically, it must selectively *objectify* 'things' in ways which render them in purely *instrumental* terms. In such circumstances the reconstruction of the original reference of signs mobilized in a representational economy in which their significance is given largely by their relation to other signs is highly problematic, to say the least.

In the pursuit of the order of instrumental systems of signification that control demands, contract with the world 'as is' is lost. Control is achieved, but that control remains of an impoverished world. Through evocative consideration of Calvino's fictional set of encounters between the Chinese emperor Kublai Khan and the Italian merchant Marco Polo we followed Jannis Kallinikos in not only demonstrating the salience of these ideas. We were also able to explore how the world could be remade and reconnected with through the powers of imbrication that experience, articulated through natural language, possesses.

▓ DISCUSSION QUESTIONS

1. What constitutes 'the system' in the Polo/Khan story?

2. Who is 'the user' of this system?

3. One of the earliest attempts at providing an 'intelligent' computer system resulted in the *Eliza* program. This program was certainly capable of passing a 'weak' Turing Test. (The Turing Test, named after the mathematician Alan Turing, suggests that we may consider a machine to be intelligent when during interaction (via suitable means so that differences in appearance, etc. are occluded) we are unable to distinguish between it and a human. A 'strong' version of the test would deliberately seek to uncover the machine by testing its 'reasoning' to the limit. A 'weak' version of the test merely seeks to ascertain whether the machine, in casual interaction with a human, can 'pass' as a human.) *Eliza* sought to mimic the behaviour of a psychoanalyst and did so very successfully with many users preferring the machine to a 'real' analyst (see www.ai.ijs.si/eliza/eliza.html, for example, if you want to have a go yourself). It did so primarily on the basis of repeating previous answers in the form of clarifying questions, with the occasional reference to 'mothers' and 'fathers' thrown in for good measure. It is, in essence, a very simple program indeed. One could postulate that the system succeeds in its deception through allowing, indeed requiring, the user to continually provide all the context required to make the interaction 'meaningful' (see Collins 1987). If, as experience of *Eliza* suggests, we are more than capable of adding 'imaginary' contexts to make a text seem 'real' (see also Garfinkel 1967), what is the status of Polo's 'experience'?

4. How is the value of a dollar defined?

5. In what other contexts can representations become more important than the reality from which they are seemingly derived?

▓ SUGGESTIONS FOR FURTHER READING

Many complex balls are kept in the air in this chapter. The ideas of semiotics—the science of signs—are, perhaps, most comprehensively articulated in Saussure's *Course in General Linguistics* (1974). They also run throughout the work of Roland Barthes (1964, trans. 1967) and Umberto Eco (1975, trans. 1976), forming an elusive and often illusory backdrop to the latter's novels, particularly *The Name of the Rose* (1983).

Information's self-generation is a consistent theme in Roszak's and Zuboff's work (see notes in Chapter 2) and also finds interesting expression in Paul Virilio's (1988) *The Vision Machine*. Bryan Rotman has applied these ideas to our contemporary international finance system in his masterful (1987) *Signifying Nothing: The Semiotics of Zero*. These ideas are also given graphic expression in the pop band U2's hit 'Better than the real thing', a title apparently derived from a response given by one of the pilots involved in the Gulf War to a reporter's question: 'What was it like?'

Sotto's evocative notion of 'spectaction' can be grasped from his 1996 article in *Studies, Organizations and Society* as well as from his earlier thesis. These ideas are of course themselves indebted to the work of Bainbridge (1983, trans. 1987). They are also well expressed in easily digestible form in Geoffrey Vickers' (1970) *Freedom in a Rocking Boat*. For a particularly entertaining illustration of the self-sealing nature of systems and their consequent retreat from the world, you could do much worse than watch Terry Gilliam's (1985) film, *Brazil*. If you would rather talk about it than watch it, you might like to note that discussions of this film have an extensive presence on the web.

10 | Handling Knowledge Management

Introduction

In this chapter we will examine how our understandings of the knowledge concept can influence the way we can handle or manage it, or at least the ways in which we think we can handle or manage it, through examination of three different theories of Knowledge Management (KM).

As we have noted throughout this text, we have witnessed an increasingly voci-ferous interest in, and proclamation of the costs and benefits of, information and its management. But in recent years, information has started to feel out of date, to be, to use the jargon back on itself, lacking in timeousness. Terms such as the 'infor-mation age' and the 'informational society' (e.g. Castells 1996: 21) are seemingly superseded by others such as 'knowledge era' and 'knowledge workers' (e.g. Drucker 1993). Interest in information has waxed and waned as developments in the technological arena have shifted expectations from a belief that it would be possible to control the flood of information and that this control would itself simply lead to the accumulation of huge amounts of 'knowledge' to a new vision of the promised land. The grail remains knowledge but since, as Mintzberg (1994: 110) observed '[f]ormal systems, mechanical or otherwise, have offered no improved means of dealing with the information overload of human brains; indeed they have often made matters worse', the new quest seeks explicitly to manage *knowledge itself* rather than expect it to arise from the mere management of information. This new discourse of KM relies very heavily upon some rather clunky distinctions, and primary amongst them are those made between data, information, and knowledge itself.

Data, information, knowledge

For Laudon and Laudon data are 'streams of raw facts representing events occurring in organizations or the physical environment before they have been organized and arranged into a form that people can understand and use' (1999: 8). The suggestion being that data their own have no meaning, but that they might be used as a basis for reasoning, discussion, or calculation in a process in which, through their orga-nization and arrangement, they become imbued with meaning. Information is thus 'data that have been shaped into a form that is *meaningful* and useful to human beings' (Laudon and Laudon 1999: 8, emphasis added). Yet already we see some of the problems of untenable division arising. Information, as we have discussed throughout this text, can best be seen as a representation which assumes an inevitably unstable partitioning between the *object* of representation and *its repre-sentation*, as well as the involvement of some*body* to produce and/or recognize this relationship (somebody to construct or interpret the representation). For Bateson (1973, 1979) information is any type of pattern or symbolically imbued object that influences the construction and alteration of other patterns or representations (something potentially perceived as a representation), and that ultimately 'infor-mation consists of differences that make a difference' (1979: 5). A difference that makes a difference is, however, a long way from Laudon and Laudon's comfortable humanistic conception of meaning. For there is nothing necessarily *meaning*ful about differences that make a difference. Such differences are, in strictly logical terms, merely *meta*differences, a distinction which itself rests solely upon our position relative to the system of differences under consideration. And if matters are messy for our terminologists when it comes to distinguishing data from information, when they come to consider knowledge a great deal of rhetorical sleight of hand is required to prevent the absolute implosion of posited levels of difference.

To avoid such an unpleasant outcome, practitioners and scholars in the field of KM tend to adopt *working*, rather than definitive, definitions for *knowledge*. For example, Turban and Frenzel (1992: 17) state that knowledge 'is information that has been organized and analysed to make it understandable and applicable to problem solving or decision-making'—a twist that all too closely resembles the dubious distinctions made between data and information. Similarly, Beckman (1997: presentation) argues that knowledge 'is reasoning about information to actively guide task execution, problem-solving, and decision-making in order to perform, learn, and teach'. The suggestion here is that information is now, in itself, limited to a building block that can be used to *produce* knowledge.

A stream of writers (amongst others Alter 1996; Tobin 1996; and van der Spek and Spijkervet 1997) have worked along these lines to attempt to sharpen and reinforce these differentiations and to create purposeful connections between them with the broad conclusion that information is data plus *meaning* and knowledge is information plus *processing*. Knowledge, then, from this viewpoint, is one step *forward* from information, and KM systems are one step *up* the hierarchy from information management systems, a comforting reassurance that progress is being made. For what remains implicit in the heady rhetoric of KM is that information management has failed to deliver on its promises of better decision-making and problem solving. An improved organizing principle is needed to ensure that the inherent virtues of our data are finally made manifest to the user.

Such calls to action, based on a revitalization of what has now come to be seen as obsolete, are an accepted part of the 'developing' canon of management literature. Take, for example, Miller and O'Leary's astute reflections upon the publication of the best-selling accounting text *Relevance Lost* (Johnson and Kaplan 1987): 'Accountancy is generally assumed to have a practical function. This function is that of guiding decisions within firms towards the end of economic efficiency. Even when this function is considered to have been lost, it is by reference to such a notion that calls for reform are made' (1993: 479). And, perhaps even more tellingly for our discussion here, they go on to argue that one of the principal problematics that underlies this discourse is that: 'the notion of accountancy's practical function is the end point of complex processes of conceptual invention, rather than an *a priori* grounding.' Accounting appears here as a 'congenitally failing' (see Miller and O'Leary 1993) technology, exactly the facet of a technology that is necessary for its continual renewal and reinvention, but perhaps most importantly, its perpetuation.

What then of knowledge management? The first, cheap shot is to point out that the cosy narrative of progress in KM suggests that several initiatives were designed in order to facilitate access to, and processing of, data/information so that it could become knowledge. Accordingly, a variety of information systems that have been labelled 'KM tools' have centred on 'electronic digital repositories' for data/information (databases) with different supporting technologies to make them accessible to different users (such as intranet, Internet, groupware services and applications, web technologies). Effectively, these 'tools' are constituted by pools of data that, it was assumed, users would be delighted to 'fill up' and 'trawl' through, in a process of information sharing, and consequently knowledge creation.

Yet this history does not stand close scrutiny. Early writers, since adopted as founding fathers of this burgeoning field, were more reporters of technological possibilities and pitfalls rather than theoreticians suggesting how principles of KM should be applied. Take, for example, Anthes' (1991: 28) recognition of the necessities of ensuring that there are 'policies, procedures and technologies employed for operating a continuously updated linked pair of networked databases' before the innumerable benefits listed above will accrue. Or, indeed, Strapko's (1990) contemporary concerns: of understanding the relationships of data; identifying and documenting rules for managing data; and assuring that data are accurate and maintain integrity. Essentially, the early history of KM is based upon the old story that progress simply rests upon more information, better organization. And so we should not be too surprised then to find that the same old problems of management information systems are revisited upon knowledge management systems '[m]ore than one company has found itself with millions of dollars invested in best practice databases that never get off the ground, or just limp along with a few stalwart contributors and users' (Allee 2003: 93; see also Chapter 8 in this volume).

Overall then it would appear that it requires more than operation upon representations of the world (data or information) to *create* modified representations of it, to create outcomes (that we might call 'knowledge') which we *expect* to be of use. For it would seem not only that something is missing with this *mechanistic* approach to knowledge, and its management, but also that, as Miller and O'Leary (1990) note, practicality is no more something that we can take for granted with regard to knowledge in general than it is with regard to that restricted financial form of the beast that is accounting. And if practicality is not something that we can take for granted, how then can we talk about managing it?

Dealing with knowledge in KM

There are three approaches to KM that draw our attention. The first considers knowledge creation to be an *individual* process that can be transmuted into a *collective* practice. The second considers knowledge creation to be *organizational* learning capacity based upon individuals, and the third as organizational learning structured on *organizations themselves*.

From individual to collective knowledge

One of the most prominent conceptualizations of Knowledge Management was developed by Nonaka (1991; 1994; see also Nonaka and Takeuchi 1995; and Von Krogh et al. 2000) and based on the differences and interrelationships between *tacit* and *explicit* knowledge.

This distinction is drawn from Polanyi (1958, 1966) who categorized tacit knowledge as personal, context-specific, derived from experience, and difficult to communicate to others; while explicit knowledge was 'codified' and thus could be readily expressed, made available, and conveyed from one person to another in systematic ways. However, Polanyi claimed that ultimately *all* knowledge is either tacit or rooted in tacit knowledge and that true discovery cannot come through application of rule-based algorithms. And so, in many ways, this serves as a romantic, humanistic exit from the totalizing problems of representation that we have encountered throughout this text. An exit route that mirrors the *working* definitions we encountered earlier.

Underlying this is an elision of the traditional definition of knowledge as 'justified truth belief', into 'justified belief', thereby downplaying any call for 'truthfulness'. So, instead of emphasizing 'the absolute, static, and non human nature of knowledge, typically expressed in propositions and formal logic', knowledge is considered '*as a dynamic human process of justifying personal belief toward the "truth"* ' (Nonaka and Takeuchi 1995: 58, emphasis in the original). The focus on the human is further drawn out in the assertion that 'an organization cannot create knowledge by itself. Tacit knowledge of individuals is the basis of organizational knowledge creation' (1995: 72).

Sadly, despite their protestations as to the nature of knowledge, Nonaka and colleagues' theories come to resemble the propositions and formal logic they abhor. They suggest an interaction between individual/personal knowledge and social/ organizational knowledge that moves through four distinct stages, or 'conversions' (socialization, externalization, combination, and internalization) through which knowledge is 'created'. In this model, knowledge moves from tacit to explicit and back to tacit, through the '*spiral of knowledge*' creation, thereby realizing four 'typologies' of knowledge (sympathized, conceptual, systemic, and operational). Table 10.1 shows the main elements of the interactions/'conversions'.

Table 10.1 The 'Knowledge Spiral'

Knowledge Changes		Conversion Processes	Contents of Knowledge
From	To		
Tacit Knowledge	Tacit Knowledge	Socialization	Sympathized
Tacit Knowledge	Explicit Knowledge	Externalization	Conceptual
Explicit Knowledge	Explicit Knowledge	Combination	Systemic
Explicit Knowledge	Tacit Knowledge	Internalization	Operational

Source: Adapted from Nonaka and Takeuchi (1995), *The Knowledge-Creating Company: How Japanese Companies Create the Dynamics of Innovation*. New York: Oxford University Press, pp. 62–72.

At the same time there are moves between individual and collective knowledge. Tacit knowledge originates with individuals, becoming 'social' through interaction with other individuals. This knowledge is then formalized and becomes explicit, which in turn allows combination with other sets of explicit knowledge. And finally, the cycle is completed as individuals internalize, and make tacit, the new knowledge. Rather forcefully, they suggest that each and every one of the modes of conversion is required for practical benefits to occur (Nonaka 1991). Moreover, five conditions must be fulfilled for this process to take place: the organization must aspire to this goal; individuals must be autonomous and self-organizing; the organization must allow creative chaos in interaction with its environment; there must be an intentional overlapping of information; and there must be requisite variety so that the organization's internal diversity matches the variety and complexity of its environment (Nonaka and Takeuchi 1995: 72–3). Finally, in order to succeed, there must be an acknowledgement that: 'the sharing of tacit knowledge among multiple individuals with different backgrounds, perspectives, and motivations becomes the critical step for organisational knowledge creation to take place. The individual's emotions, feelings and mental models have to be shared to build mutual trust' (Nonaka and Takeuchi 1995: 85).

We return to these tendentious conditions and claims at the end of the chapter.

Organizational learning

The organizational learning approach was developed under the aegis of organizations gaining competitive advantage from their enhanced deployment of information and knowledge, but can be seen as having two distinct foundations: that organizations learn from individuals; and that organizations themselves can learn—see, for example, the work of Cyert and March (1963); Weick (1969; 1977; Weick and Westley 1996); Argyris and Schön (1974; 1978; Argyris 1982; Schön 1983); Senge (1990; 1991; Senge et al. 1999); and Garvin (1993).

Organizations learning from individuals

The interest in the 'learning organization' may be tentatively suggested to have started with Cyert and March (1963), who described a process whereby organizations, as communal groups, learnt, or at least patterned themselves and their conduct, through ongoing interaction with their surroundings. According to Kim (1993) individual members of an organization operate as 'learning agents', reacting to changes in the internal and external environments of the organization, and, through interacting with other members of the organization, share their experiences and insights.

Senge (1990) takes what is, in some way, a more radical line by suggesting that: 'A learning organization is a place where people are continually discovering how they create their reality. And how they can change it.' (1990: 13). His approach is essentially systems-based (see Chapter 3 of this volume) especially when he suggests that in the unimproved organization, 'events' merely induce individuals to 'react' (creating an initial level of understanding). But by moving to the recognition of behaviour patterns, which 'focus on seeing long-term trends and assessing their implications' (Senge 1990: 52), individuals can break away from the 'reactive trap' and become 'responsive'. And, at the seemingly deepest level of explanation there is, Senge contends, both the existence and possibility of knowledge of a systemic structure that allows examination of what 'causes' these patterns of behaviour. Action here allows individuals to become 'generative' in their thinking about both their own and organizational behaviour, with (beneficial) change following. Indeed:

> [t]he practice of organizational learning involves developing tangible activities: new governing ideas, innovations in infrastructure, and new management methods and tools for changing the way people conduct their work. Given the opportunity to take part in these new activities, people will develop an enduring capability for change. The process will pay back the organization with far greater levels of diversity, commitment, innovation and talent. (Senge et al. 1999: 33)

This learning process identifies five learning disciplines (see Table 10.2) and relies on individuals understanding how organizations function (through 'system thinking', the *chief discipline*) and how they (first as individuals and then as an organization) can change working practices to be more effective. It is based on *individuals* changing to *improve* and *achieve* personal and, ultimately, organizational goals, mirroring much of the rhetoric of the new wave management we encountered in Chapter 6. Perhaps the exemplar of this individualized gospel of self-directed achievement is Stephen Covey (1990; but see also Jackson 2001: 94–117), whose message is distinctly messianic in its appeal. Indeed, '[e]ach of the disciplines alters its practitioner in certain very basic ways. This is why we refer to them as *personal* disciplines, even those that must be practiced collaboratively' (Senge 1990: 374–5). Senge sees a virtuous cycle, as empowered individuals act to change organizational structure, for 'Structure produces behavior, and changing underlying structures can produce different pattern of behavior' (Senge 1990: 53).

Ultimately, organizational learning here is derived from individual members within the organization. The organization itself does not strictly 'learn' but, through structural changes caused by individuals, then 'influences' individuals towards particular 'behaviors' (Senge 1990: 43–7). And, at its best, organizations apparently 'purposefully adopt structures and strategies to encourage learning' (Dodgson 1993: 387). Thus, this approach is 'foreshadowed by indigenous individual learning' (Weick 1991: 122; cf. Dodgson 1993).

Learning at an organizational level

Gherardi (1997: 542) also runs with biological metaphors drawn from systems thinking, but at a different level. She sees the organization as 'a subject which learns, which processes information, which reflects on experiences, which is endowed with

Table 10.2 The Five Learning Disciplines

Learning Disciplines	Levels	Activities / Theories / States of being

1. Personal mastery
Discipline of aspiration
(what an individual
wishes to achieve)
	Practices
	(activities)
		Clarifying personal vision
		'Holding' creative tension
		   —Focusing on the result
		   —Seeing current 'reality'
		Making choices

	Principles (theories)	Vision Creative tension versus emotional tension Subconscious
	Essences (state)	Being Generativeness Connectedness
2. Mental models Discipline of reflection and enquiry (refinement of thinking and development of awareness)	Practices (activities)	Distinguishing 'data' from abstraction based on data Testing assumptions 'Left-hand' column
	Principles (theories)	Espoused theory versus theory-in-use Ladder of inference Balance inquiry and advocacy
	Essences (state)	Love of truth Openness

3. Building shared vision
Discipline of collectiveness
(common sense of purpose
and actions to achieve it)
	Practices
	(activities)
		Visioning process
		   —Sharing personal visions
		   —Listening to others
		   —Allowing freedom of choice
		Acknowledge current 'reality'

	Principles (theories)	Shared vision as 'hologram' Commitment versus compliance
	Essences (state)	Communality of purpose Partnership
4. Team learning Discipline of group interaction (collective thinking and action to accomplish common goals)	Practices (activities)	Suspending assumptions Acting as colleagues Surfacing own defensiveness 'Practicing'
	Principles (theories)	*Dia logos* Interactive dialogue and discussion Defensive routines
	Essences (state)	Collective intelligence Alignment
5. System thinking Discipline of understanding (methodology for seeing wholes, recognizing patterns and interconnections / interdependencies)	Practices (activities)	System archetypes Simulation
	Principles (theories)	Structure influences behaviour Policy resistance Leverage
	Essences (state)	Holism Interconnectedness

Source: Adapted from Senge (1990), *The Fifth Discipline: The Art and Practice of the Learning Organization*. New York: Doubleday/Currency, pp. 139–272, 373–7.

a stock of knowledge, skill and expertise'. Thus, organizations can themselves learn: from their own past experiences (such as with production processes) and from other organizations' experiences. These 'learned' proceedings can then be incorporated in equipment, procedures, accounts, patents, and other artefacts of organizational life.

For this 'learning' to occur, organizations need some kind of 'shared memory' or 'repositories of knowledge' (Schön 1983: 242; but see Chapter 8 of this volume for alternative perspectives on organizational memory). From an economic point of view, 'business firms are organizations that know how to do things [. . .]. In fact [. . .] a particular firm at a particular time is a repository for quite specific range of productive knowledge' (Winter 1988: 175). Here, learning is explicitly linked to the ability to hoard knowledge. But the make-up of these 'repositories' affects how and what may be stored within, acting as a 'screen' that determines the ability to gather knowledge, to filter or to select the knowledge that will be accumulated, and, ultimately, to influence what may be learned. Indeed, Weick and Westley (1996: 456) suggest that:

> Different forms of organizing create different problems for learning. Adhocracies explore, create and align with changes but, in embracing disorder with disorderly forms, they risk integrity, a loss of identity, and a loss of lessons learned from past that undergird current efficiencies. Bureaucracies exploit lessons from the past as well as past identities. Adhocracies trade away retention for variation, bureaucracies trade away variation for retention. Adhocracies embody disorder, bureaucracies embody order. Only as each form adopts some of the other, or imitates the other, is it possible to achieve repunctuation [learning] that persists.

But how, from such a perspective, does learning happen? It occurs when there is a 'revision' of the shared memory or repository's content. The revision can either be by adding new knowledge to what exists; or by changing the way in which knowledge is added. Argyris and Schön (1978), drawing upon Bateson's (1973) models of 'Learning I' and 'Learning II', name these two types of revision single- and double-loop learning. In the single-loop process, new knowledge is incrementally added to the 'repositories' without altering the norms, standards, procedures, or routines already in place. In the double-loop process organizations—via a feedback system— query, challenge, or rethink their values and assumptions, allowing them to modify their objectives, policies, norms, or procedures. In the words of Argyris and Schön:

> Organizational learning involves the detection and correction of error. When the error detected and corrected permits the organization to carry on its present polices or achieve its present objectives, then that error-detection-and-correction process is single-loop learning. Double-loop learning occurs when error is detected and corrected in ways that involve the modification of an organization's underlying norms, polices and objectives. (1978: 3)

What about organization?

But we have been presumptuous here. Before we can explore what is meant by 'learning', we perhaps need to consider what is meant by *organization*. If we start with a fairly naive model of organization, 'a social arrangement for achieving controlled performance in pursuit of collective goals' (Buchanan and Huczynski 1985: 5), then we are able to suggest, as Huysman (1999: 61) does, that the learning organization is 'a form of organisation that enables the learning of its members in such a way that it creates positively valued outcomes, such as innovations, efficiency, better alignment with the environment and competitive advantage'.

But what if we do not accept the contention that we live in such a 'just-so', static world, inhabited by 'just-so', static organizations?. If instead we follow Pettigrew (1999: 1):

> In describing new forms of organizing, the use of the active word 'organizing', instead of the passive term 'organization', is important. In the present competitive situation, few firms see organization change as a move from one static structure to another. Rather, innovations in organizing are seen as strategic activity designed to improve flexibility, creativity and responsiveness of the company. The active term organizing thereby recognizes the dynamic and perpetual and simultaneous character of the process of changing. Organizing also entails a much more inclusive process with alterations in structural form being continuously shaped alongside movements in organization process and boundaries.

Then we can move to a more dynamic model, such as that of Garvin (1993: 80), who suggests that the learning organization is a congruence of organizational skills and processes, more precisely, it is 'an organization skilled at creating, acquiring, and transferring knowledge, and modifying its behaviours to reflect new knowledge and insights'. And to an account that emphasizes the *process* of learning itself rather than the organizational *structure* that supposedly enables it.

Different representations of organization confront us with different representations of what the learning organization can be and, consequently, different theoretical conceptualizations of it. Indeed, we may even note, with Weick and Westley (1996: 440) that the concepts of 'organization' and 'learning' are contradictory. Organization stands for order, uniformity, and stability, amongst other characteristics; while learning requires change, diversity, and unpredictability. Yet Weick and Westley only distinguish between structure and process while remaining within a clearly managerialist frame of analysis. What if we open the door of opportunity a little wider? What if we give up notions of organization as the pursuit of 'collective goals' via 'controlled performance'? What if we, heaven forbid, allow our differing experiences of organizations and life within them to come to bear upon our (consequently differing) definitions of them?

If we, for example, take the representation of organization as a rigid bureaucratic establishment (Morgan's 1986 metaphors of 'machine' or 'psychic prison', for instance), it seems that the contradiction holds and learning in such an environment would be particularly restricted, if not inexistent. But if organization is seen, anthropomorphically, as a 'human brain' (Morgan 1986) then learning seems entirely appropriate. And, as we have seen, some of our theoreticians explicitly draw upon such representations in order to create an environment in which it *does* make sense to talk about the learning organization. But such formulations are clearly contingent, never stable. And such simple shifts alert us to the possibilities of more radical deconstruction of the terms employed. Take, for example, the allegoric introduction to a more 'linguistic' and intricate view of the representation at work in the processes and structuring of organization, made explicit by Lilley (2001: 80, our emphasis): '*Organi*zations, as their very name suggests, consist of, exaggerate and extend *organs*—lines of sight, auditory channels, arbitrations of taste, specified 'wings' and 'arms'—sensors and effectors of all sorts'.

As our metaphors become more fanciful, but also perhaps more informative, any pretension to a grounded reality for the 'learning organization' becomes ever more difficult to hold. Indeed, the learning organization is revealed as conceptually mired within a particular, narrow system of representation. One that not all the actors have yet been enrolled in. And yet here we have only critiqued organization. In a chapter about KM, perhaps we should examine the status of knowledge itself.

Understanding knowledge

Knowledge is not a straightforward concept to deal with, as millennia of debate concerning its status and nature attest. Even in everyday use, the term 'knowledge' is employed in a variety of ways to mean very different things. And it is our contention that knowledge can only appear as *manageable* if one actively maintains ignorance of this diversity and its history.

Two key contexts of consideration have historically attempted to handle 'knowledge': the philosophical and what might be loosely described as the sociological.

A philosophical bent

Enquiries into the nature of knowledge with a philosophical bent have traditionally been organized under the banners of both epistemology and the so-called philosophy of mind. The former has tended to concentrate upon the nature and derivation of knowledge, the scope of knowledge, and the validity, limits, and reliability of claims to knowledge; whereas the latter turns around the nature of the knower and its mental concepts (consciousness, emotion, imagination, introspection, intention, thinking, will, mind and matter, feeling, etc.).

The epistemological, or theory of knowledge, view is far from a settled one and itself contains, or has had imputed to it by commentators, innumerable distinctions of its own. For what has become known as 'rationalism'—proponents of which include, for example, Plato (*c*.427 BC–*c*.347 BC), René, Descartes (also known as 'Cartesius' 1596–1650), Gottfried Wilhelm von Leibniz (1646–1716), and Benedictus (also known as 'Baruch') de Spinoza (1632–1677)—the central claim would seem to be that the 'only source' of knowledge is that 'reason' seen to arise from conscious thought, which is intrinsic to the mind. *In extremis*, the senses that connect us to an outside of mind have no role to play. The formal demonstrations of logic and mathematics constitute the basis for the rationalist's model of certainty. Rationalism sought to build the entirety of human knowledge through use of 'pure' reasoning from unquestionable axioms. Thus, Descartes argued that it would be possible to question all beliefs apart from the existence of the questioner and was able, in a delightfully reductivist move, to arrive at just one unquestionable axiom: *cogito ergo sum* (I think therefore I am).

For many commentators, and indeed significant numbers of the protagonists in this ongoing debate, the contraposition is that of empiricism. Claimed luminaries include such figures as Aristotle (384–322 BC), Francis Bacon (also known as Baron Verulam and Viscount St. Albans, 1561–1626), John Locke (1632–1704), George Berkeley (also known as Bishop Berkeley, 1685–1753), and David Hume (1711–1776). In an inversion of the rationalists' fundamentalism, 'sense experience' is the most important strand of knowledge, and again, *in extremis*, the human mind nothing but a blank sheet or *tabula rasa* (Locke 1690, reprint 2003), containing nothing but the potential to be embossed by sensorial experience.

As we have none too subtly hinted, there is far from full agreement about these distinctions and indeed the mapping of individuals upon them. So, for example, Borges (1970) claims Berkeley and, in the extension of his ideas, the scepticism of Hume, as idealist (while this scepticism itself may be seen to derive from Plato's writing of Socrates). In this sense Berkeley and Hume might appear 'radically empiricist', but not in the way in which the term 'empiricist' is generally used in contemporary circumstances.

Eighteenth-century philosophy was seen to witness the emergence of a Third Way, with Immanuel Kant (1724–1804), grappling with Hume's problematic, adopting the Giddensian position. Kant argued that there could, indeed had to, be synthetic a priori knowledge (innate ideas and concepts), such as a framework of basic organizing concepts (space, time, causality, and others) which was necessary for human minds to make sense of and interpret their experiences of the world (Kant 1781, trans. 1998).

In its more modern forms epistemology has taken the analysis of the meaning and the status of claims to knowledge as its quarry. Consequently, writers such as Bertrand Arthur William Russell (also known as the third Earl Russell, 1872–1970), George Edward Moore (1873–1958), and Ludwig Joseph Johann Wittgenstein (1889–1951) have attempted to delineate three kinds of knowledge:

1. *Knowledge that*, or 'factual knowledge'. There is fairly general agreement amongst analytical philosophers that the following are necessary and sufficient conditions of X's knowledge that *p*.
   (a) *p* must be true.
   (b) X must believe that *p*, in the sense that he sincerely asserts, or is ready so to assert, that *p*.
   (c) X must be in a position to know that *p*.

Nevertheless, Edmund Gettier (born 1927), amongst others, has challenged the sufficiency of these conditions of 'knowing that' (a = truth, b = belief, and c = justification) and suggested therefore that it would not be possible to ever provide a proper definition of knowing (Gettier 1963). The impossibility of defining knowledge here seems fundamental, to say the least, and KM's retreat into *working* definitions may not in consequence *work*. However, all may not be lost for our practical epistemologists for:

2. *Knowledge how*, or 'practical knowledge', is predicated upon the claim that 'efficient practise precedes the theory of it' (Ryle 1949: 30). Gilbert Ryle (1900–1976) argued that 'knowledge that' cannot be the basis of 'knowledge how', challenging the 'traditional' assumption that knowledge of what something *is* precedes knowledge of what to *do* with it. Thus, although belief undoubtedly has a 'propositional character', it depends upon activity, and not vice versa. It is a mere legend—the *intellectualist legend*—to presume 'knowledge that' is reducible to a knowledge of truths. For as Ryle argued the requirement that intelligent acts be the product of the conscious application of mental rules results in an infinite regress of thought (see also Collins 1987).

> According to the legend, whenever an agent does anything intelligently, his act is preceded and steered by another internal act of considering a regulative proposition appropriate to his practical problem. [. . .] Must we then say that for the hero's reflections on how to act to be intelligent he must first reflect how best to reflect how to act? The endlessness of this implied regress shows that the application of the appropriateness does not entail the occurrence of a process of considering this criterion. (Ryle 1949: 31)

Such 'pragmatism', mirrored in the work of Charles Sanders Peirce (1839–1914), William James (1842–1910), John Dewey (1859–1952), and Richard Rorty (born 1931), would seem to constitute the ideal philosophical framework upon which to hang contemporary understandings of KM. But it too, of course, is not without its own complications. For example, noting that there is an infinite regress involved in claims to 'knowledge that', while of course erudite, in no way inoculates 'knowledge how' against similar outcomes. Pragmatism can only note the shifting sands upon which other claims to knowledge stand by accepting them as its own, which *it* may be happy to do, but such acceptance seems ill-equipped to provide for KM.

3. *Knowledge of people, places, and things*, or 'knowledge by acquaintance', frequently entails knowledge of types 1 and 2, but not necessarily so. Bertrand Russell, in his earlier writings (1910, 1912, 1914), considered 'knowledge by acquaintance' to be knowledge only of that of which human beings are immediately aware of via their 'senses', in something of a reinvigoration of the empiricist tradition. For Russell knowledge is primarily—and all knowledge depends upon—the 'knowledge by acquaintance of sensations'; but when this is uttered in language, and organized by common sense or science, human beings have 'knowledge by description'. Distinguishing 'knowledge by acquaintance' from 'knowledge by description', he claims that many instances of what would normally be regarded as 'knowledge by acquaintance', for example knowledge of a person or a place, are really instances of

the more formalized 'knowledge by description'. To muddy waters still further, at least James and Peirce, claimed above as 'pragmatists', have produced work which would happily sit within the borders of a rigorous categorization of 'knowledge by acquaintance'.

A sociological bent

More sociological conceptions of knowledge move beyond the seeming absolutisms of some of the claims of some of the philosophical traditions towards a relativization of knowledge claims, via the study of the social factors involved in the origin of ideas and systems of belief (see, for example, Kuhn 1962, for an exploration of the impact of such a view on those bastions of knowing that we call 'science'). Sociologists stress that the study of social factors is inseparable from study of the broad history of ideas.

Since Auguste Comte (also known as Isidore Marie Auguste Francois Xavier Comte, 1798–1857), theorists have sought to provide an explicitly *social history* of knowledge (Comte 1853; see also Castoriadis 1987). Articulation of the relationship between social relations and knowledge—both of those relations, and indeed in general—is perhaps most explicit in the work of Karl Marx (1818–1883; see, for example, Marx and Engels 1846, trans. 1970; Marx 1867, trans. 1990). Marx saw the ideologies that enable knowledge as inevitably associated with (the) social relations (of production), giving a very novel spin to the notion of 'political economy'. In somewhat simplified terms (see Chapter 1) the proletariat (almost) inevitably perceive the world in one way while the bourgeoisie perceive it in another, with these different understandings of 'reality' deriving from how each 'class' experiences the productive process.

Similarly, although less explicitly politically, Emile Durkheim (1858–1917) argued that the ways human beings order the world are based upon the basic mental categories with which they organize society and that 'the determining cause of a social fact should be sought among the social facts preceding it and not among the state of individual consciousness' (Durkheim 1912, trans. 1964: 110). Durkheim, then, provides a socially based repetition of Kant's mentalist Third Way. Indeed, Durkheim and Mauss (1903, trans. 1963) attempt to scrutinize fundamental 'collective representations' of humankind's social attitudes and behaviours—such as time, space, and religious dogmas—in order to highlight their social 'imprinting'. Moreover, they claim that the 'social' classification of 'people' is replicated in the classification of 'things' (Worsley 1956; Lukes 1973; Lamo de Espinosa, González García, and Torres Albero 1994: 205–26). For Durkheim 'social facts' constrain people in their actions, even their actions upon natural or inanimate objects, and thus 'social external' circumstances are not only the context of human knowledge but potentially its ultimate source or explanation. Max Weber (1864–1920), with an empirical comparison of social structures and normative orders, was able to describe the development of forms of rationality and legitimization (Weber 1922, trans. 1947) and, in so doing, establish the grounds for a specifically sociological hermeneutic tradition.

György Lukács (also known as György Szegedy von Lukács, 1885–1971) and the Frankfurt School revisited Hegel (also known as Georg Wilhelm Friedrich Hegel, 1770–1831) in their work with Marxist theory to suggest that it is the *form* of knowledge rather than its content that is significant. For Lukács wished to reappropriate a Hegelian dialectic to apprehend a knowledge of the 'totality', suggesting that antinomies (categories such as subject and object) share a fundamental unity which is hidden by the predominance of bourgeois thought. And, as a romantic Marxist, Lukács believed that the views of a class-conscious proletariat came closest to 'objective' truth.

By contrast, Karl Mannheim (1893–1947) claimed that not only 'social class' but other social positions determine forms of knowledge, and no one position can be granted greater truth-value than another (Mannheim 1929, trans. 1936). However, happily, intellectuals were granted leave to arbitrate, and thus generate a closer approximation to knowledge, by virtue of their 'free-floating' (*freischwebend Intelligenz*) social status.

But two new 'contenders' enter the ring with structuralism—in which loose category we sometimes find, for example, Ferdinand de Saussure (1857–1913), Leonard Bloomfield (1887–1949), Vladimir Propp (1895–1970), Roman Jakobson (1896–1982), Claude Levi-Strauss (born 1908), Jean-Pierre Vernant (born 1914), Roland Barthes (1915–1980), Louis Althusser (1918–1990), Noam Chomsky (born 1928)—and poststructuralism—an even more inappropriate grouping that might include, say, Jacques Lacan (1901–1981), Jean François Lyotard (1924–1998), Gilles Deleuze (1925–1995), Michael Foucault (1926–1984), Pierre-Félix Bourdieu (1930–2002), Jacques Derrida (born 1930), Félix Guattari (1930–1992), Bruno Latour (born 1947)—radically challenging the status of the very distinction between philosophical and sociological approaches with which we have been operating up to now.

But what is important here is not the categorization, but the general premise of these two approaches that humankind has no direct, or unmediated, access to the 'real world' about which its theories claim to have knowledge. Any human experiences or observations of the 'real world' depend upon some prior form of conceptual or linguistic ordering. It is not possible to get away from 'language' or 'discourse', a claim made most explicitly by the later Wittgenstein (1953), which therefore makes it impossible to verify whether the 'discourse' is consistent with 'reality'. And consequently a strong articulation of this position refuses to allow 'knowability' of any 'reality' that may lie outside discourse.

Foucault (1966, trans. 1970) called attention to the 'discursive practices' or 'serious speech acts' that lay claim to revealing knowledge and examined them in terms of their 'history' or 'genesis' instead of their 'truth'. Since the mechanisms of power and the development of knowledge were seen by Foucault to be interrelated, 'it was contended that the search for knowledge does not merely reveal pre-existing 'objects'. It creates them. And primary amongst the objects so born is 'man' (1966, trans. 1970), the humanist core of the practicalities of KM.

Similarly, Derrida argues that 'text' structures human interpretation of the world and, thus, humankind. 'Binary oppositions' (such as mind versus matter, speech versus writing, man versus woman, or good versus evil) are the bedrock of Western thought (cf. Descartes' dualism). But such oppositions are not equal—one 'element' is a 'corruption' of the other—and this creates hierarchies: hierarchies that continue to run through all text. As such, text can be reinterpreted through interrogation, inversion, and oscillation of these hierarchies and therefore there can be no end-point of interpretation, a final 'truth' that stands outside the text. There will always be more than one interpretation and meaning never finally settled.

Such arguments are typically accused of epistemological relativism (that human judgements are always conditioned by, relative to, the specific social environment (Rorty 1991)); conventionalism (that virtues such as truth, good, and beauty are merely a matter of social convention); or scepticism (that they deny all claims of knowledge; Sim 2000). But this 'realist' attack merely serves to hide other ways of understanding 'knowledge', such as, for example, through Derrida's exploration of *difference* (rather than essence) through deconstruction. For the inevitability of more than one possible reading of a text does not automatically mean that *any* reading goes; far from it, the point is rather that there is no one settled reading of the text available, if we are to take the task of *reading* seriously. For Derrida, meaning (and indeed, all manner of other things) is put into question not by *indeterminacy*, but by *undecidability*: 'undecidability is always a *determinate* oscillation between possibilities (for example, of meaning, but also of acts). These possibilities are themselves highly *determined* in strictly *defined* situations' (Derrida 1988:148, original emphases; see also Jones 2003: 13–56).

However, our goal here is not to arbitrate, nor to claim that one way of 'knowing' is better than another, but merely to acknowledge the ongoing debate around the problem of determining 'knowledge'. An acknowledgement that seems to be missing in the KM literature to which we now return.

And back to KM

With knowledge and organization both revealed as so vehemently disputed, does it make any sense to even *try* to talk of KM in an organizational context? Well, in some ways, perhaps not: not when it relies upon so much slippery allusion in order to even bring the terms to hand. But our game has never been to try and rule who should, and who should not, be allowed to play. Instead, we prefer to take the role of Mannheim's noble academics, sifting through the different histories presented before *us*, much as you, the reader, are encouraged to pick and choose from the platter laid before *you*.

Even at first blanche, we see that despite its avowedly practical turn, the conceptualizations of KM continue to fall back into the morass of philosophical and sociological debate over the nature of knowledge. Take, for example, Nonaka and colleagues' tacit–explicit 'conversions' of knowledge. Surely here we see made clear Derrida's haunting, hierarchical binary oppositions, where explicit knowledge is a 'corruption'[1] of tacit knowledge? But that is just the first connection we could make: Nonaka suggests that tacit knowledge can only be exchanged through socialization, exemplifying Russell's slide of 'knowledge by acquaintance' into 'knowledge by description'. But this also implies that knowledge is socially constructed, leading us back to Durkheim. And Nonaka unreservedly tries to counter Marx's assertion that class positions influence the way knowledge is shaped by emphasizing the importance of workers' autonomy (a more ambitious take would be to suggest that this also reflects Lukács's claim that this must be so, because workers are closer to objective truth, at least once they have become/been made class conscious). Externalization turns attention explicitly to language, as well as pointing to Descartes' division between the human subject (knowledge within the human being) and non-human object (knowledge in a non-human 'format'). And once we turn to language, inherent in the combination of explicit knowledge, we are faced with Wittgenstein's 'language games' and if that language forms 'text' (which it must), once more with Derrida's deconstruction. The internalization phase draws us both back to Russell's 'knowledge by description', and puts at centre stage the structuralist/post-structuralist questions about the relation of knowledge and 'reality'.

Indeed, if we take tacit knowledge to be the only 'fundamental' knowledge, the whole process aimed to *create* knowledge may instead 'impoverish' it. In the move to explicit knowledge through the *formalization* of tacit knowledge, much would be lost in *translation*, for the explicit must always be representational and thus etiolated (think back to emperor Kublai Khan and his appropriation of Marco Polo's adventures in Chapter 9). When knowledge gets 'impoverished' at each cycle, the 'spiral of knowledge' may end up a drill. And at an individual level, perhaps, the shift has other repercussions. For what is KM if not a means of controlling part of the Labour Process (see Chapter 1) that had hitherto been resistant to inclusion within such systems of control while that knowledge remained tacit? And if such knowledge is, indeed, impoverished by its translation, then what might be the consequences of the shift from human to organization? Does the move to the virtual, to the Internet or groupware systems (see Chapter 8), not represent the intermingling of explicit knowledge, writ large?

If so then perhaps the future may not be so bleak. As we have seen, in such networks participants actively seek out and deploy new strategies to manage their own accountability within their changed surroundings. For once knowledge is made explicit, it migrates across organizations, ready to be enrolled in new networks, should *any* potential enunciator (see Chapter 4) be able to mobilize it.

The second theorization of KM, which stressed learning by individuals within an organizational structure (Senge and colleagues), also seems a motley collection of concepts drawn from empiricist, pragmatist, social constructivist, and structuralist/ post-structuralist, as well as the obvious behaviourist, underpinnings. Of course, for Senge and his followers, organizations are both a 'construct' of the individuals that populate them and a 'determinant' of those selfsame individuals' behaviour. But such a Third Way may not be the only route out of the debates that flow around structuralism and post-structuralism, in all their forms. For we may be able to avoid a retreat into the tidy categories of individual and organization by simply paying more attention to them. For once we make the binary opposition of individual and organization visible, we can attempt to seek out the histories of such categorizations, and the effects that they bring with them (Foucault 1966, trans. 1970; 1975, trans. 1977). And we can then see that knowledge management cannot be, and never has been, a neutral term and that its enrolment into organizational learning will always be accompanied by significant additional baggage.

The third approach to knowledge management, which pictures organizational learning as a group or collective activity (Argyris et al.), seems to return to the *mechanistic* approach to 'knowledge' we tackled at the beginning of this chapter, where knowledge can be 'created' through *processing* representations. However, although knowledge still comes through processing representations of individual knowledge, we find that we have come to an unusual turn, with individuals, in conjunction with information systems, providing the necessary *processing power*. This leads us down a convoluted path, upon which 'momentous miracles of transformation can take place' (Burke 1969: 24). For our final conceptualization knowledge management can be analysed in five 'alchemic' (Burke 1969: 24) stages:

(1) *separation* of the object—knowledge—from the (knowing human) subject;
(2) *imaterialization* of the separated 'object';
(3) via storage, *transformation* of the 'object' into an 'artefact' (knowledge—'that', 'how', and 'by acquaintance'—are amalgamated within 'repositories' as 'knowledge by description', bringing with them norms, procedures, processes, methods, recipes, patents, inventions, evaluations, communications, reports, computers, equipments, and so forth);
(4) via redistribution of the 'object' from the 'repositories' to individuals, *collective transformation* of one 'object' (one representation of knowledge) into another (an altered representation); and, finally,
(5) *recollection* of the transformed 'object' into 'repositories' once more.

And, although at first sight, this seems to require us to uncomplainingly accept a series of what seem to be illusions (such as that we can 'store' knowledge outside of individuals), are we not also in the process approaching what Law asked for? The ability to 'find a way of talking about the-social-and-the-technical, all in one breath' (Law 1991b: 8; see Chapter 4)? Being critical of the banalities that permeate the knowledge management literature, is it possible that we ourselves have been seeking knowledge in all the wrong places?

For although the concept of knowledge is intricate and complex to grasp, we cannot hope to handle it through the categorization of the way in which it informs or is collected. 'To conceive of knowledge as a collection of information seems to rob the concept of all of its life . . . Knowledge resides in the user and not in the collection. It is how the user reacts to a collection of information that matters' (Churchman 1971: 10).

As Burke (1969) notes, where knowledge is created and deployed, practices of division function around the notion of the *substance* of that which is to be known. But as the etymology of 'substance' makes clear, matters are far from simple here. 'Literally a person's or a thing's sub-stance would be something that stands beneath or supports the person or thing' (Burke 1969: 22). For this means that the word 'used to designate what a thing is derives from a word designating something that a thing *is not*' (Burke 1969: 23, original emphasis). 'Here . . . the intrinsic and extrinsic can change places' (Burke 1969: 24) and perhaps where knowledge is concerned, it is not information but *material trans*formation that is of the essence.

▥ SUMMARY

The chapter examined distinctions between data, information, and knowledge, particularly the ways in which such distinctions are enrolled in accounts of knowledge management. Indeed, all manner of other distinctions were also revealed as essential to the functioning of that body of literature, including amongst others: that between tacit and explicit knowledge, that between organization and individual, that between order and disorder, that between learning and memory, and even that between learning and organization. Consideration was given to the paucity of theorization of organization and indeed of knowledge within the 'knowledge management' literature, a paucity that was illustrated with a whistle-stop tour of the intellectual history of theorizations of knowledge from other disciplinary bases. Battles from the history of knowledge's conceptualization were re-enacted on the terrain of knowledge management to reveal the precariousness of its positions, before a rather more optimistic conclusion: a view of knowledge management literature as a potential opening with which to articulate the power of *trans*formation.

▥ DISCUSSION QUESTIONS

1. What are the practical implications of Ryle's 'infinite regress of thought' (the intellectualist legend) and the representational attempts to correlate data, information, and knowledge in a mechanistic processing approach?

2. How can individuals influence their organizational environment so that they themselves might enjoy a virtuous 'spiral of knowledge' creation?

3. What happens with the 'system thinking' approach to knowledge management if we take a different system as our starting point?

4. Are 'repositories of knowledge' value free, or does knowledge always come at a price?

5. Which individuals structure organizations?

▓ SUGGESTIONS FOR FURTHER READING

Burke, P. (2000). *A Social History of Knowledge: from Gutenberg to Diderot*. Cambridge: Polity Press—provides a good introduction into sociological approaches to knowledge.

Grant, R. M. (2001). 'Knowledge and Organization', in I. Nonaka and D. J. Teece (eds.), *Managing Industrial Knowledge: Creation, Transfer and Utilization*. London: Sage—explores further the interrelations between knowledge and organization.

Pedler, M., Burgoyne, J. G., and Boydell, T. (1991). *The Learning Company: A Strategy for Sustainable Development* (1997—2nd edn.). London: McGraw-Hill—looks at a range of other approaches to organizational learning and includes a number of practical examples.

Nonaka's theoretical approach to knowledge creation is well explained in Nonaka, I., Toyama, R., and Konno, N. (2001). 'SECI, Ba and Leadership: A Unified Model of Dynamic Knowledge Creation', in I. Nonaka and D. J. Teece (eds.), *Managing Industrial Knowledge: Creation, Transfer and Utilization*. London: Sage.

▨ POSTSCRIPT

Rather than end this text with a neat tying up of all the threads we have loosened, into a bundle of hope for a more manageable future, much as we would like to stop writing, we feel we cannot *conclude*. For to conclude is to close, but it is more than mere finish, it is also to settle, worse still, to confine. And that, we have argued, is precisely what much that passes for theorization of the management of and through knowledge and information seeks to do and precisely what we have tried to resist. But such theorization can only seek; it cannot do. As we have seen, only the slightest tug causes the whole rug, on which such simplicities sit, to unravel. For if information does anything, it expands, multiplies, flows. And trumping these dispersions with a calming invocation of knowledge does nothing to turn them back or hold them in check, particularly when that claim on knowledge itself rests upon similarly shifting sands. Our mixing of metaphors here reveals perhaps the inescapability of a representational turn, and to pretend that organization can avoid this turn is to bury our heads in those shifting sands. There are no oases in these deserts, only mirages.

▓ NOTES

Introduction

1 See, for example, www.post-gazette.com/obituaries/20010210simon2.asp (consulted 1 July 2003). One should also note, however, that a certain Marvin Minsky might dispute this claim (for the view from the horse's mouth, see web.media.mit.edu/~minsky, consulted 1 July 2003).

1 Management, Information, and the Labour Process

1 Although not of course unusual. Consider for example the sale made on products like 'home banking'.

2 See also Noble, D. F. (1984), *Forces of Production: A Social History of Industrial Automation* (reprint 1986 edn.).

3 There are of course many other 'processes' involved in successfully capitalizing upon the production of clothing and other textile-based products. Such 'processes' include financing; sourcing, shipping, and preparation of raw materials; dyeing, washing, and other production processes; administration; labour relations; design; outbound logistics; and indeed, marketing in its entirety, to name but a few. The last example in our list, while not central to our concerns here, should not be overlooked. When we are taught the 'history' of the industrial revolution in our schooldays, there tends to be much too little focus on the importance of pre-existing markets as a spur to technological innovation in a capitalistic system. We explore further these complex relations between 'technologies' and 'societies' in Chapter 4.

4 Of course, the weavers' demands are merely those of the market for final products back-flushed through the value chain. If extensive market demand is not present, nor are the bottlenecks we describe.

5 Process technologies 'make' technological products.

6 Presumably three axes following the 'normal' three dimensions of space and two rotational axes.

7 More detail on this example is available in Ezzamel, Lilley, and Willmott (1996), 'Practices and Practicalities: Changing Human Resource Management', *Human Resource Management Journal*.

2 Information, Representation, and Organization

1 It is, it seems to us, no accident that the recent flurry of interest in ideas of Business Process Re-engineering (see Hammer and Champy 1993) follows an intense period of systems investment in the commercial world. The practices of BPR, the desire to 'take a machine gun' to organizational processes, and to not 'automate but obliterate', bear a striking resemblance to the processes Zuboff describes. While for Zuboff (1988), at the time of her study at least, informating was something of a pleasant by-product of informational automation, for the proponents of BPR this is precisely the explicit opportunity to invoke ideals of business revolution.

2 This idea of 'human limits' is prevalent throughout the social sciences. Indeed it can even be found beyond this realm in the work of evolutionary theorists such as Stephen Jay Gould (2002). Bounded Rationality itself emerged as Simon attempted to wrestle with the inhuman assumptions of perfectable information that lay beneath classical economic theory. It re-emerges in perhaps its simplest form in Miller's famous work (1956) on the scale (and limitations) of short-term memory, 7 +/− 2.

3 Think back to the example of the multidivisional company. Managers here can 'enjoy' career paths that take them throughout the conglomerate's organizational network (at least once they have reached a certain level of seniority) while certain administrative functions may be centralized for the group as a whole. 'Discrete' business units are only discrete in some regards here. In others the overarching corporate network is pre-eminent.

4 The emergence of so-called ethical investment funds, although not an entirely novel idea, is changing this picture slightly. But it is important to note that the structural characteristics of a representational economy are not affected by such moves. Instead, what we will witness is merely a larger scorecard—one that perhaps includes an abstract value for a country or organization's human rights record. In European football, the away goals rule performs a similar function.

5 That is, one whose value could be manipulated by the very act of trading.

6 There is an important distinction here with the UK mortgage market where the majority of loans are made on a variable interest basis.

7 Obviously, particularly to the more astute amongst the trading community, large, 'strategically' significant, private sector organizations are implicitly and effectively guaranteed against risks of dissolution by the state, and hence the potential for near total loss on the part of investors is minimal.

8 This 'power' is slightly different from the forms of the beast we considered in the previous chapter. Indeed we can delineate at least four ways in which the notion of power was mobilized in the previous chapter. 'Mechanical power' is the notion most consonant with our common sense ideas of power. Such power was embodied in the machines that populated the machine shops that Noble describes. The familiarity with these machines gained through extensive training and experience then gives us a second notion of power, that associated with the operation of such devices, perhaps best captured by the notion of 'know-how'. Craft-labour is the wielder of this power, it being seen as a product of knowledge and embodied skill built up through experience. The third notion of power we confronted was that associated with managers. The basis of this ability to influence events comes from the widely shared ideology of private ownership, which in modern enterprise is translated into the mantra of managers' right to manage. In certain renderings this form of power may also be justified through reference to built up experience, knowledge, and technique, but it is also structurally determined. Owners grant certain rights to make resource allocation decisions to certain organizational bodies. It is important to note here that all of these forms of power are deeply relational, although in everyday talk these aspects are frequently elided. Mechanical power derives from the arrangement of materials to concentrate and disperse energy; skilled labour may only be skilled with particular technologies at its disposal and managers cannot manage without some form of acquiescence from those who are managed. The fourth notion of power we came across, that associated with empowerment, often makes precisely the elision we have alluded to. It is not clear the managers 'hold' power that they can differentially distribute, rather a complex of relations enables certain positions within a hierarchy to act as points of decision and

hence power, but crucially such positions of power only hold for as long as the relations upon which they depend can be sustained. 'Real' empowerment, changes in the relative power of different hierarchical positions, only occurs when relations change and it is crucial to note this rather than assume that one position can change independently of another.

3 The Conceptual Basis of Information Systems: Modelling the World

1 These are seemingly favoured by punters but one should never forget that a bookmaker likes nothing more than a customer who believes in a system.

2 This idea is also central for the body of transdisciplinary work that has come to be known as 'Actor Network Theory' (see, for example, the work of Law, Callon, and Latour, and the associated work of historians of technology such as Hughes). We will deal with this material in a little more detail in Chapters 4 and 5.

3 Although this is the most popular form of the story, it is important to note that it can be very dangerous to impute origins to ideas. GST *may* have emerged out of von Bertalanffy's readings of work in the biological sciences. But where did that come from? Both hosts may have been infected by a common carrier!

4 There is something of an irony here. The disinterestedness of evolution's selection processes renders them bloodless, forever above and beyond the conscious chimera of individual concerns. For the more reductionist readings (such as Dawkins) suggest that it is only the information carried by the code of genes that is seen to be important, the flesh and the desires to which it gives rise being seen as nothing more than carrier or host. Yet, our most vivid metaphorical mapping of the 'progress' of such forces is that of 'nature red in tooth and claw'.

5 The explosion of interest, in the late 1980s and early 1990s, in the notion of 'end-user' computing may be seen as both restatement and putative solution to both of these questions. As should be clear by now, such solutions are doomed to remain putative, their complete realization forever deferred, precisely because they do not solve 'the problem' of the gap between design and use, merely move it around. A computer system that allows users to design their own systems through construction of their information needs and interrogative strategies still requires prior design in terms of both the range of interrogative strategies potentially available and in terms of the type of information that may be held. In practice, moreover, there will always be pre-imposed limits on the amounts and sources of information that may be gathered or accessed for subsequent interrogation or 'processing'.

6 Indeed, the situation is more complex. Much absorption relies upon the co-action of foreign bodies, organisms that exist within our digestive tract in a symbiotic relationship with their hosts. Are they to be seen as part of the system?

7 Foucault's (1975, trans. 1977) reflections upon the penal system may be read as suggesting that this outcome was precisely what was required of disciplinary incarceration. A Marxian interpretation such as that hinted at by Foucault in parts of this work would emphasize the functionality of such an outcome for the overall system of capitalism, with its overall objective of perpetuation. However, at no point is this requirement seen to be the product of an intentional, individual mind.

8 Representational games abound here too. *The Times* table of university 'performance' reduces all this muddle to the tidiness of a single figure: the rank.

9 The broadness we have just been considering is somewhat narrowed in the seemingly more practical domain of business enterprise but still manages to maintain much of its laughable nature. This is most apparent in the platitudes of mission statements. It is unclear what senior managers of, say, Microsoft (copyrighted) expect to be delivered when they inform their workforces that their mission is 'To Be First': for if we take the statement to be meaningful, a fairly stiff proposition, we are more likely to find it at odds than in consonance with our knowledge of the history of the organization it supposedly encapsulates. And if we do not take it to be meaningful, a much easier option, it is unclear as to why one would bother promulgating it in the first place.

10 Indeed, it is just such an understanding of the differential relations of a variety of actors to systems that provides the *raison d'être* for the seemingly enlightened practices of soft systems methodology (see, for example, Checkland 1981).

11 Of course, Einstein's infamous equation, $e = mc^2$, allows us to translate between matter and energy, enabling an integration of this troubling distinction at, presumably, another level of description. Whether such a move avoids the problem we are highlighting or merely moves it around is a moot point.

12 As should be more than apparent from both previous chapters and what follows, this distinction is *entirely* arbitrary. Modelling, particularly 'world' modelling, *technicizes* the social and *socializes* the technical. Indeed, it is increasingly difficult to sustain a serious social/technical distinction in any meaningful talk about any aspect of the world (see, for example, Latour 1991*a*, trans. 1993).

13 A centre for much of the early work involved in the development of the digital computer. Think about Noble's argument in Chapter 1.

14 'Feedback control centres on the idea of monitoring the output of a particular piece of equipment and feeding back—electrically—selected information about the behaviour of the device, comparing actual behaviour with some reference point and effecting action to eliminate any discrepancy between the two. One early application was in fire-control devices for weapons systems and Forrester's work proved a notable contribution to the field' (Bloomfield 1986: 2).

'[A] simple example of a closed-loop [feedback] system is that of a heating system and thermostat. (The thermostat receives information about the temperature in a given room and "decides" whether or not to start up the boiler; if it does so, it monitors the increasing temperature of the room before eventually shutting off the boiler at some pre-selected temperature)' (Bloomfield 1986: 4).

15 This was linked to the idea of *low performance*, a state to which complex systems were seen to tend to move. Worse still, the system could itself act to counteract 'corrective' problems, to serve 'higher' system ends.

16 This 'conclusion' came out of Forrester's WORLD 2 and 3 models that grew out of a meeting with the Club of Rome—an international group of scientists, businessmen, and policy-makers.

4 Speaking for Information Systems: Analysing and Prescribing Material Information

1 As we will see the dual terms 'innofusion' and 'diffusation' (see Fleck 1986) may be better here, given our subsequent valorization of the translation approach.

2 The 'seven sisters' is a term that has been used for most of this century to describe the major, vertically integrated, transnational players in the oil industry. Recent commercial imperatives have resulted in a reduction in the number of sisters seen to rule this roost.

3 Names have been changed to protect the confidentiality of informants. Where commentary on the organization is available in the business press, we have utilized it but, of course, have not provided full reference details to meet similar confidentiality concerns.

4 Such as, for example, supermarkets.

5 And one could add its similarly impoverished efforts to accommodate other fleshy non-human animals in its universe, or indeed the human as animal.

6 The point is made most clearly by Iain Banks in his novel *The Crow Road*: 'Who makes up real things, dad?' 'Nobody and everybody; they make themselves up. The thing is that because the real stories just happen they don't always tell you very much. Sometimes they do, but usually they're too . . . messy' (Banks 1992: 236).

7 Organizational structure is itself perhaps best apprehended as a 'technology' as writers following Herbert Simon's lead seek to demonstrate (Boland 1987; Cooper 1992). However, this is to prefigure much of our subsequent argument.

8 Yet another change of name.

9 The title 'Rotterdam spot market' with it's geographically situated connotations is perhaps something of a misnomer. The name derives from the fact that much of the product trading carried out in the market is dependent on the movements of products, by barge, up and down one of the main north European rivers, the Rhine, which emerges in the vicinity of Rotterdam. The Rotterdam spot market is the European instantiation of these developing intermediate markets. Other regions in the world have their own spot markets.

'Rotterdam has a high concentration of refineries. It's at this end of the Rhine, hence it's the focal point for much of the supply system into Germany and for that reason it's the largest centre for oil movement in North West Europe, and hence people use this term, the Rotterdam spot market. There was a little cartoon in one of the papers when oil prices hurtled up which had these two dear old souls in their car, and he's driving and she says to him "Are you sure that if we find the Rotterdam spot market it will still be cheaper?" And that says it all, people use this term but the place, you know, there is no such thing' (Interview with Production Planning Leader and Ex-trader, Oiltown Refinery).

10 Which may themselves be equally well rendered as 'technical' reasons. Think of how the 'administrative machine' of bureaucracy is rendered as an 'iron cage' in Max Weber's account of the beast (see Weber 1922, ed. 1968).

11 Another pseudonym.

12 'Ontology' is the branch of metaphysics dealing with the nature of 'being', what we see as actually 'existing' in the world, independently of our modes of looking at it. The notion of ontology also entails claims about the statuses of various 'beings'. In the example we are considering here, we seem to be trapped in a game in which we can either give *agency* to technical artefacts, or to people and their social arrangements, but not to both at the same time.

13 Latour (1991*b*); other renderings of the enunciator or primary actor include the *Prince* (Latour 1988*b*); the *heterogeneous engineer* (Law 1987); and the *system builder* (Hughes 1983).

14 One must bear in mind that it is likely that the enunciator and its enunciation will also have been translated through this process. Translation entails negotiation between

putative entities in the mutual mediation of a workable network. Workable is an operative word here. As Latour puts it, the truth or reality of a network is an effect of enrolment. These relations are 'true' because they hold. That is, they are workable and will remain 'true' for as long as they remain workable.

5 Representation 2: Representation and Simulation

1 As we noted earlier: 'All representations originate in the instability of the body'. It is the extension of this process and recombination of the subjects/objects so produced that distinguishes modern technologies/representations.

2 See also Perrow's (1984) conception of 'normal accidents'.

3 As perhaps should be obvious, there are two 'gigantics' at work here. At Cobber attempts to pull everything together in a seamless system creates a system so complex that it cannot function. In the group as a whole, attempts to standardize, albeit fairly modestly (50% local, 50% generic), are wrecked on the rocks of differing local contingencies. In both cases however the logic is the same: bringing too much disparity too tightly together results in explosive destabilization of the entire system.

4 This 'implosion' is merely the logical corollary of the 'explosion' delineated in the previous note. If we retain attachment to 'the real', our systems explode as they attempt to capture its manifold difference. If we privilege order, that which systems require to be systematic, over reality, the latter is simply folded in to a dimensionless point of abstraction.

6 New Management Practices: Empowerment, Information, and Control

1 Tom Peters is perhaps the exemplar here; see, for example, Peters and Waterman (1982), Peters (1988). For consideration of the management guru and management fads and fashions phenomenon more broadly, consider, for example, Huczynski (1993), Jackson (1994, 1996, 2001), Collins (2000, 2001), or Lilley (1997).

2 Or, more realistically, at least at one level of remove.

3 For obvious reasons we provide no identifying details here. Indeed, we might go as far as to suggest that . . . the events, characters, and forms depicted in this paper are fictitious. Any similarity to actual persons, living or dead, or to actual events or forms, is purely coincidental.

4 Our shoppers reported that being checked on these latter two occasions had been extremely irritating. The check had felt like an affront, a questioning of integrity, an illegitimate singling out. According to a number of Safeway's checkout staff that we have informally spoken to about this, this sort of reaction, varying from the mild to the extreme, is not uncommon.

7 Accountability and Systems Success

1 Notable *bêtes noires* here for the management and information systems community include the Taurus share dealing and clearance system and indeed its 'successor' (Currie 1997; *Guardian*, 7 April 2000; *Observer*, 9 April 2000), boo.com's website which was seen as a significant contributory factor in that company's very public

demise (*Observer Business*, 28 May 2000), and perhaps the most infamous of all in the United Kingdom at least, the Wessex Health Authority debacle (HMSO 1993).

2 'Oiltown'; 'Oiltown's' parent group, 'Mexaco'; and the moniker given to the system design company, 'ITCo.', are all pseudonyms.

3 Unfortunately, it was impossible to involve ITCo. staff in the study as they insisted on charging the refinery full consultancy rates for any time spent talking to the researcher.

4 Most clearly expressed in the mantras of the 'End User Computing' fraternity, first seen in the introduction to this volume (Chapter 1).

5 In philosophy 'ontology' is the study of what actually exists as opposed to 'epistemology', the study of how we come to know what exists.

6 David Hume probably provides the most damning indictment of such a view, although many others have followed his path (Harrison 1976; Sim 2000).

8 The Virtual Organization?

1 The study (groupware: computer mediated meetings and the mediation of memory) was carried out by Steve Brown and Geoff Lightfoot under the ESRC's *Virtual Society?* initiative (ESRC award: L132251042).

2 All contributors have been anonymized.

3 A fictional acronym that could stand for The Conferencing System. TCS is 'a service which allows like minded individuals to converse with each other easily on a group basis, and discuss similar topics of interest together. This level of discussion is achieved by "joining" electronic conferences, each of which is related to a particular subject. You can post new messages to a conference, read other conference members' messages and reply to them' (TCS website). In more general terms, TCS is a UK version of the more famous WELL (Whole Earth Lectronic Link) discussion community in San Francisco. Like WELL, the population of TCS places great store by the notion of an online 'community'—to the extent of holding regular meets and get-togethers for the users.

4 Typographical mistakes are from the original message(s).

9 Representation 3: Risk, Control, and the Escape of Uncertainty

1 For example, goods are represented by a value, which is represented by money, which is represented by a cheque, which is represented by an entry on a statement, which is represented on a screen, which is represented by a piece of data, which is represented by a series of noughts and ones, which is represented by differences in the conductivity of different silicon sites.

2 People can appear as either here. All subjects are people within this 'humanist' view (see, for example, Brown and Lightfoot 1998). They are the masters. But sometimes the things they master (including themselves!) are also people. Such a view is the basis of management and governance of all sorts.

3 Somewhat strangely, we can witness counter trends in the present to this understanding, although this notion of reversal requires some careful handling. Even though we increasingly see advertisements calling for 'hybrid managers' and witness the ever-growing salience of the 'MBA' as *the* training in the combinatory techniques seemingly required of our modern managers, these combinatorial positions remain precisely that. They rely

upon the prior separation that specialization requires, before any subsequent recombination can be considered and valorized.

4 Think about the way in which Mexaco made problems for itself to solve, seeking control as it simultaneously created the 'need' for such control.

5 The italicized text that follow is the text of Calvino's that Kallinikos draws upon to illustrate his argument. Kallinikos draws upon the 1979 Picador imprint of the English translation of this text.

6 And just as in the idealizations of principal–agent theory, the asymmetries that pertain to this situation are likely to be exploited by all sides.

7 Think of how often discussion of the 'offside rule' or the 'penalty shoot-out' interfere with representations of the game of football on TV.

10 Handling Knowledge Management

1 Perhaps it might be better to consider the differentiation of knowledge into *tacit* and *explicit* as a *pharmakon*, as both poison and cure (following Derrida's 1981 reading of Plato), for the distinction both obscures and illuminates that which it seeks to apprehend.

■ BIBLIOGRAPHY

Aglietta, M. (1979). *A Theory of Capitalist Regulation: The US Experience*. London: New Left Books.

Akrich, M. (1992). 'The De-Scription of Technical Objects', in W. E. Bijker and J. Law (eds.), *Shaping Technology-Building Society: Studies in Sociotechnical Change*, Inside Technology. Cambridge, MA: MIT Press.

Allee, V. (2003). *The Future of Knowledge: Increasing Prosperity Through Value Networks*. Burlington, MA: Butterworth-Heinemann.

Alter, S. (1996). *Information Systems: A Management Perspective* (2nd edn.). Menlo Park, CA: Benjamin/Cummings.

Anthes, G. H. (1991). 'A Step Beyond a Database'. *Computerworld*, 25/9: 27–31.

Argyris, C. (1982). *Reasoning, Learning, and Action: Individual and Organizational* (1st edn.), Jossey-Bass Social and Behavioral Science Series and Jossey-Bass Management Series. San Francisco, CA: Jossey-Bass.

Argyris, C. and Schön, D. A. (1974). *Theory in Practice: Increasing Professional Effectiveness* (1st edn.). San Francisco, CA: Jossey-Bass.

—— (1978). *Organizational Learning: A Theory of Action Perspective*. Reading, MA: Addison-Wesley.

Armstrong, P. (2000). 'Designing Accountability: The Managerial Semiotics Project'. *Critical Perspectives on Accounting*, 11/1: 1–22.

—— (2002). 'The Politics of Management Science: An Inaugural Lecture'. *International Journal of Management and Decision-Making*, 3/1: 2–18.

—— 'Styles of Illusion'. *Sociological Review*, still forthcoming.

—— and Tomes, A. (1996). 'Art and Accountability: The Languages of Design and Managerial Control'. *Accounting, Auditing and Accountability Journal*, 9/5: 114–25.

—— (2002). 'Growth by Design: A Model for Design-led Businesses?'. *Business Strategy Review*, 13/2: 74–9.

Ashby, W. R. (1958). 'Requisite Variety and its Implications for the Control of Complex Systems', in G. J. Klir (ed.), *Facets of Systems Science* (reprint 1991 edn.), International Federation for Systems Research International Series on Systems Science and Engineering. New York: Plenum Press.

Bainbridge, L. (1983). 'Ironies of Automation'. *Automatica*, 19/6: 775–9. Reprinted (1987) in J. Rasmussen, K. Duncan, and J. Leplat (eds.), *New Technology and Human Error*. Chichester: Wiley, pp. 276–83, also available at www.bainbrdg.demon.co.uk/Papers/Ironies.html, consulted July 1 2003.

Banks, I. (1992). *The Crow Road*. London: Abacus.

Barnes, B. (1988). *The Nature of Power*. Cambridge: Polity Press.

Barthes, R. (1964). *Éléments de Sémiologie*, Bibliothèque Médiations. Paris: Éditions Conthier.

—— (1967). *Elements of Semiology*. London: Johnathan Cape.

Bateson, G. (1973). *Steps to an Ecology of Mind: Collected Essays in Anthropology, Psychiatry, Evolution, and Epistemology* (ed. C. Vern), Chandler Publications for Health Sciences Series. San Francisco, CA: Chandler.

—— (1979). *Mind and Nature: A Necessary Unity*. New York: Dutton.

Bateson, J. E. G. (1989). *Managing Services Marketing: Text and Readings* (reprint 1999—4th edn.), The Dryden Press Series in Marketing. London: Dryden Press.

Baudrillard, J. (1983). *Simulations* (tr. Paul Foss, Paul Patton, and Philip Beitchman). New York: Semiotext(e).

—— (1989). *America* (tr. C. Turner). New York/London: Verso

—— (1990). 'The Ecliptic of Sex', in P. Foss and J. Pefanis (eds.), *The Revenge of the Crystal: Selected Writings on the Modern Object and its Destiny 1968–1983*. London: Pluto Press.

—— (1993). *Symbolic Exchange and Death* (tr. Iain Grant). London: Sage.

—— (1994). *Simulcra and Simulation* (tr. S. F. Glaser). Ann Arbor: University of Michigan Press.

—— (1995). *The Gulf War Never Took Place* (tr. P. Patton). New York: Power.

Beckman, T. J. (1997). 'A Methodology for Knowledge Management', AI and Soft Computing Conference at Banff, International Association of Science and Technology for Development (IASTED).

Bentham, J. (1787). *Panopticon: or, The Inspection-house* (reprint 1791 edn.), in a series of letters written in the year 1787. Dublin. Reprinted and sold, London: T. Payne.

Bey, H. (1996). 'The Information War', in T. Druckrey (ed.), *Electronic Culture: Technology and Visual Representation*. New York: Aperture, pp. 369–75.

Blackburn, P., Coombs, R., and Green, K. (1985). *Technology, Economic Growth, and the Labour Process*. Basingstoke: Macmillan.

Bloomfield, B. P. (1986). *Modelling the World: The Social Constructions of Systems Analysts*. Oxford: Basil Blackwell.

—— and Vurdubakis, T. (1992). 'A Note on the Role of Technology in Accounts of the Labour Process', paper presented at Labour Process Conference, Lancaster.

—— (1994). 'Re-presenting Technology: IT Consultancy Reports as Textual Reality Constructions'. *Sociology*, 28/2: 123–46.

Böhme, G. and Stehr, N. (eds.) (1986). *The Knowledge Society: The Growing Impact of Scientific Knowledge on Social Relations*, Sociology of the Sciences Series. Norwell, MA: D. Reidel.

Boland, R. J. (1987). 'The In-formation of Information Systems', in R. J. Boland and R. A. Hirschheim (eds.), *Critical Issues in Information Systems Research*, John Wiley Information Systems Series. Chichester: John Wiley.

Borges, J. L. (1970). 'A New Refutation of Time', in D. A. Yates and J. E. Irby (eds.), *Labyrinths: Selected Stories and Other Writings* (2nd edn.). London: Penguin, pp. 252–69.

Boulding, K. E. (1956). 'General Systems Theory—The Skeleton of Science'. *Management Science*, 2: 197–208.

Brown, P. L. (1982). *Managing Behavior on the Job*. New York: Wiley.

Brown, S. D. and Lightfoot, G. (1998). 'Insistent emplacement: Heidegger on the technologies of informing'. *Information Technology and People*, 11/4: 290–304.

—— (2002). 'Presence, Absence and Accountability: E-mail and the Mediation of Organizational Memory' in S. Woolgar (ed.) *Virtual Society?: Technology, Cyberbole, Reality*. Oxford: Oxford University Press, pp. 209–29.

Buchanan, D. A. and Huczynski, A. (1985). *Organizational Behaviour: An Introductory Text* (2001—4th edn.). Harlow: Financial Times/Prentice Hall.

Burchell, G., Gordon. C., and Miller, P. (eds.) (1991). *The Foucault Effect*. Brighton: Harvester Wheatsheaf.

Burke, K. (1966). *Language as Symbolic Action: Essays on Life, Literature, and Method*. Berkeley, CA: University of California Press.

—— (1969). *A Grammar of Motives*. Berkeley, CA: University of California Press.

Burnham, J. (1941). *The Managerial Revolution: What is Happening in the World*. New York: The John Day Company.

Callon, M. (1986). 'Some Elements of a Sociology of Translation: Domestication of the Scallops and the Fishermen of St Brieuc Bay', in J. Law (ed.), *Power, Action, and Belief: A New Sociology of Knowledge?*, Sociological Review Monograph 32. London: Routledge and Kegan Paul, pp. 196–233.

—— (1991). 'Techno-economic Networks and Irreversibility', in J. Law (ed.), *A Sociology of Monsters: Essays on Power, Technology, and Domination*, Sociological Review Monograph 38. London: Routledge, pp. 132–64.

Callon, M. and Latour, B. (1981). 'Unscrewing the Big Leviathan: How do Actors Macrostructure Reality and How Sociologists Help Them', in K. Knorr-Cetina and A. V. Cicourel (eds.), *Advances in Social Theory and Methodology: Toward an Integration of Micro- and Macro-Sociologies*. Boston: Routledge and Kegan Paul, pp. 277–303.

Calvino, I. (1972). *Le città invisibili*. Torino: Einaudi.

—— (1979). *Invisible Cities*. London: Picador.

Castells, M. (1989). *The Informational City: Information Technology, Economic Restructuring, and the Urban–Regional Process*. Oxford: Blackwell.

—— (1996). *The Rise of the Network Society—The Information Age*, The Information Age: Economy, Society and Culture Series. Oxford: Blackwell.

Castoriadis, C. (1987). *The Imaginary Institution of Society* (reprint 1997 edn.). Cambridge: Polity Press.

Checkland, P. (1981). *Systems Thinking, Systems Practice*. Chichester: John Wiley.

Chia, R. (ed.) (1996). *In the Realm of Organization: Essays for Robert Cooper*. London: Routledge.

—— (1998). 'From Complexity Science to Complex Thinking: Organization as Simple Location'. *Organization*, 5/3: 341–69.

Chomsky, N. (1972). *Language and Mind*, New York: Harcourt, Brace, Jovanovich.

Churchman, C. W. (1971). *The Design of Inquiring Systems: Basic Concepts of Systems and Organization*. New York: Basic Books.

Clarke, S. (1992). 'What in F__'s Name is Fordism?', in N. Gilbert, R. Burrows, and A. Pollert (eds.), *Fordism and Flexibility: Divisions and Change*. Basingstoke: Macmillan.

Collins, D. (2000). *Management Fads and Buzzwords: Critical–Practical Perspectives*. London: Routledge.

Collins, D. (2001). 'The Fad Motif in Management Scholarship'. *Employee Relations*, 23/1, 2: 146–63.

Collins, H. M. (1987). 'Expert Systems, Artificial Intelligence and the Behavioural Co-ordinates of Skill', in B. P. Bloomfield (ed.), *The Question of Artificial Intelligence: Philosophical and Sociological Perspectives*. London: Croom-Helm, pp. 258–81.

Comte, A. (1853). *Cours de Philosophie Positive* (reprint 1974 edn.). Paris: Bachelier.

Cooper, D. (1983). 'Tidiness, Muddle and Things: Commonalities and Divergences in Two Approaches to Management Accounting Research'. *Accounting, Organizations and Society*, 8: 269–86.

Cooper, R. (1989). 'Modernism, Postmodernism and Organizational Analysis 3: The contribution of Jacques Derrida'. *Organization Studies*, 10/4: 479–502.

—— (1992). 'Formal Organization as Representation: Remote Control, Displacement and Abbreviation', in M. I. Reed and M. Hughes (eds.), *Rethinking Organization: New Directions in Organization Theory and Analysis*. London: Sage, pp. 254–72.

—— (1993). 'Technologies of Representation', in P. Ahonen (ed.), *Tracing the Semiotic Boundaries of Politics*. Berlin: Mouton de Gruyter, pp. 279–312.

Covey, S. R. (1990). *The Seven Habits of Highly Effective People: Restoring the Character Ethic*. New York: Fireside Books.

Currie, W. (1997). 'Computerising the Stock Exchange: A Comparison of Two Information Systems'. *New Technology, Work and Employment*, 12/2: 75–83.

Cyert, R. M. and March, J. G. (1963). *A Behavioral Theory of the Firm*, Prentice Hall Behavioral Sciences in Business Series. Englewood Cliffs, NJ: Prentice Hall.

Dawkins, R. (1976). *The Selfish Gene*. Oxford: Oxford University Press.

—— (1986). *The Blind Watchmaker*. Harlow: Longman Scientific and Technical.

Deleuze, G. (1986). *Foucault* (ed. and tr. Sean Hand). Minneapolis, MN: University of Minnesota Press.

—— (1988). *Le Pli: Leibniz et le Baroque*. Paris: Minuit.

—— (1993). *The Fold: Leibniz and the Baroque* trans. Tom Conley, Minneapolis, MN: University of Minnesota Press.

Derrida, J. (1972). *La Dissémination*. Paris: Seuil.

—— (1981). 'Plato's Pharmacy', in *Dissemination* (tr. Barbara Johnson). London: Athlone.

—— (1981). *Dissemination* (tr. Barbara Johnson). London: Athlone.

—— (1988). *Limited Inc.* (tr. Samuel Weber). Evanston, IL: Northwestern University Press.

Dodgson, M. (1993). 'Organizational Learning: Review of Some Literature'. *Organization Studies*, 14/3: 375–94.

Drew, P. and Heritage, J. C. (1992). *Talk at Work: Interaction in Institutional Settings*. Cambridge: Cambridge University Press.

Drucker, P. F. (1947). *Big Business: A Study of the Political Problems of American Capitalism*. London: W. Heinemann Ltd.

—— (1967). 'Technology and Society in the Twentieth Century', in M. Kranzberg and C. W. Pursell (eds.), *Technology in Western Civilization*. New York: Oxford University Press.

—— (1988). 'The Coming of the New Organization'. *Harvard Business Review*, 66/1 (Jan–Feb): 45–53.

—— (1993). *Post-capitalist Society*. Oxford: Butterworth Heinemann.

du Gay, P. (1994). 'Colossal Immodesties and Hopeful Monsters: Pluralism and Organizational Conduct'. *Organization*, 1/1: 125–48.

—— (1996). *Consumption and Identity at Work*. London: Sage.

Durkheim, É. (1912). *Les Règles de la Méthode Sociologique* (6th edn.), Bibliothèque de Philosophie Comtemporaine Series. Paris: F. Alcan.

—— (1912). *The Rules of Sociological Method* (reprint 1964—8th edn.), Free Press Paperback Series. New York: Free Press of Glencoe.

—— and Mauss, M. (1903). 'De Quelques Formes Primitives de Classification'. *L'Année Sociologique 1901–1902*. Paris: F. Alcan.

—— (1903). *Primitive Classification* (reprint 1963 edn.) (ed. R. Needham). Chicago: University of Chicago Press.

Eco, U. (1975). *Trattato di Semiotica Generale*, Il Campo Semiotico. Milano: Bompiani.

—— (1976). *A Theory of Semiotics*. Bloomington, IN: Indiana University Press.

—— (1983). *The Name of the Rose*. San Diego, CA: Harcourt Brace Jovanovich.

Emery, F. E. and Trist, E. L. (1969). 'Socio-technical Systems', in F. E. Emery (ed.), *Systems Thinking: Selected Readings* (reprint 1976 edn.), Penguin Modern Management Readings Series. Harmondsworth: Penguin.

Ezzamel, M., Lilley, S., and Willmott, H. (1993). 'Be Wary of New Waves'. *Management Today*, Oct: 99–101.

—— (1994). ' "The New Organization" and "The New Managerial Work" '. *European Management Journal*, 12/4: 454–61.

—— (1996). 'Practices and Practicalities in Human Resource Management'. *Human Resource Management Journal*, 6/1: 63–80.

—— (1996). 'The View from the Top: Senior Executives' Perceptions of Changing Management Practices in UK Companies'. *British Journal of Management*, 7/2: 155–64.

—— (1997). 'Accounting for Management, Managing Accounting'. *Journal of Management Studies*, 34/3: 439–64.

—— (in press). 'Accounting Representation and the Road to Commercial Salvation'. *Accounting, Organizations and Society*.

—— Wilkinson, A., and Willmott, H. (1996). 'Practices and Practicalities in Human Resource Management'. *Human Resource Management Journal*, 6/1: 63–80.

Fine, B. (1979). 'Struggles Against Discipline: The Theory and Politics of Michel Foucault'. *Capital and Class*, 9: 75–96.

Fisher, P. (1978). 'The Recovery of the Body'. *Humanities and Society*, 1: 133–46.

Fleck, J. (1986). 'Innofusion or Diffusation? The Nature of Technological Development in Robotics'. PICT Working Paper Number 4. Edinburgh: Edinburgh University.

Forrester, J. W. (1969). *Urban Dynamics* (reprint 1995 edn.). Portland, OR: Productivity Press.

Foucault, M. (1966). *Les Mots et les Choses: Une Archéologie des Sciences Humaines*, Bibliothèque des Sciences Humaines Series. Paris: Gallimard.

—— (1970). *The Order of the Things: An Archaeology of Human Sciences*. London: Tavistock.

Foucault, M. (1975). *Surveiller et Punir: Naissance de la Prison*, Bibliothèque des Histoires. Paris: Gallimard.

—— (1976). *Histoire de la Sexualité*, Bibliothèque des Histoires Series. Paris: Gallimard.

—— (1977). *Discipline and Punish: The Birth of the Prison* (tr. A. Sheridan) London: Allen Lane

—— (1979). *The History of Sexuality, Volume I: An Introduction*. London: Allen Lane.

—— (1980). *Power/Knowledge: Selected Interviews and other Writings, 1972–1977* (ed. C. Gordon). Brighton: Harvester Press.

—— (1982). 'The Subject and the Power', in H. L. Dreyfus and P. Rabinow (eds.), *Michel Foucault: Beyond Structuralism and Hermeneutics*. Brighton: Harvester Press.

—— (1991). 'On Governmentality', in G. Burchell, C. Gordon, and P. Miller (eds.), *The Foucault Effect: Studies in Governmental Rationality*. Hemel Hempstead: Harvester Wheatsheaf.

Fournier, V. and Grey, C. (1999). 'Too Much, Too Little and Too Often: A Critique of du Gay's Analysis of Enterprise'. *Organization*, 6/1: 107–28.

Galbraith, J. (1974). 'Organization Design: An Information Processing View'. *Interface*, 4/3: 28–36.

Garfinkel (1967). *Studies in Ethnomethodology*. Englewood Cliffs, NJ: Prentice Hall.

Garvin, D. A. (1993). 'Building a Learning Organization'. *Harvard Business Review*, 71/4 (Jul–Aug): 78–91.

Gettier, E. (1963). 'Is Justified True Belief Knowledge?'. *Analysis*, 23: 121–3.

Gherardi, S. (1997). 'Organizational Learning', in A. Sorge and M. Warner (eds.), *Handbook of Organizational Behavior* (1st edn.), International Encyclopedia of Business and Management Handbook Series. London: International Thomson Business Press, pp. 542–51.

Goody, J. (1986). *The Logic of Writing and the Organization of Society*, Studies in Literacy, Family, Culture, and the State. Cambridge: Cambridge University Press.

Gould, S. J. (2002). *The Structure of Evolutionary Theory*. Cambridge, MA: Belknap Press of Harvard University Press.

Gribbin, M. and Gribbin, J. (1995). *Being Human*. London: Phoenix.

Gutek, B. A. (1995*a*). 'In the Future: Transacting with Strangers and Not-so-strange Machines'. *Organization*, 2/3 and 4: 539–45.

—— (1995*b*). *The Dynamics of Service: Reflections on the Changing Nature of Customer/Provider Interactions*. San Francisco, CA: Jossey-Bass.

Hammer, M. and Champy, J. (1993). *Reengineering the Corporation: A Manifesto for Business Revolution*. New York: HarperBusiness.

Haraway, D. J. (1991). *Simians, Cyborgs and Women: The Reinvention of Nature*. London: Free Association Books.

Harrison, J. (1976). *Hume's Moral Epistemology*. Oxford: Clarendon Press.

Harvey, D. (1989). *The Condition of Postmodernity*. Oxford: Blackwell.

Heidegger, M. (1962). *Being and Time*. Oxford: Basil Blackwell.

—— (1977). *The Question Concerning Technology, and other Essays*. New York: Harper and Row.

Hesse, H. (1943). *Das Glasperlenspiel: Versuch Einer Lebensbeschreibung des Magister Ludi Josef Knecht Samt Knechts Hinterlassenen Schriften*. Zürich: Fretz and Wasmuth.

—— (1969). *Magister Ludi: The Glass Bead Game*. New York: Bantam Books.

Hiltz, S. R. and Turoff, M. (1978). *The Network Nation: Human Communication Via Computer*. Cambridge, MA: MIT Press.

HMSO (1993). 'Wessex Regional Health Authority Regional Information Systems Plan', London: HMSO, Committee of Public Accounts Sixty-third Report, House of Commons, Session 1992–3.

Hoskin, K. (1995). 'The Viewing Self and the World We View: Beyond the Perspectival Illusion'. *Organization*, 2/1: 141–62.

—— (1996). 'The 'Awful Idea of Accountability': Inscribing People into the Measurement of Objects' in R. Munro and J. Mouritsen (eds.), *Accountability: Power, Ethos and the Technologies of Managing*. London: International Thomson Business Press, pp. 265–82.

Huczynski, A. A. (1993). *Management Gurus: What Makes Them and How to Become One*. London: Routledge.

Hughes, T. P. (1983). *Networks of Power: Electrification in Western Society, 1880–1930*. Baltimore: Johns Hopkins University Press.

Huysman, M. (1999). 'Balancing Biases: A Critical Review of the Literature on Organizational Learning', in M. Easterby-Smith, L. Araujo, and J. G. Burgoyne (eds.), *Organizational Learning and the Learning Organization: Developments in Theory and Practice*. London: Sage, pp. 59–74.

Jackson, B. G. (1994). 'Management Guru as Guarantor: The Implications and Challenges for Management Research', paper presented at the Annual Conference of the British Academy of Management, Lancaster, September.

—— (1996). 'Reengineering the Sense of Self: The Manager and the Management Guru'. *Journal of Management Studies*, 33/5: 571–90.

—— (2001). *Management Gurus and Management Fashions: A Dramatistic Inquiry*. London: Routledge.

Jacques, R. (1996). *Manufacturing the Employee: Management Knowledge from the 19th to 21st Centuries*. London: Sage.

Jenkins, G. A. (1969). 'The Systems Approach'. *Journal of Systems Engineering*, 1/1: 1–21.

Johnson, H. T. and Kaplan, R. S. (1987). *Relevance Lost: The Rise and Fall of Management Accounting* (reprint 1991 edn.). Boston: Harvard Business School Press.

Jones, C. (2003). Resistances of Organization Studies. Unpublished Ph.D. Dissertation, Keele University.

Kallinikos, J. (1993). 'Identity, Recursiveness and Change' in P. Ahonen (ed.), *Tracing the Semiotic Boundaries of Politics*. Berlin: de Gruyter.

—— (1994). 'Predictable Worlds: On Writing, Rationality and Organization', paper presented at the Workshop on Writing, Rationality and Organization, European Institute for Advanced Studies in Management, Brussels.

—— (1995). 'The Archi-tecture of the Invisible: Technology is Representation'. *Organization*, 2/1: 117–40.

Kant, I. (1781). *Kritik der Reinen Vernunft* (reprint 1998 edn.), Philosophische Bibliothek Series. Hamburg: F. Meiner Verlag.

—— (1998). *Critique of Pure Reason*, ed. P. Guyer and A. W. Wood, The Cambridge Edition of the Works of Immanuel Kant Series. Cambridge: Cambridge University Press.

Kanter, R. M. (1989). 'The New Managerial Work'. *Harvard Business Review*, 67/6 (Nov–Dec): 85–8.

Kanter, J., Schiffman, S., and Faye Horn, J. (1990). 'Let the Customer Do It'. *Computerworld*, 27 August: 75–8.

Kast, F. E. and Rosenzweig, J. E. (1972). 'General Systems Theory: Applications for Organization and Management'. *Academy of Management Journal*; 447–65. Reprinted in J. C. Wetherbe, V. T. Dock, and S. L. Mandell (1988) (eds.), *Readings in Information Systems: A Managerial Perspective*. Volume 15, St Paul, MN: West.

Keat, R. and Abercrombie, N. (eds.) (1991). *Enterprise Culture*, International Library of Sociology Series. London: Routledge.

Keenoy, T. (1990). 'HRM: A Case of the Wolf in Sheep's Clothing?' *Personnel Review*, 19/2: 3–9.

Khoshafian, S. and Buckiewicz, M. (1995). *Introduction to Groupware, Workflow and Workgroup Computing*. New York: John Wiley.

Kim, D. H. (1993). 'The Link between Individual and Organizational Learning'. *Sloan Management Review*, Fall: 37–50.

Kirkpatrick, D. (1993). 'Groupware goes Boom'. *Fortune*, 27 December: 63–7.

Knights, D. and Vurdubakis, T. (1994). 'Foucault, Power, Resistance and All That', in J. M. Jermier, D. Knights, and W. R. Nord (eds.), *Resistance and Power in Organizations*, Critical Perspectives on Work and Organization Series. London: Routledge.

Kuhn, T. S. (1962). *The Structure of Scientific Revolutions* (1st edn.). Chicago: University of Chicago Press.

Lamo de Espinosa, E., González García, J. M., and Torres Albero, C. (1994). *La Sociología del Conocimiento y de la Ciencia*, Alianza Universidad. Madrid: Alianza Editorial.

Large, P. (1984). *The Micro Revolution Revisited*. London: Frances Pinter.

Latour, B. (1986). 'The Powers of Association', in J. Law (ed.), *Power, Action, and Belief: A New Sociology of Knowledge?*, Sociological Review Monograph 32. London: Routledge and Kegan Paul, pp. 264–80.

—— (1987). *Science in Action: How to Follow Scientists and Engineers Through Society*. Milton Keynes: Open University Press.

—— (1988a). *The Pasteurization of France*. Cambridge, MA: Harvard University Press.

—— (1988b). 'The Prince for Machines as Well as for Machinations', in B. Elliott (ed.), *Technology and Social Process*. Edinburgh: Edinburgh University Press, pp. 20–43.

—— (1991a). *Nous n'avons jamais été Modernes: Essai d'Anthropologie Symétrique*. Paris: Editions La Découverte.

—— (1991b). 'Technology is Society Made Durable', in J. Law (ed.), *A Sociology of Monsters: Essays on Power, Technology, and Domination*, Sociological Review Monograph 38. London: Routledge, pp. 103–31.

—— (1993). *We Have Never Been Modern*. New York: Harvester Wheatsheaf.

Laudon, K. C. and Laudon, J. P. (1999). *Essentials of Management Information Systems: Transforming Business and Management*. Upper Saddle River, NJ: Prentice Hall.

Law, J. (ed.) (1986). *Power, Action, and Belief: A New Sociology of Knowledge?*, Sociological Review Monograph 32. London: Routledge and Kegan Paul.

—— (1987). 'Technology, Closure and Heterogeneous Engineering: The Case of The Portuguese Expansion', in W. E. Bijker, T. P. Hughes, and T. J. Pinch (eds.), *The Social*

Construction of Technological Systems: New Directions in the Sociology and History of Technology. Cambridge, MA: MIT Press, pp. 111–34.

—— (ed.) (1991*a*). *A Sociology of Monsters: Essays on Power, Technology, and Domination*, Sociological Review Monograph 38. London: Routledge.

—— (1991*b*). 'Introduction: Monsters, Machines and Sociotechnical Relations', in J. Law (ed.), *A Sociology of Monsters: Essays on Power, Technology, and Domination*, Sociological Review Monograph 38. London: Routledge, pp. 1–23.

—— (1994). *Organising Modernity*. Oxford: Blackwell.

Legge, K. (1995). *Human Resource Management: Rhetorics and Realities*, Management, Work and Organisations Series. Basingstoke: Macmillan Business.

Letiche, H. (1993). 'Ex-change', paper presented at the 11th International SCOS Conference on Organizational Symbolism, Organizations and Symbols of Transformation, Barcelona: EADA-Collbato.

Lévi-Strauss, C. (1962). *La Pensée Sauvage* (reprint 1995 edn.), Agora Series. Paris: Plon.

—— (1966). *The Savage Mind*, The Nature of Human Society Series. London: Weidenfeld and Nicolson.

Lewis, M. (1989). *Liar's Poker: Two Cities, True Greed*. London: Hodder and Stoughton.

Lilley, S. (1993*a*). Discourse and Sociotechnical Transformation: The Emergence of Refinery Information Systems. Ph.D. Thesis. University of Edinburgh, Edinburgh.

—— (1993*b*). 'Moving Management Around the Organisation, or How to Make Jobs for the Boys', in F. A. Stowell, D. West, and J. G. Howell (eds.), *Systems Science: Addressing Global Issues*, The Language of Science. London: Plenum Press, pp. 181–6.

—— (1995). 'Disintegrating Chronology'. *Studies in Cultures, Organizations and Society*, 2: 1–33.

—— (1996). 'Refining Accountabilities: Opening the Black Box of Management Systems Success', in R. Munro and J. Mouritsen (eds.), *Accountability: Power, Ethos and the Technologies of Managing*. London: International Thomson Business Press, pp. 118–43.

—— (1997). 'Stuck in the Middle with You?' *British Journal of Management*, 8/1: 51–60.

—— (1998). 'Regarding Screens for Surveillance of the System'. *Accounting, Management and Information Technologies*, 8: 63–105.

—— (2001). 'The Language of Strategy', in R. I. Westwood and S. Linstead (eds.), *The Language of Organization*. London: Sage.

Locke, J. (1690). *Essay Concerning Human Understanding* (1959 reprint of the 1st edn.). New York: Dover.

—— (1690). *Essay Concerning Human Understanding*. Reproduced at www.netLibrary.com/urlapi.asp?action=summary&v=1&bookid=1085946, consulted 01 July 2003.

Luchsinger, V. P. and Dock, V. T. (1976). 'An Anatomy of Systems', in J. C. Wetherbe, V. T. Dock, and S. L. Mandell (eds.) (1988), *The Systems Approach: A Primer*. Dubuque, IO: Kendall/Hunt. Reprinted as *Readings in Information Systems: A Managerial Perspective*. St Paul, MN: West.

Lukes, S. (1973). *Émile Durkheim, his Life and Work: A Historical and Critical Study*. London: Allen Lane.

Machlup, F. (1962). *The Production and Distribution of Knowledge in the United States*. Princeton, NJ: Princeton University Press.

Machlup, F. (1980). *Knowledge, its Creation, Distribution, and Economic Significance*. Princeton, NJ: Princeton University Press.

Macintosh, N. B. (2002). *Accounting, Accountants and Accountability: Poststructuralist Positions*, Routledge Studies in Accounting Series. London: Routledge.

MacKay, D. M. (1969). *Information, Mechanism and Meaning*. Cambridge, MA: MIT Press.

MacKenzie, D. A. and Wajcman, J. (1985). 'Introduction', in D. A. MacKenzie and J. Wajcman (eds.), *The Social Shaping of Technology: How the Refrigerator Got its Hum*. Milton Keynes: Open University Press.

Mannheim, K. (1929). *Ideologie und Utopie*, Schriften zur Philosophie und Soziologie. Bonn: F. Cohen.

—— (1936). *Ideology and Utopia: An Introduction to the Sociology of Knowledge* (reprint 1991 edn.), Routledge Sociology Classics. London: Routledge.

Marx, K. (1867). *Das Kapital: Kritik der politischen Ökonomie*. Berlin: Dietz.

—— (1990). *Capital: A Critique of Political Economy*, Penguin Classics Series. London: Penguin in association with New Left Review.

—— and Engels, F. (1846). *Die deutsche Ideologie; Kritik der neuesten deutschen Philosophie in ihren Repräsentanten, Feuerbach, B. Bauer und Stirner, und des deutschen Sozialismus in seinen verschiedenen Propheten* (reprint 1960 edn.), Bücherei des Marxismus-Leninismus Series. Berlin: Dietz.

—— (1970). *The German Ideology* (ed. C. J. Arthur). London: Lawrence and Wishart.

McKinlay, A. and Starkey, K. (eds.) (1998). *Foucault, Management and Organization Theory: From Panopticon to Technologies of Self*. London: Sage.

Meyer, J. and Rowan, B. (1977). 'Institutionalised Organizations: Formal Structure as Myth and Ceremony'. *American Journal of Sociology*, 83: 340–63.

Miller, G. A. (1956). 'The Magical Number Seven, Plus or Minus Two: Some Limits on our Capacity for Processing Information'. *Psychological Review*, 63: 81–97.

Miller, P. (1992). 'Accounting and Objectivity: The Invention of Calculating Selves and Calculable Spaces'. *Annals of Scholarship*, 9/1 and 2: 61–86.

—— and O'Leary, T. (1987). 'Accounting and the Construction of the Governable Person'. *Accounting, Organizations and Society*, 12/3: 235–65.

—— (1990). 'Making Accountancy Practical'. *Accounting, Organizations and Society*, 15/5: 479–98.

—— (1993). 'Accounting Expertise and the Politics of the Product: Economic Citizenship and Modes of Corporate Governance'. *Accounting, Organizations and Society*, 18/2 and 3: 187–206.

Mintzberg, H. (1994). *The Rise and Fall of Strategic Planning: Reconceiving Roles for Planning, Plans, Planners*. New York: Free Press.

Morgan, G. (1986). *Images of Organization*. Newbury Park, CA: Sage.

Mumford, E. (2003). *Redesigning Human Systems*. Hershey, PA: Information Science.

Munro, R. and Kernan, D. (1993). 'Governing the New Province of Quality: From Presentations of Economic Reality to Re-presenting the Customer', paper presented at the 11th International SCOS Conference on Organizational Symbolism, Organizations and Symbols of Transformation, Barcelona: EADA-Collbato.

—— and Mouritsen, J. (eds.) (1996). *Accountability: Power, Ethos and the Technologies of Managing*, London: International Thomson Business Press.

Neimark, M. (1990). 'The King is Dead, Long Live the King'. *Critical Perspectives in Accounting*, 1: 103–14.

Noble, D. F. (1979). 'Social choice in Machine design', in A. Zimbalist (ed.), *Case Studies on the Labor Process*, New York/London: Monthly Review Press.

—— (1984). *Forces of Production: A Social History of Industrial Automation* (reprint 1986 edn.). New York: Oxford University Press.

—— (1985). 'Social Choice in Machine Design: The Case of Automatically Controlled Machine Tools', in D. A. MacKenzie and J. Wajcman (eds.), *The Social Shaping of Technology: How the Refrigerator Got its Hum*. Milton Keynes: Open University Press.

Nonaka, I. (1991). 'The Knowledge Creating Company'. *Harvard Business Review*, 69/6 (Nov–Dec): 96–104.

—— (1994). 'A Dynamic Theory of Organizational Knowledge Creation'. *Organization Science*, 5: 14–37.

—— and Takeuchi, H. (1995). *The Knowledge-creating Company: How Japanese Companies Create the Dynamics of Innovation*. New York: Oxford University Press.

Noon, M. (1992). 'HRM: A Map, Model or Theory?', in P. Blyton and P. J. Turnbull (eds.), *Reassessing Human Resource Management*. London: Sage, pp. 16–32.

Norris, C. (1992). *Uncritical Theory: Postmodernism, Intellectuals, and the Gulf War*. Amherst, MA: University of Massachusetts Press.

Parker, M. (2002). *Against Management: Organization in the Age of Managerialism*. Oxford: Polity.

Pedler, M., Burgoyne, J. G., and Boydell, T. (1991). *The Learning Company: A Strategy for Sustainable Development* (1997—2nd edn.). London: McGraw-Hill.

Perrow, C. (1984). *Normal Accidents*. New York: Basic Books.

Peters, T. J. (1988). *Thriving on Chaos*. London: Pan in association with Macmillan.

—— and Waterman, R. H. (1982). *In Search of Excellence: Lessons from America's Best Run Companies*. New York: Harper and Row.

Pettigrew, A. M. (1999). 'Organizing to Improve Company Performance'. *Hot Topics*, 1/5(Feb). Warwick: Warwick Business School.

Pinker, S. (1994). *The Language Instinct: The New Science of Language and Mind*. London: Allen Lane, Penguin Press.

Polanyi, M. (1958). *Personal Knowledge: Towards a Post-critical Philosophy*. London: Routledge and Kegan Paul.

—— (1966). *The Tacit Dimension* (reprint 1996 edn.). London: Routledge and Kegan Paul.

Poster, M. (1990). *The Mode of Information: Poststructuralism and Social Context*. Cambridge: Polity Press and Basil Blackwell.

Reason, J. (1994). 'Latent Errors and System Disasters', in C. Huff and T. Finholt (eds.), *Social Issues in Computing: Putting Computing in its Place*. New York: McGraw-Hill, pp. 128–76.

Rice, R. and Love, G. (1987). 'Electronic Emotion: Socioemotional Content in a Computer Mediated Communication Network'. *Communication Research*, 4/1: 85–103.

Robb, F. F. (1988). 'Prescription for the Support of Groups Addressing Novel Organizational Problems'. *International Journal of Information Management*, 8: 275–88.

—— (1990). 'In Defence of Conversation: A Polemic Against Information Technology and an Agenda for its Future'. *SCIMA*, 19/1 and 2: 15–25.

—— (1993). 'Suprahuman Systems and Management: Steering in Jeopardy?', in F. A. Stowell, D. West, and J. G. Howell (eds.), *Systems Science: Addressing Global Issues*, The Language of Science. London: Plenum Press, pp. 97–102.

Robson, K. (1993). 'Accounting Policy Making and "Interests": Accounting for Research and Development'. *Critical Perspectives on Accounting*, 3: 1–27.

Robson, W. (1994). *Strategic Management and Information Systems: An Integrated Approach* (1997—2nd edn.). London: Pitman.

Rorty, R. (1991). *Objectivity, Relativism, and Truth*. Cambridge: Cambridge University Press.

Rose, N. S. (1988). 'Calculable Minds and Manageable Individuals'. *History of the Human Sciences*, 1/2: 179–200.

—— (1990). *Governing the Soul: The Shaping of the Private Self*. London: Routledge.

Rosen, M. and Baroudi, J. (1992). 'Computer-based Technology and the Emergence of New Forms of Managerial Control', in A. Sturdy, D. Knights, and H. Willmott (eds.), *Skill and Consent: Contemporary Studies in the Labour Process*, Critical Perspectives on Work and Organization. London: Routledge.

Rosenberg, N. (1976). *Perspectives on Technology*. Cambridge: Cambridge University Press.

Roszak, T. (1986). *The Cult of Information: The Folklore of Computers and the True Art of Thinking*. Cambridge: Lutterworth.

Rotman, B. (1987). *Signifying Nothing: The Semiotics of Zero*, Language, Discourse, Society. Basingstoke: Macmillan.

Rubin, M. R., Huber, M. T., and Taylor, E. L. (1986). *The Knowledge Industry in the United States, 1960–1980*. Princeton, NJ: Princeton University Press.

Russell, B. (1910). 'Knowledge by Acquaintance and Knowledge by Description', *Proceedings of the Aristotelian Society*. London: Aristotelian Society, pp. 108–28.

—— (1912). *The Problems of Philosophy*. London: Oxford University Press.

—— (1914). *Our Knowledge of the External World: As a Field for Scientific Method in Philosophy* (reprint 1929—2nd edn.), Lowell Institute Lectures—1914. Chicago: Open Court.

Ryle, G. (1949). *The Concept of Mind*. London: Hutchinson's University Library.

Saussure, F. D. (1974). *Course in General Linguistics* (eds. Bally, C., Sechehaye, A., and Riedlinger, A.). London: Fontana.

Scarry, E. (1985). *The Body in Pain: The Making and Unmaking of the World*. New York: Oxford University Press.

Schmandt-Besserat, D. (1992). *Before Writing*. Austin, TX: University of Texas Press.

Schmitz, J. and Fulk, J. (1991). 'Organizational Colleagues, Media Richness and Electronic Mail: A test of the Social Influence Model of Technology Use'. *Communication Research*, 18/4: 487–523.

Schön, D. A. (1983). *The Reflective Practitioner: How Professionals Think in Action*. New York: Basic Books.

Schotter, A. (1981). *The Economic Theory of Social Institutions*. Cambridge: Cambridge University Press.

Senge, P. M. (1990). *The Fifth Discipline: The Art and Practice of the Learning Organization*. New York: Doubleday/Currency.

—— (1991). 'The Learning Organization Made Plain'. *Training and Development*, 45/10 (Oct): 37–44.

—— Kleiner, A., Roberts, C., Ross, R., Roth, G., and Smith, B. (1999). *The Dance of Change: The Challenges of Sustaining Momentum in Learning Organizations*. London: Nicholas Brealey.

Sewell, G. and Wilkinson, B. (1992). ' "Someone to Watch Over Me": Surveillance, Discipline and the Just-in-time Labour Process'. *Sociology*, 26/2: 271–89.

Shannon, C. E. and Weaver, W. (1949). *The Mathematical Theory of Communication*. Urbana, IL: University of Illinois Press.

Sim, S. (2000). *Contemporary Continental Philosophy: The New Scepticism*. London: Hutchinson.

Simon, H. A. (1947). *Administrative Behavior: A Study of Decision-making Processes in Administrative Organization*. New York: Macmillan.

—— (1955). 'A Behavioural Model of Rational Choice'. *Quarterly Journal of Economics*, 69: 99–118.

Sisson, K. (1994). 'Personnel Management: Paradigms, Practice and Prospects', in K. Sisson (ed.), *Personnel Management: A Comprehensive Guide to Theory and Practice in Britain* (revised 2nd edn.). Oxford: Blackwell Business, pp. 3–50.

Smart, B. (1985). *Michel Foucault*, Key Sociologists Series. London: Tavistock.

Sotto, R. (1990). Man Without Knowledge: Actors and Spectators in Organizations. Ph.D. Thesis, Department of Business Administration, Stockholm University.

—— (1996). ' "Spect-Action" Technical Control and Organizational Action'. *Studies in Cultures, Organizations and Societies*, 2/1: 131–46.

Sproull, L. and Keisler, S. (1998). *Connections: New Ways of Working in the Networked Organization* (6th edn.). Cambridge, MA: MIT Press.

Stone, A. R. (1995). *The War of Desire and Technology at the Close of the Mechanical Age*. Boston: MIT Press.

Strapko, W. (1990). 'Knowledge Management'. *Software Magazine*, 10/13: 63–6.

Theroux, P. (1993). *Millroy the Magician* (reprint 1994 edn.). London: Penguin.

Tobin, D. R. (1996). *Transformational Learning: Renewing Your Company through Knowledge and Skills*. New York: John Wiley.

Townley, B. (1993). 'Foucault, Power/Knowledge, and its Relevance for Human Resource Management'. *Academy of Management Review*, 18/3: 518–45.

Turban, E. and Frenzel, L. E. (1992). *Expert Systems and Applied Artificial Intelligence*. New York: Macmillan.

Turkle, S. (1997). *Life on the Screen*. New York: Simon and Schuster.

van der Spek, R. and Spijkervet, A. L. (1997). 'Knowledge Management: Dealing Intelligently with Knowledge', in J. Liebowitz and L. C. Wilcox (eds.), *Knowledge Management and its Integrative Elements*. Boca Raton, FL: CRC Press.

Vickers, G. (1970). *Freedom in a Rocking Boat: Changing Values in an Unstable Society*. London: Allen Lane.

Virilio, P. (1988). *The Vision Machine*. London: British Film Institute.

—— (2000). *The Information Bomb*. London: Verso.

Vogel, D. and Nunamaker, J. (1990). 'Group Decision Support System Impact: Multi-methodological Exploration'. *Information and Management*, 18: 15–28.

von Bertalanffy, L. (1950*a*). 'An Outline of General Systems Theory'. *British Journal of Philosophy of Science*, 1: 134–64.

—— (1950*b*). 'The Theory of Open Systems in Physics and Biology'. *Science*, 111: 23–9.

Von Krogh, G., Ichijo, K., and Nonaka, I. (2000). *Enabling Knowledge Creation*. New York: Oxford University Press.

Vonnegut, K. Jr. (1969). *Slaughterhouse 5; or, The Children's Crusade: A Duty-Dance with Death*. New York: Delacorte/Seymour Lawrence (reprint 1991 edn.).

Watson, T. J. (1994). *In Search of Management*. London: Routledge.

Weber, M. (1922). *Wirtschaft und Gesellschaft* (1976—5th edn.), Grundriss der Socialökonomik. Tübingen: J.C.B. Mohr.

—— (1947). *The Theory of Social and Economic Organization: Being Part I of Wirtschaft und Gesellschaft* (reprint 1964 edn.; ed. T. Parsons). London: Collier Macmillan.

—— (1968). *Economy and Society; An Outline of Interpretive Sociology* (tr. E. Fischoff et al., ed. G. Roth and C. Wittich). New York: Bedminster Press.

Weber, S. M. (1996). *Mass Mediauras: Form, Technics, Media* (ed. A. Cholodenko). Stanford, CA: Stanford University Press.

Weick, K. E. (1969). *The Social Psychology of Organizing* (reprint 1979—2nd edn.). Reading, MA: Addison-Wesley.

—— (1977). 'Enactment Processes in Organizations', in B. M. Staw and G. R. Salancik (eds.), *New Directions in Organizational Behavior*. Chicago: St Clair Press, pp. 67–300.

—— (1991). 'The Nontraditional Quality of Organizational Learning'. *Organization Science*, 2/1(Feb): 116–24.

—— and Westley, F. (1996). 'Organizational Learning: Affirming an Oxymoron', in S. Clegg, C. Hardy, and W. R. Nord (eds.), *Handbook of Organization Studies*. London: Sage, pp. 440–58.

Wetherbe, J. C., Dock, V. T., and Mandell, S. L. (eds.) (1988). *Readings in Information Systems: A Managerial Perspective*. St Paul, MN: West.

Wiener, N. (1948). *Cybernetics: Or, Control and Communication in the Animal and the Machine*. Cambridge, MA: Technology Press.

Williams, M. and Farnie, D. A. (1992). *Cotton Mills in Greater Manchester*. Preston: Carnegie.

Williamson, O. E. (1975). *Markets and Hierarchies, Analysis and Antitrust Implications: A Study in the Economics of Internal Organization*. New York: Free Press.

Winter, S. G. (1988). 'On Coase, Competence and the Corporation'. *Journal of Law, Economics and Organization*, 4/1(Spring): 163–80.

Wittgenstein, L. (1953). *Philosophische Untersuchungen—Philosophical Investigations*. New York: Macmillan.

Wood, S. (1989). 'New Wave Management?'. *Work, Employment and Society*, 3/3: 379–402.

Woolgar, S. (1991). 'Configuring the User: The Case of Usability Trials', in J. Law (ed.), *A Sociology of Monsters: Essays on Power, Technology, and Domination*, Sociological Review Monograph 38. London: Routledge, pp. 57–99.

—— (ed.) (2002). *Virtual Society: Technology, Cyberbole, Reality*. Oxford: Oxford University Press.

Worsley, P. (1956). 'Emile Durkheim's Theory of Knowledge'. *Sociological Review*, 4: 47–61.

Yeats, W. B. (1916). 'Easter Rising', in A. Martin (ed.), *W. B. Yeats: Collected Poems* (reprint 1990 edn.). London: Arena.

Zuboff, S. (1988). *In the Age of the Smart Machine: The Future of Work and Power*. New York: Basic Books.

▓ NAME INDEX

▨ SUBJECT INDEX